SICILY

Other books by the author

Discovering the Hilltowns of Italy
The AA Tour Guide to Italy

SICILY

A Traveller's Guide

◆ ◆ ◆

PAUL DUNCAN

JOHN MURRAY

© Paul Duncan 1992

First published in 1992
by John Murray (Publishers) Ltd.,
50 Albemarle Street, London W1X 4BD

The moral right of the author has been asserted

A catalogue record for this book is available from the British Library

ISBN 0–7195–4820 9

Typeset in 11/12 pt Garamond by
Colset Pte Ltd, Singapore

Printed and bound in Great Britain by
Biddles Limited, Guildford and King's Lynn

For my parents

Contents

Illustrations

The author and publishers wish to thank the following for permission to reproduce illustrations: Frank Horvat, Plates 1, 9, 10; Toby Glanville, Plates 2, 7; Tim Benton, Plates 3, 4, 19, 20, 21; Joseph Rykwert, Plates 5, 6, 13; David Gilmour, Plates 8, 12; Enzo Sellerio Editore, Palermo/Società italiana per la storia patria, Palermo, Plate 11; Serge Chirol, Plates 15, 18; Leeds City Art Galleries, Plate 16; Melo Minella, Plates 14, 17.

Acknowledgements

I would never have gone to Sicily in the first place had it not been for Emma-Louise O'Reilly who dragged me there in the summer of 1987. Together we picked over the carcass of Palermo, and a great many of our finds were accompanied by the mournful wail, 'If only we could club together and buy it, we could save it . . .'. Well, we didn't, and we haven't, and Palermo is still very much as we found it. Thanks to Emma, I can think of no better place to spend the odd spare fortnight.

A great many people helped and advised me in various ways. A huge thank you most of all to Anne Engel and Joseph Rykwert (who read the text), Paola Greco, Piermichele Tafi and Gigliola Lantini of the Italian State Tourist Office (who arranged my visits to Sicily), Lia Verdina (of the Palermo Tourist Office), Marcus von Ackermann and Johnnie Shand Kydd (both of whom at various intervals drove me around Sicily), Gaia Servadio, Duncan Fallowell and Flandina di Cutò (all of whose letters of introduction were invaluable), Kris Mancuso, Gioacchino and Nicoletta Lanza Tomasi, Gioacchino and Marina Lavanco, Toti Corleone, Antonio Bartolo (who took me on a Tour of the Dead in the catacomb at Savoca), Aldo Bevacqua, Carlo Ducci, Judith Watt (and Beattie), Patrick Deedes-Vincke, Frank Horvat, Toby Glanville, Guy and Betsy de Lotbinière, Diana Scarisbrick, Joan Kent, Elena and Daniela Inga (of Ausonia travel agency), and Susie and Jonathan Smailes and Gabriel (who was conceived in the Albergo Orientale in the Palazzo Cutò, Palermo). Oh, and the London Library whose collection of obscure Italian travel books is unsurpassed.

Introduction

There is probably less Italian blood in Sicilian veins than there is Greek, Arabic, Norman or Spanish. For better or worse, Sicilians have been the victims for centuries of their island's location. Positioned on east-west and north-south routes in the Mediterranean Sea, their island has always been much coveted and for two thousand years its valleys and plains have resounded to the tramp of foreign feet. Fertile, and in antiquity extremely rich, Sicily also has excellent natural harbours which have been usefully employed as trading posts and watering holes halfway between Africa and Europe.

Without delving into the island's Paleolithic, Neolithic or even Bronze Age past, and leaving aside the native Siculi in the west, the Sicani in the east and the oddball Elymians at Erice and Segesta, I shall treat Sicily's history as starting when a series of trading posts were established by the Phoenicians (mostly in the north-west) probably in the 8th century BC. At the same time the Greeks were arriving in the east. The Greek period was something of a 'golden age', particularly during the days of the Tyrants of Syracuse, and in the 5th and the 4th centuries the island was reknowned for its power and enormous wealth. In fact in 413 BC Syracuse was responsible for puncturing the power of Athens.

After the Greeks, and following the First Punic War, the Romans arrived, followed nearly seven centuries later by the Vandals, who in turn were ejected by the Goths. These were followed by colonists from Byzantium and then by Arabs; for two hundred years Sicily flourished under Islam. In 1060 the Norman conquest of Sicily began, and for the next 150 years the island, and particularly Palermo, was culturally very active. Visiting foreigners at the time of Roger II noted that no other prince ruled a realm so peaceful and flourishing as the King of Sicily. Apart from intermittent periods of prosperity under the Hohenstaufen Emperor Frederick II, who succeeded the Normans, this was the last time in its history that

1

Sicily was itself the centre of an empire, and was treated to home rule.

Later, under the Angevins and the Spanish – in fact right up until 1947 – Sicily was ruled from abroad. The island was marginal to the political, social and artistic development of Europe, and indeed is still on the fringes of Italian politics. The community spirit so necessary for the creation of a sense of national identity was lacking as well. Centuries of almost unbroken Spanish rule – from the Sicilian Vespers which replaced Angevins with Aragonese in the 13th century to the removal of the Spanish Bourbons of Naples in 1860 – put paid to that. One would have thought unification with the Italian mainland after the Risorgimento in 1860 might have brought an end to Sicily's problems; not a bit of it. One foreign monarch, Francis II, was replaced by another, Vittorio Emanuele II, and even though every Sicilian town has its Via Garibaldi and its Corso Vittorio Emanuele, the advantages of unification which showered on the rest of Italy, passed Sicily by. Autonomy was denied, taxation was oppressive, and promises of land reform in favour of the peasants were left unfulfilled. The situation has been relieved somewhat nowadays by autonomous government – set up in 1947. But the centuries of neglect have taken their toll, and the result is that the Mafia is nowadays the strongest force to be reckoned with in Sicily.

With its concepts of private loyalty, private justice, the value it attaches to personal strength and violence used effectively as the best guarantee of survival in a cruel world, the Mafia is the inevitable product of a repressive state, an exploitative nobility, and the severest poverty. Family solidarity transcends the rule of law and the Mafia, though deeply interwoven with the framework of society, operates outside it. Cesare Mori, Mussolini's Prefect of Palermo, claimed that he would 'clear the ground of nightmares, threats and dangers which are paralysing, perverting and corrupting every kind of social activity'. Well, the Fascist government was ruthless enough to overpower, though not to destroy, the Mafia, but the *mafiosi* saw their chance to help the Allies take Sicily in 1943 and at the same time reinstate themselves. Today, nothing has really changed; in fact matters are if anything worse and apart from its interests in drugs, construction and real estate, the Mafia, true to its tradition of flagrant disregard for the administration, has been targeting officials of state in a campaign of murder and terror designed to prevent close scrutiny of its activities. Have no fear, though, a traveller on the island is unlikely to find the Mafia at all interested in him.

Was Goethe right to say that without seeing Sicily it is impossible to have a clear idea about the true nature of Italy? Is it true that each Italian characteristic can be seen magnified there? It is not as simple as that. The fact that Sicily is an island has intensified the cultural impact of each succeeding occupier. The resulting mixture – exotic, spicy and highly inflammable – has created a separate nation at the foot of Italy. And there are nuances within Sicily itself. The island's westerners, who have more in common with the Arabs, are at odds with its easterners, in particular those in the south-east, whose Greek inheritance is stronger; the former (in my opinion) exist in what Norman Lewis calls a 'sullen mental climate' while the latter have a happier approach to life. Goethe would agree with Lewis that Sicily is a morose place; I say this is true more of the west than the east. But while Goethe blames the 'hopeless struggle of men with the . . . malice and treachery of their times, and the rancours of their own rival factions', Lewis sees in it a survival from 'Roman antiquity, when a ground-down multitude of slaves produced nothing but corn for export'. Both are right. And the violence of interminable wars of conquest and of earthquakes which reduce cities to dust in seconds, plus the poverty of land deforested and desiccated, have created a psyche unlike any other in the Mediterranean.

If you know this, then you are halfway to understanding the frustratingly unfathomable, complicated character of a people who by habit have enveloped themselves in intrigue and adopted all forms of escapism as relief from the heavy hand of their overlords. In Sicily you will find a fierce mythology and a stoic belief in the power of magic and saintly intercession. It's as though the quiet transposition from classical polytheism to Christianity happened in name only; as if while paying lip service to a Christian god the islanders never really gave up their belief in the classical divinities revered by their ancestors. And yet, perversely, the greatness of Sicily lies in the wealth of sensibility, feeling and imagination contributed by the many races who colonized the island and subjugated its people, and whose traces have persisted thanks to the tenacious conservatism of the Sicilians. In this light must be read the islanders' customs, mythology, peculiar brand of Christianity, dialects, art, architecture, even cooking.

The early history of Sicily can be seen as a microcosm of a youthful civilised world. As conquerors came and went they left behind them on this tiny triangular island a deposit of art and architecture, customs and language. All this was assimilated, then reproduced in a uniquely Sicilian form. Eclecticism, quirky and unusual, is characteristic of the Sicilian vernacular in virtually every field. The Sicilian language, for example, has, since the Romanization of the island, been a Latin one. But it absorbed elements from the Byzantines, the Arabs, the Normans, and most particularly the Spanish, and today there is nothing quite like the Sicilian dialect anywhere in the Mediterranean. In general, the cultural material left behind by the departing overlords was of inferior quality. To the Romans for example, Sicily was only another outpost in an already overstretched empire. But their predecessors the Greeks, more than all the other early colonists, left a great deal that was of enormous cultural significance. To them, Sicily was anything but a far-flung outpost in an expanding empire. There was regular traffic between Athens and the island which kept up the swift flow of ideas, and culturally there cannot have been much difference between the two. In fact a visitor from Athens in, say, the 5th century BC, would probably have felt very much at home among the monumental Doric temples dotted about the Sicilian landscape, or the agora of somewhere like Akragas (Agrigento) or Syracuse. And today the remains of these cities of Magna Graecia are amongst the most magnificent ruins of the ancient Greek world.

During their time, the Arabs and the Normans actually held court in Palermo, and it is no coincidence that the years of their power were the most brilliant period of Sicilian artistic achievement. Strangely though, there are few purely Arabic buildings left in Sicily, yet Arab influence emanates very strongly from the Norman remains and can be read along with Byzantine Greek influences in any buildings spanning the Norman and Hohenstaufen periods. The Normans, having been so totally assimilative and having welded together and respected the heterogeneous nature of the island's population – Greeks, Arabs, Jews, Normans – engendered a great efflorescence of literature, art, architecture and political thought which was not to be matched on Sicilian soil ever again.

By contrast, the long period of Spanish rule had a stultifying effect. Sicily became an obscure backwater, and even the Renaissance had only a minimal effect. Much that was Spanish was imported – customs, architecture, people, language – but the very insularity of this period, in particular of the 17th and the 18th centuries, also induced an odd and brief flowering of an architecture peculiar to Sicily. Sharpened up from time to time by local practitioners who had been to Rome, Sicily in these years produced a baroque style in response to the elaborate ritual of the Viceregal court. Families rivalled one another in pomp and splendour of which the backdrop, the buildings, was the most important ingredient.

The elaborate adornments to be seen piled up on these buildings, the lavish display and the rich materials, fit a continuing Sicilian artistic tradition – a love of decorative embellishment which harks back to the splendid mosaics and polychromatic materials of the Normans, Arabs and Byzantine Greeks. Even the buildings of Ernesto Basile (1857–1932, see Appendix II) at the turn of the century carry on this tradition as if in an effort to keep alive an idiosyncratic symbol of Sicily's individuality.

Visitors to Sicily nowadays will notice one striking characteristic about the island: the peculiar difference between the west and the east, and more specifically between Palermo and Syracuse. By contrast to the anarchy of Palermo, Syracuse is temperate; industry thrives in the south-east while the north-west is spectacularly lethargic and troublesome. This contrast is thought to reflect the diverse pattern of colonization in the two regions way back in the mists of time.

One might think this is a fearful generalisation, but it is often said that there are two Sicilies and that this stems from the fact that while Palermo was traditionally where the Phoenicians, the Carthaginians and the Arabs had important bases, Syracuse was – and is – Sicily's Greek city *par excellence*.

Sicily is a world apart from the rest of Europe, even now. Marooned halfway between Africa and Europe, belonging to neither, only within the last fifty years has it been given official acknowledgement of its own identity. In Italy's statute books, Sicily is now an autonomous region with its own parliament holding the power to legislate on all matters regarding the island. New laws distributed to small farmers land expropriated from the vast hereditary estates, and in 1950 the Italian government created a financial agency – the Cassa del Mezzogiorno (discontinued in 1983) – to 'finance and execute a programme of special works' favouring the economy of southern Italy. Those who led the uprising of the

Sicilian Vespers in the 13th century and the separatist fighters of this century – who toyed with the idea of a Sicily annexed to America as its 53rd state – could not have hoped for better. And yet development was not uniform across the island, and in the 1950s and 1960s large-scale migration took place to the industrialised north of Italy. Even now that Italy belongs to the EEC, Sicily, one of its so-called problem regions (with high unemployment exacerbated by the closure of hitherto easy channels of migration), can expect further marginalisation as its economy – particularly agriculture – faces stiff competition from countries like Spain and Greece.

It is the culture of Sicily and the mentality of its people that are partly to blame; centuries of oppressive and stifling foreign rule have taken their toll. The legacy of the past is redolent throughout Sicily. If you could not beat the occupiers, you went underground. Thus it is that history must be held to account for the subversion and intrigue which characterize business and government, (Sicily has had over thirty governments in the last forty years) as well as the social life of modern Sicily, suffocating attempts at progress or enmeshing them in a web of corruption. Even the Mafia is thought to have originated as a 'self-help' organisation against foreign overlords.

Cynics have a field day in Sicily. They maintain that nowadays the only things to flourish here are bureaucracy and the Mafia. Tourism could flourish also. Sicily has abundant summer sunshine, magnificent beaches, some of the best archaeological sites in the Mediterranean (and the best Greek ruins outside Greece), and amongst Europe's richest and most varied architecture. It is possibly the most splendid of all the Italian regions.

This guide pays considerable attention to Palermo which in my opinion is an underrated city. Its monuments may be the backdrop to unpleasant crimes; its palaces and villas subject to the whims of attendants more concerned about their lunch than the footsore traveller who, arriving 'too late' in the morning for a visit, will find them frustratingly and inexplicably closed. But perseverance is the key, and – particularly if you speak a little Italian – someone nearby will be only too pleased to help, and will undoubtedly know the person to turn to for the name of the man who can tell you who holds the key. Such is life in Sicily.

This section of the book is divided into three walking tours around Palermo, each with its own map. The text I hope illuminates the story of each place – architectural, human and historical. A note of caution here: do not walk around Palermo with a large bag and wearing favourite jewellery. You may return with neither.

The rest of the book follows a variety of routes through the island, picking out principally architectural and archaeological sites of interest and importance. Chapter 9 (Mistretta to Enna) would be best covered at Easter; it illustrates some of the most fascinating – and bizarre – Easter celebrations held in that region.

PART ONE

PALERMO

1

The City

If you had floated into Palermo with Goethe and his companion
Christoph Heinrich Kniep in 1787, you would have seen, as he did,
the 'delicate contours of Monte Pellegrino to the right ... with
bays, headlands and promontories ... far away to the left'. This
view has not changed, but Palermo itself certainly has. You can still
view it from a boat, though perhaps less romantically now, since it is
more likely you will be on the deck of a rusting Tirrenia ferry from
Genoa or Naples.

In the distance to the south, Goethe and Kniep would have seen,
rising behind Palermo, the high mountains sheltering Monreale
and San Martino delle Scale. This rocky arc forms the gently sloping
flank of the Conca d'Oro, Palermo's protective 'Golden Shell', and
between it and the sea is a plain which at one time was immensely
fertile. At its edge, on the shore, is the city.

Like a smaller version of Rome, Palermo's centre is sprinkled with
domes and dotted with the pedimented façades of churches rising
above the rooftops of surrounding palaces and houses. Patrick
Brydone (traveller and author, 1741–1818) wrote in 1770, in a letter
to William Beckford, that he was 'every day more delighted with
[Palermo], and shall leave it with much regret'. He thought it a
'great capital ... which in our opinion in beauty and elegance is
greatly superior to Naples'. Praise indeed.

But Palermo nowadays is a shadow of its former self. Although
the Marina, for example, the once fashionable promenade lining
the city's northern boundary with the sea, still exists (as the three
lane Foro Italico) and has kept its fringe of magnificent palaces
(mostly now in a state of advanced dilapidation), Palermo has
turned its back on the sea and the bay Goethe called 'incomparable'.

Wartime bombing, severe neglect and a whole host of more
subtle problems have beset Palermo over the last fifty years. Perversely, the traveller who may once have come to admire a city
renowned as a showcase of palaces, monasteries and churches now

11

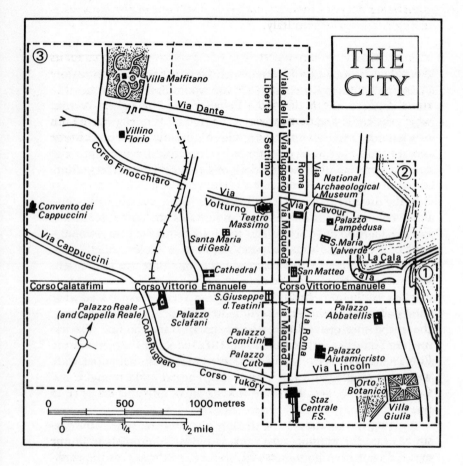

THE
CITY

③

Villa Malfitano

Via Dante

Libertà

Viale della Via Ruggero

Villino
Florio

Corso Finocchiaro

Via
Volturno

Settimo

Roma

Via

National
Archaeological
Museum

②

Convento dei
Cappuccini

Teatro
Massimo

Via
Cavour

Palazzo
Lampédusa

Via Maqueda

Santa Maria
di Gesù

S.Maria
Valverde

La Cala

Via Cappuccini

Cathedral

San Matteo

Cala

①

Corso Calatafimi

Corso Vittorio Emanuele

Corso Vittorio Emanuele

Palazzo Reale
(and Cappella Reale)

Palazzo
Sclafani

S.Giuseppe
d.Teatini

Palazzo
Abbatellis

Co Re Ruggero

Palazzo
Comitini

Via Maqueda

Via Roma

Palazzo
Cutò

Palazzo
Aiutamicristo

Corso Tukóry

Via Lincoln

Orto
Botanico

Staz
Centrale
F.S.

Villa
Giulia

0   500   1000 metres

0   ¼   ½ mile

comes to pick over its carcass, to unearth the forgotten façade or courtyard that the guidebook missed. But Palermo's former beauty is not quite gone and the best of her surviving treasures – like the Serpotta stuccos, the Norman mosaics, the baroque palaces and villas, the Cathedral – become more magnificent the sharper the contrasting decay of their setting. This is still one of the most fascinating cities in southern Italy.

Palermo has always been a port. The site of the city was chosen for its natural harbour (the Cala), an inlet which in the very earliest history of the city cut deep into the mainland extending two arms – the rivers Papireto and Maltempo – up either side of a peninsula on which the earliest settlement was to be found. The rivers have both now disappeared, but examine a map of the *centro storico* (historic centre) and you will find ample evidence of where they ran. The course of the Papireto for example, as the north-western boundary of the city, is the Via Venezia leading out of the west side of the Via Roma, just after the latter's junction with the Corso Vittorio Emanuele. It then crosses the Via Maqueda, becoming first the Via Candelai and then the Via Isidoro before it vanishes into the labyrinth of Palermo's ancient Capo region.

The settlement's southern edge followed the Maltempo, which was a seasonal torrent active only in the winter. You can follow its original course from the Piazza Bellini (between the southern end of the Via Roma and the Via Maqueda), along the Via dell'Università, the Rua Formaggi and finally the Via Porta di Castro. The Papireto met the Maltempo at the tip of the peninsula roughly where the Via Roma cuts the Corso Vittorio Emanuele, Palermo's main street which lies on the peninsula's spine, and flowed into the sea via the Cala. Neither river was ever very large and during the course of time both dried up.

Plotting the ancient course of these rivers in this way is an oversimplification; nothing can be exact nearly 3000 years after the event. But it is rather interesting that during the disastrous earthquake of 1726, the greatest damage was sustained along the dried up river beds, and as a result cartographers were able to piece together a good enough version of the ancient topography of Palermo.

In antiquity, the settlement lay at the 'neck' of the peninsula, at its join with the mainland – in the region of the present day Palazzo Reale. Fortified in the 6th century BC, this was called Paleopolis (the

city's Greek name) and it had a later extension called Neapolis.
Paleopolis was the highest part of the peninsula. Although it is not
very obvious, Palermo is built on land which tilts towards the sea. To
get some idea of the extent of the fall you have to stand at the foot of
the Corso and look back up towards the Palazzo Reale through the
Porta Felice.

Phoenician Palermo, which existed from the 8th century BC, was
the predecessor to Paleopolis. Also occupying the higher part of the
peninsula and so easily defendable, it was an important trading
settlement situated conveniently close to a fertile plain and not
too far from the other Phoenician colonies at Motya (see Chapter 7)
and Solus (see Chapter 8), the present day Solunto. It seems odd,
enveloped in choking exhaust fumes, to imagine the Phoenicians
worshipping Baal and Astarte where the narrow streets now are.
Strangely, Palermo's Phoenician name hasn't survived though
scholars have made stabs at a range of possibilities from Mackoshbim
to Ziz. Not a single stone of Phoenician Palermo remains either, and
not a great deal more is known about it. However some fragments of
sculpture, a couple of sarcophagi and the Pietra di Palermo, a diorite
slab on which a hieroglyphic inscription records the delivery of forty
shiploads of cedarwood to Pharoah Snefru around 2700 BC, can be
seen in the city's National Archaeological Museum.

Not much more survives from the Greek occupation. The Greeks
first reached Sicily in the 8th century BC but despite its site, Palermo
never attracted them. They tended to confine their activities to
central, eastern and southern Sicily, and Palermo had to wait until
the Muslim invasion in AD 831 to become a great metropolis. Even
the Romans, whose city was called Panormus (the All-haven, a reference to its natural harbour) left only a few paltry ruins behind them
as evidence of their occupation. Some rather uninteresting late
Roman houses were unearthed in the 19th century in the Villa
Bonanno in the Piazza della Vittoria at the top of the Corso, just
below the castle. A mosaic pavement from one of these found a
permanent home in Palermo's National Archaeological Museum.
After the First Punic War (241 BC) Sicily became a Roman province,
and was treated as a granary for the Roman legions on their almighty
tramp across Europe. The Romans peopled the province largely with
slaves who whiled away their days naked in the fields sowing and
harvesting grain for Rome.

All of this would explain Palermo's lack of significant classical
ruins – temples, theatres and so on – in contrast to Syracuse,

Agrigento, Taormina or even Catania (not to mention vast ruined and uninhabited sites like Selinunte and Segesta). Yet examine the city plan again: you will notice that the grid of streets on the ancient waterbound peninsula is very regular, quite unlike the labyrinth that is the rest of the city. This is the one very discreet survivor from Palermo's classical past and it is very easy to overlook it.

After the Romans, a fog descends on the history of Palermo until the advent of the Muslims. As far as anybody can make out, in the intervening years it was bandied about as loot by foreign invaders including Theodoric and, in AD 535, Belisarius who captured it for the Eastern Empire, at that time ruled by Justinian. One would have thought that a city protected on three of its sides by water would have been spared offensive action. Well it might, but Belisarius sent his ships into the old harbour and hoisted his archers up into their mastheads to shoot over the low ramparts and kill the defenders.

Later, still under the Byzantine rule, Palermo provided Rome with a handful of popes, and an important church was built between 598 and 604 on, or very near, the site of the present Cathedral. This and the castle were the two important locations in the ancient city. This church was to become the Great Mosque of the Islamic rulers of the city, and eventually the Cathedral of a Christianized capital. Interestingly, both this and the castle site still represent the principal poles of the region's power: the Palazzo Reale is the seat of the Regional Government of Sicily, the Cathedral the seat of the Archbishopric of Palermo.

Palermo really began to develop during its Arabic phase. The principal city sites began to take shape and the city began to expand beyond the confines of the 'All-haven'. Though few buildings survive from this period, there are many descriptions of the city from travellers amazed at its splendour. Around the middle of the 10th century Palermo was divided into four distinct quarters. There was the fortified al-Qasr which corresponds roughly with Cassaro today. This took the place of the old walled Neapolis and at its centre was what became known as the Via Cassaro Vecchio – a name in use until it became the Via Toledo in 1564, and later the Corso Vittorio Emanuele. Here lived the town's merchants and the nobility. There was also the al-Halqah, corresponding with Paleopolis and from the 11th century called the Galca. Here the Arabs constructed the nucleus of what would become the Palazzo dei Normanni and later the Palazzo Reale. In all probability they built on the even more ancient remains of Phoenician fortifications. This citadel was the residence of the Emirs until about 938, when another was built down near the sea to house the ruler, the government offices, the prisons and the arsenal. That new region was called al-Halisah and today is known as the Kalsa. This, the al-Halqah and the Cassaro were the élite regions of the city, which itself was given the same name as the city of the Prophet, al-Madinah, an honour not usually conferred by Islam on cities it had conquered.

There were other, lesser regions: one, known later as the Albergheria, lay to the south-east and was unfortified and filled with buildings for trade and industry. Another, in the south-west, was inhabited mostly by slave traders and slaves, the latter imported to Palermo for their skill at piracy. They served in the Muslim navy and were adept at harassing the coastal regions of western Italy.

Some records of Arab Palermo have survived. The globe-trotting geographer Ibn-Hawqal, who visted Sicily in 872–3, seems to have walked around the city with his eyes on stalks and sour lemons in his mouth. He found Palermo a licentious place; its inhabitants' houses were dirty and dark and their diet consisted excessively of raw onions. There were about 300,000 inhabitants at the time – a mixed population not only of Arabs but of Berbers, Greeks, Lombards, Jews, Slavs, Persians, Turks and Negroes. And there was a market which 'crossed the city from east to west . . . paved in stone from one end to the other; a fine emporium of various kinds of merchandise'. For its nearest equivalent visit the Vucciria, the medieval market place which today perhaps is not too far – geographically or visually – from the one Ibn-Hawqal saw. There were also more mosques in Palermo than in any other Arab city Ibn-Hawqal had ever visited: families often had their own.

A description survives of the Great Mosque itself. It lay very slightly north of the present Cathedral, though its enclosures will have extended over the Cathedral site itself. Tiny fragments have survived here and there, the most substantial (the remains of columns and pilasters some of which support horse-shoe arches) at the back of Cappella degli Incoronati – you can see them if you go down the Via Papireto from the Corso, just beyond the main entrance to the Cathedral. And you can also see re-used bits from the Mosque scattered about the Cathedral itself.

Again it is the intrepid Ibn-Hawqal who has left us descriptions of the Great Mosque; though some of what he says seems rather puzzling now: 'in this . . . mosque, formerly an infidel church . . . is a large sanctuary. I have heard it said ... that the ancient Greek philosopher ... Aristotle lies in (a coffin) made of wood suspended in this sanctuary that the Muslims have transformed into a mosque ...'. Another visitor, Il Idrisi, describes it during King Roger's time (early 12th century); he went there just before it was transformed into a cathedral and clearly he found it very beautiful 'owing to the fantasy of the art, the singularity of the work and the rare and very new kinds of figures, gilding, columns, and calligraphic (decorations)'.

Although physical remains of the Arab period may be rare, its artistic and cultural legacies are important. You would be forgiven for thinking that the Zisa, the Cuba, San Giovanni degli Eremiti, San Cataldo, the external façade of the Cathedral's main apse, or the cloister of Monreale Cathedral pre-dated the Normans. In fact they are not Islamic at all but were built under the Normans with the help of Islamic craftsmen. The intense interest in surface decoration these buildings exhibit (their most obvious Islamic attribute) lasted far longer into the future; in fact it has entered Sicilian vernacular.

When Count Roger I captured Palermo in 1072, instead of massacring the vanquished Arabs he allowed them to continue living there as they had always done, with assurances that their lives, religion and laws would be protected. The early Norman rulers were so tolerant that at least one – Roger II – was suspected at the time of being a crypto-Muslim. These rulers all spoke Greek as well as Arabic and they steeped themselves in Arab-Byzantine culture.

Under the Normans, Palermo became a powerful and flourishing capital as industry and trade developed. It was ringed by an extensive park in which were castles and hunting lodges such as the Zisa and the Cuba. The royal castle itself grew on the remains of the palace of the Emirs in old Paleopolis, incorporating two of the Muslim watchtowers into the new fabric. A group of artists and craftsmen erected and decorated deep within it the splendid Cappella Reale, a royal chapel whose magnificence reflected the luxury of the Norman court.

Under the Angevins and the Aragonese, in the 13th and the 14th centuries, Palermo's importance was eclipsed as Sicily succumbed to rule from abroad. The long War of the Sicilian Vespers (1282–1302) left the island wasted and culturally stagnant and, although it ousted the hated French, it heralded the arrival of the Spanish House of Aragon. This warlike, unhappy period left Palermo with some celebrated fortified (and practically impregnable) palaces of which the two most important were those of the Chiaramonte and the Sclafani families. Both still survive.

Of the two families the Chiaramonte were the more powerful. They controlled Palermo from the end of the 13th century until 1392 when the head of the family, Andrea Chiaramonte, was beheaded by King Martin the Younger of Aragon for opposing his rule. He met his end in front of his palace (sometimes called the Steri, from *hostarium* meaning fortified palace), erected by his ancestor Manfredi I within the confines of the old al-Halisah district. Much restored, the building is today a part of the university. You can see it in the huge Piazza Marina, a grim symbol of private power.

The Sclafani palace was erected in 1330 by Matteo Sclafani in an effort to outshine Manfredi Chiaramonte's. It survives in the Piazza Vittorio. Both had superb gardens; indeed there were many at that time, as much within as without the walls of Palermo. Their origins were Arabic as was the irrigational infrastructure, which brought water down to them from springs in the hills. These sadly are only known today from old records and descriptions.

In the 15th century two other important fortified mansions were built: one in 1490–5 for Guglielmo Aiutamicristo, the other in 1490–3 for Francesco Abbatellis. Both were the work of Matteo Carnelivari (see Appendix II). Like those of the Steri and the Sclafani, they dominate their own particular quarters of the city. The Palazzo Abbatellis is now put to good use as the Galleria Nazionale della Sicilia while the Aiutamicristo palace is divided into flats.

The 15th century saw Palermo taking second, even third place after Messina and Catania in the league of big Sicilian cities. In 1434 Catania even founded a university, which resulted in Palermo being left behind in a cultural wilderness. (Messina's followed in 1550 and Palermo's only in 1805.) From our point of view Palermo is at this time full of puzzling contradictions. Why for example was the great fresco called *The Triumph of Death*, painted in the middle of the 15th century in the courtyard of the Palazzo Sclafani (but now housed in the Galleria Nazionale) and surely in the vanguard of European late Gothic painting, commissioned? It exhibits heads foreshortened in a way no contemporary Italian would have attempted. And yet none of the best works of Antonello da Messina (1430–79, see Appendix II), perhaps the greatest Sicilian painter, were painted for Palermo.

Only towards the end of the 15th century did the city begin to transform itself into a vigorous and energetic capital once more. This was the period of Spanish vice-rule which was to last until 1713, and it brought in its wake a long period of relative calm. The government bureaucracy (with its office for the Inquisition) was efficient if terrifying, and religious orders gained power and property. New churches, chapels, monasteries and hospitals flooded the capital, and there was a new sense of civic identity to impose order on the haphazard fabric of the old city.

When the Viceroy Don Ferrante Gonzaga took over in the 16th century, the walls of Palermo were still Norman and Hohenstaufen, if not in part Arab as well. The city, even after five centuries, had hardly extended beyond these early confines. The fortifications had to be modernized and new bastions built. By the late 1530s work was well under way and the results rival Sangallo's work at Florence (1526), Sanmicheli's at Verona (1527) or Peruzzi's at Siena (1528).

In the 1580s the Via Cassaro became the Via Toledo and the old street was extended right down to the seafront, which it faced through the new Porta Felice. At the opposite end of the street, beside the Palazzo Reale, another gate, the Porta Nuova, was built. Expansion came hand in hand with a desire to formalize the city, when it was cut into four. A great new thoroughfare named after Viceroy the Duke of Maqueda now crossed the old Via Cassaro at a point called the Quattro Canti. Here four splendid, grandiose architectural screens divided into zones of the three orders – Doric, Ionic and Corinthian – mask the buildings behind them. This is still the most magnificent spot in old Palermo and, long before wild traffic rendered it a danger zone, it functioned as the centre of outdoor social life.

The opening up of the Via Maqueda was an invitation to the nobility to inaugurate a lavish building programme, lining the new route with magnificent palaces which also hid the squalid reality of the old quarters behind. Because under Spanish and subsequent Neopolitan Bourbon rule the ritual attendant on being a titled personage was so complex and required so much space for pomp and display, these palaces became bigger, grander and ever more extravagantly decorated. Every nobleman had to house not only himself and his immediate family but all the cadets of the house, who would live on the mezzanine floors or in small apartments around the courtyard. These palaces were enormous – the Palazzo Santa Croce stretches fifteen bays down the Via Maqueda, and the Palazzo Butera has thirty bays on the Via Butera. The size of these palaces is easily matched by the wealth of carving and decoration displayed inside them.

The 18th century saw the restructuring of certain areas of Palermo, principally the Piazza San Domenico and the Piazza Sant' Anna. The former was the work of Tommaso Mario Napoli (1655–1725, see Appendix II), one of the principal architects of the Sicilian baroque (and better known for his villas – Valguarnera and Palagonia at Bagheria). After the Quattro Canti, this piazza is the most important urban project of the time but it was simply imposed on the old street plan. Imagine your surprise when you squeezed out of the medieval market, the Vucciria (as you still do, though this was in the days before the Via Roma was opened up) suddenly to find yourself in an imposing piazza dominated by the twin towers of a vast church.

In 1734 another ambitious urban programme was initiated by the Marquis of Regalmici. Its motive was to speed up traffic to the country, in particular out to the Piana dei Colli which along with Bagheria was beginning to fill with summer villas for the nobility. The Via Maqueda was extended to where the Piazza Sant' Oliva is now. About forty years later the Marquis decided that the city should have a public garden. And so the Villa Giulia was added on the eastern flank of the city, down by the sea on the Foro Italico. This garden was inaugurated in 1778, not only the very first such place in Palermo but among the first in the whole of Italy. It was a welcome addition to the Marina parade which lay between it and the sea, and became the spot at which the daily *passeggiata* of the fashionable took place overlooked by two of the most magnificent palaces in the whole of Palermo – the Butera and the Torremuzza.

Thus the scene was set for the arrival in 1770 of Patrick Brydone and his gossiping pen. It was he who introduced Palermo and the world to each other. Later J. Houell published his *Voyage Pittoresque des Iles de Sicile, de Malte et de Lipari* in Paris in 1782–7, Goethe arrived in 1787, and after him Henry Swinburne whose accounts, *Travels in the Two Sicilies, 1777–80*, were published in 1790. It was no accident that in the 1770s a bookseller opened in the city selling translations of Pope, Hume, Voltaire, Diderot and Montesquieu. If one could choose, one would have visited Palermo in the 18th century. But perhaps this is because the contemporary descriptions of the city and its customs are so lavish and so lively, and so full of riveting incidental detail reflected through the eyes of foreigners, and northerners at that.

One opportunity for the lavish display the 18th century loved was the Festival of Santa Rosalia, Palermo's most revered saint and patroness of the city. Her shrine is on Monte Pellegrino – the Santuario di Santa Rosalia. If you ask about the origins of Santa Rosalia, Palermitans will present all kinds of stories as true accounts of her life and the reasons for her blessed status. Even Brydone found himself listening to 'the most fabulous legends'; in fact they differed so widely that he concluded she possibly never existed at all.

According to one popular account Rosalia was the niece of King William the Good (which if true would make her a relative by marriage of Richard Coeur de Lion, William's brother in law). She left home at an early age and disappeared on to Monte Pellegrino, to the west of the city, to lead a life of prayer as a hermit. Nothing more was heard of her until about 500 years later in 1624, when a local visionary claimed to have seen, in a dream, her mortal remains on the mountain. Sure enough a search party discovered a pile of bones in a cave which has since become a sanctuary, one that Goethe thought was naïvely decorated and touchingly venerated. While this drama unfolded Palermo was languishing under the cloak of plague. Luckily the visionary was able to refer back to his dream and let the stricken citizens know that the bones, if carried three times around the city walls, would deliver them. It seems they did.

Unimpressed, Brydone believed the relics were nothing more than the bones of 'some poor wretch that was probably murdered, or died for want in the mountains'. Other cynics say that the plague was most probably on the wane anyway. Perhaps the authorities needed to rally a wretched and depressed populace whose faith in the Church's power to end a ghastly period of suffering and death was seriously diminishing. In fact whatever the truth about her saintliness, and in spite of the monuments the churches built in her honour, the chapels dedicated to her memory, the prayers imploring her intervention (she even gave a local ducal family its title, the Duchess of Santa Rosalia having been, in the 19th century, a Palermitan society matron to be reckoned with), it was proved not too long ago that the bones in her sacred reliquary were in fact those of a goat.

Perhaps a veil is best drawn over that discovery. Each 15 July Palermitans still drag her reliquary in procession around their city on the back of a large and ornate cart. Magnificently vulgar in the past, this cart – like the festival of which it was an essential prop – is now much reduced in scale and pomp. In the 18th century the Festival of

Santa Rosalia was one of Europe's most spectacular events, and it obviously fascinated Patrick Brydone because he wrote an almost daily account of its side attractions in his letters home.

Had you been present with Brydone, you would have seen the 'carozza', a huge vehicle like a gigantic pram, teetering through the streets accompanied by a deafening, crunching sound, the grinding of its metal wheels. The friction often made them red hot and buckets of water had to be thrown in an effort to avoid the ultimate calamity – fire.

That 'carozza' was seventy feet long, thirty wide, and eighty high. Brydone noticed that 'as it passed along it over-topped the loftiest houses of Palermo. The form of its underpart is like that of the Roman gallies, but it swells as it advances in height; and the front assumes an oval shape like an amphitheatre, with seats placed in the theatrical manner. This is the great orchestra, which was filled with a numerous band of musicians placed in rows, one above the other: Over this orchestra and a little behind it, there is a large dome supported by six Corinthian columns, and adorned with a number of figures of saints and angels; and on the summit of the dome there is a gigantic silver statue of Santa Rosalia . . .'. And as if this was not enough, 'The whole machine is dressed out with orange trees, flower pots, and trees of artificial coral'. And if you do not believe this, there are plenty of contemporary engravings and paintings as well as a large wooden model in the Museo Pitré to back up Brydone's story. Like a great portable junkyard it was drawn, heaving and wobbling, by fifty-six mules. (A print dated 1686 shows it drawn by elephants and bears – though this may be wishful thinking on the part of the artist.) The procession took about three hours in all and ended with magnificent illuminations down on the Marina. Today's version is rather unglamorously hauled by a team of oxen or sometimes by an old tractor, resplendent in a coat of funereal gladioli (Sicilians' best-loved flowers); the cart itself looks suspiciously like plastic.

But now as then the whole town joins in the celebrations. There used to be fireworks, street decorations and a wildly animated crowd. Brydone found his heart 'dilating and expanding itself' for the event. Lucky for him it did only that. A dodgy heart nowadays might simply give up at the thought of a band of unruly Palermitans let loose in the municipal fireworks chest, or of being squeezed into the narrow streets between the traffic jams and the faithful.

The best days of festival ended in the 19th century, due to the waning influence of the nobility whose precedence, power and wealth it conveniently underlined with its splendour and magnificence. A great deal else about Palermo changed considerably at this time. The Viale della Libertà with its surrounding suburbs was opened up under the revolutionary government, after 1860, as a further extension of the Via Maqueda. Land was expropriated in order to build it, originally '*dar lavoro al popolo e di adornare la città*' – to give work to the people and to adorn the city. The latter it certainly did although today you may be pressed to imagine it as it was, so built up is the area. For people wanting to escape from the confines of the old city and live in open, suburban surroundings though, it was in its day ideal. Gardens were laid and Ernesto Basile was kept busy building Liberty (Art Nouveau) style villas for the nobility and for the rich bourgeoisie (like the tuna fish canners the Florio and the Marsala millionaires the Whitakers). Gradually the cultural, commercial and administrative activities of Palermo began to move away from the old city centre.

If you had come to Palermo in the early years of the 20th century, you would have witnessed the dying spasms of the Belle Epoque. Palermo, with all its exotica, its intriguing position as a capital halfway between Europe and Africa, and its rich, feudal aristocracy with endless illustrious and pseudo-illustrious titles (one princess had so many that she was able to give one to her lover), attracted international visitors, not a few belonging to the various European royal families. It was not unusual at the time to see a Tsar or a Kaiser, or even George V and Queen Mary, chatting to local notables on the terrace of the Princess of Trabia's Palazzo Butera, at the Whitakers' Villa Malfitano, or the Florios' Villa Igiea. This period was Palermo's last conspicuous fling before it sank into the quagmire of the 20th century and the grip of the Mafia.

What strike you nowadays about Palermo's historic centre are its dilapidated splendour and its silence after 8 pm. The '*vita*' of the city happens elsewhere after dark, leaving its old neighbourhoods a black labyrinth of uninhabited houses and crumbling palaces, often boarded up and forgotten. Here and there a baroque tendril on the façade of a defunct church stands out against the night sky, and old courtyards are black and still. Few people work here during the day and even fewer now live here. Allied bombing reduced parts to rubble in 1943 and much of the rest has suffered from neglect and abandonment.

Ancient city centres are allowed an element of decay. Like Rome
or Venice they can grow old gracefully. But both to outsiders and to
Palermitans old Palermo is dead, choked by its own modern expansion in concrete over the Conca d'Oro, the 'fertile plain' that so
enchanted Goethe. And nowadays the centre of the city is virtually a
no-man's land, a transit zone for traffic. The Via Maqueda, for
example, is like an *autostrada*, packed with free-wheeling cars and
lined with beautiful baroque buildings blackened by pollution.

A web of Mafia intrigue touching on property deals, civic
administration, and the diversion of public money from restoration
projects to more profitable private works, is at the heart of the
problem. Cynics will tell you that the Mafia and the *centro storico*
can never co-exist in Palermo. But they will also tell you that the
administration in charge of its welfare is composed of ill-educated
first generation city dwellers (often non-Palermitans) for whom
Palermo's architectural patrimony and historic environment have
no meaning.

The city's remarkable 17th century achievements, its range of
buildings from Arabic and Norman to baroque and Art Nouveau,
are without comparison in Sicily. There are Roman and medieval
street patterns and once there were traditional zones for different
artisans. While there are of course many monuments in the *centro
storico* in good condition and well looked after (some preserved by
the efforts of an admirable organization called Salvare Palermo or
Save Palermo), more are crumbling into ruin. Most of the artisans
have gone and their old workshops are closed for good.

For example, some of the most prominent buildings in the Corso
Vittorio Emanuele are the 18th century ones, most notably those by
Venanzio Marvuglia (1729–1814, see Appendix II), a conspicuous
and successful architect of his day. Yet the most splendid of his
palaces, the Palazzo Belmonte-Riso, placed where the Corso cuts
through a side of the Piazza Bologni, is a ruin. Although it was
bombed by the Allies in 1943 (it was the Fascist headquarters in
Palermo), its façade was left standing – luckily, as it happens,
because it is a vital part of one of the city's most elaborate urban
vistas. Yet until 1989 wartime debris was still lying about in its
courtyard and behind the hoarding that sealed off its entrance, and
only by some quirk of fate did the façade remain upright. At last,
forty-seven years on, an attempt is being made to rescue the remains
of this important building.

Next door to it is the Palazzo Geraci, another of Marvuglia's works and many times more ornate. This time only a half of its façade survives (some of the muscular women holding up the window pediments have been snapped in two), and if you peer through the hoardings you will see the rest lying where the bombs scattered it.

Even Marvuglia's Palazzina Cinese, a chinoiserie pavilion in the Parco Favorita, shut for years, is decaying. Eighteenth century buildings still containing their purpose-made furnishings, textiles and interior decoration are few and far between in southern Italy. You could say that the Palazzina Cinese is unique. That it survived the war is fortunate, as it was requisitioned as billeting for the Allied army. Immediately after the war its Chinoiserie furniture was in perfect condition. Exiled Ferdinand IV and Queen Maria Carolina's 'Oriental' frescos and silk hangings were also intact and the Queen's bedroom was still jewel-like with filigreed woodwork and gilding.

But ownership by the *comune* gave it the kiss of death: nowadays, if you are lucky enough to get inside, you will see the gilded seats and the consoles lying broken in heaps, the silk hangings in tatters and the Queen's bedroom propped up against collapse. The *'chiuso per restauro'* notice seems in this case to be a screen behind which an uncaring owner has hidden. Maybe it's just that the local council's hands are tied by lack of funds. But whatever the reasons, the only hope now is an international restoration effort. Soon there will be nothing left.

Less important architecturally, but significant none the less for its associations, is the 18th century Villa Lampedusa, once the home of Giuseppe di Lampedusa, author of *The Leopard*. Even if your hunt for it among the rubbish of an old farm happens to be successful, a total ruin will greet you. It too manages to remain upright by some remarkable chance. More recent buildings have suffered just as much: Ernesto Basile's florid Liberty villa, the Villino Florio, for example, while intact externally, is a wreck inside – the victim of a mysterious fire.

These are selected highlights, but the list is endless and the story is the same all over Palermo. Parts of the ancient Castellammare and Kalsa quarters down by the port are filled with rubbish, and wastelands of empty, ancient houses are in an advanced state of ruin. Vast murky palace courtyards are filled with old abandoned Fiats and whole streets are walled off, their adjacent buildings too dangerous to approach.

After the war much of the population moved out from the centre,

attracted by newly built suburbs on the periphery. The richer inhabitants went in search of the creature comforts that their ancient
family homes could not provide. (They often simply closed their
palaces or off-loaded them to the highest bidder who, finding he
had bitten off more than he could chew, would chop them into flats
or leave them to decay.) Meanwhile the poor were shunted off into
new concrete apartment blocks even further out. And so Palermo
set off rapidly on the road to decline.

The real incentives for developing the periphery of town, at the
expense of the regenerating of the centre, were as it turned out
somewhat sinister. An official commission discovered that about
eighty per cent of the building contracts for the new apartments had
been awarded by the administration to the Mafia who, in return,
were supporting corrupt officials with controlled votes.

And that's not all: the new apartments were built on the edge of
the city on land which had fallen into the hands of speculators,
many of whom were also Mafia. The boom was on and the profits
piled up. Planning regulations were ignored (probably with the
help of Mafia partisans in the local planning departments) and
apartment blocks mushroomed. The wonderful Liberty villas with
their big gardens around the Viale della Libertà and the historic
parks on the outskirts of Palermo were decimated overnight by
mysterious fires.

This situation prevails even now. Even more sinister, apartments
were built as the quickest way to launder Mafia drug trafficking
profits. The suburbs have now absorbed so many people that in a
city of roughly 800,000 inhabitants (Palermo has the highest demo-
graphic growth in southern Italy, ensuring the need for new apartment blocks in the immediate future), only some 4000 remain in
the old centre where about 200,000 lived immediately after the
Second World War.

Some of the new suburban inhabitants regret moving and
would like to go back. But even the most corrupt administration
would never allow that. Within the last two years, old houses in the
ancient quarters have been known to collapse after severe rainstorms.
(Inadequately maintained, their sandstone fabric quickly erodes.)
On one occasion all the inhabitants of one house were killed.

What is being done about this? From time to time, and more so
recently, the fate of Palermo's *centro storico* is linked to its capacity
to attract votes in local elections. Bearing in mind that a united front
against the scourge of the Mafia emerged in recent years with some

show of strength, and that the Mafia are to a large extent to blame for the appalling condition of the *centro storico* today, politicians periodically find it expedient to discuss plans for its salvation. But how the administration could satisfy the electorate as well as the crooks, who are a fact of life in modern Palermo, especially bearing in mind the symbiotic relationship between politicians and the Mafia, is a question with no answer.

In 1989 and 1990, a rehabilitation plan known as the *Piana particolareggiato esecutivo*, was put forward and discussed in a local evening newspaper, *L'Ora*. The plan, known as the Ppe, would establish a commercial and residential environment in the centre of the city, its guiding visual principle being, rather idealistically, that the city should revert to its appearance at the end of the 19th century – the Palermo of *The Leopard*. Tunnels would be built under the port to remove the ever mounting pressure of traffic, war-time bomb sites would be cleared for new housing in styles sympathetic to their surroundings, and the old city fabric would be restored. To an outsider this sounds wonderful. Yet the vociferous opposition is fearful that the *centro* would never again be a viable commercial centre so long as one existed in the suburbs. Palermo would simply become a museum, they say. Some wonder whether funds for the Ppe's implementation would in fact ever reach their targets. Others are optimistic: they say that there is now no room outside Palermo for further development. The *centro* must inevitably be given a second chance. But would a regional government ever provide for a project that aims to demolish late 20th-century apartment blocks because they do not match the city's appearance at the turn of the century? In fact the inevitable political prevarication, and the intransigent idealism of its creators, make it unlikely that the Ppe will ever be put into practice. Thirty years on, everyone will still be discussing its merits and demerits. Such is the way of life in the city of Palermo.

Meanwhile, come and see what is left of it before it is too late.

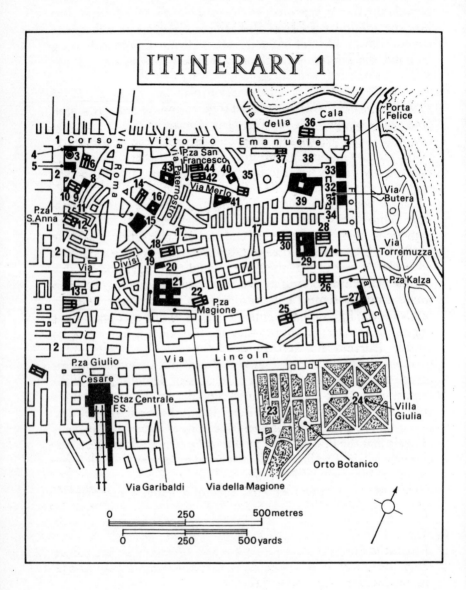

ITINERARY 1

Corso Vittorio Emanuele

Via della Cala

Porta Felice

Via Roma

P.za San Francesco

Via Paternostro

Via Merlo

P.za S.Anna

Via Divisi

Via Butera

Via Torremuzza

P.za Kalza

P.za Magione

Via Lincoln

P.za Giulio Cesare

Staz Centrale F.S.

Via Garibaldi

Via della Magione

Orto Botanico

Villa Giulia

Foro Italico

| 0 | 250 | 500 metres |
| 0 | 250 | 500 yards |

Itinerary One
The Eastern Quarter

The Lattarini, Fieravecchia and Kalsa regions: Quattro Canti,
Via Maqueda, Piazza Pretoria, Fontana Pretoria, Palazzo
Pretorio, Santa Caterina, Piazza Bellini, Teatro Bellini, La
Martorana, San Cataldo, Via Calderai, San Nicolò da Tolentino,
Palazzo Santa Croce-Sant'Elia, Sant'Anna, Palazzo Gangi,
Convent of Sant'Anna, Via Alloro, Piazza Rivoluzione, Fontana
di Panormus, Palazzo Scavuzzo, Palazzo Aiutamicristo, La
Magione, Orto Botanico Tropicale, Villa Giulia, Spasimo, Santa
Teresa, Palazzo Forcella, Madonna della Pietà, Palazzo
Abbatellis, Santa Maria degli Angeli, Casa Lampedusa, Hotel
Trinacria, Palazzo Butera, Marina, Piazza Marina, Santa Maria
della Catena, San Giovanni dei Napolitani, Zecca, Palazzo
Chiaramonte, Santa Maria dei Miracoli, Palazzo Fatta, Santa
Maria di Porto Salvo, Palazzo Mirto, San Francesco, Palazzo
Cattolica, Oratorio di San Lorenzo

This itinerary begins in the **Quattro Canti (1)** (also called the Piazza
Vigliena), the formal intersection of the Via Maqueda and the older
Corso Vittorio Emanuele. Planned by Giulio Lasso in 1608, its four
façades were each ornamented with Doric, Ionic and Corinthian
decoration, a fountain and statues of monarchs and Virtues. It was
built under the direction of Mariano Smiriglio (see Appendix II).
The whole scheme is not far removed from Sixtus V's Quattro
Fontane in Rome, another crossroads with a fountain at each corner.
From the Quattro Canti, walk south-east down the **Via Maqueda (2)**
in the direction of the railway station.

The **Piazza Pretoria (3)** is dominated by the **Fontana Pretoria (4)**,
a monumental construction originally destined for the Florentine

villa of Don Pietro di Toledo (a former Spanish viceroy), and designed in 1544 by Francesco Camilliani and Michelangelo Naccherino in a deranged Mannerist style. The piazza is also known as the Piazza della Vergogna – 'Place of Shame' – as the forty nude figures, both male and female, with which the fountain is decorated look with shameless interest at each other. Partisans of Mannerist sculpture will understand its quirks and the exaggeratedly affected stances of the figures and beasts surrounding it. But others will quite understand why Don Pietro's son chose to flog it to the Palermitans for 30,000 scudi in 1573. The piazza had to be remodelled to accommodate it. You may notice that the noses of various deities have been replaced. As the story goes, a gang of Messinese youths, insulted by the Palermitani who chopped off Neptune's penis on the Fountain of Neptune in their city, retaliated against the noses of the Fontana Pretoria figures.

Facing the fountain to the south-east is the **Palazzo Pretorio (5)**, the seat of the Mayor of Palermo. Crowding around its front door you will always see groups of dark-suited bureaucrats and demonstrators making points, presumably beneath the mayor's own windows. This rather stuffy looking building, conspicuous by its uniquely (for Palermo) spruced up condition, has been altered so many times that its original form is no longer recognisable. It is thought that a building for local government was first built on this site around 1300. If you can get into the courtyard you will see an elaborate baroque doorway by Paolo Amato (1634–1714, see Appendix II) and some 16th century frescos of the Crucifixion and the Virgin by Giuseppe Albina, known locally as 'the Dirty'. The building was Garibaldi's headquarters for a while, and from the balcony at the front he spoke to the Palermitani on 30 May 1860, after his initial successes. In fact Garibaldi was often to be seen sitting about on the steps of the fountain in front during lulls in the battle for the city.

On the east of the piazza is the side of the massive baroque church of **Santa Caterina (6)** which you enter from adjacent Piazza Bellini. It was begun in 1566, but its internal decoration is mostly 17th and 18th century and it is one of the most original churches in Palermo – a good place for the uninitiated to experience the full thwack of the Palermitan baroque. In fact, if time is short, and you have to limit yourself to one church only, this should be it. Anthony Blunt says 'the main lines of the architecture are left so clearly visible and so sharply defined that they impose an order on the exuberant colour and carving. This is indeed Sicilian Baroque in one of its most typical manifestations'. Orgiastic ceiling frescos, and wall surfaces rippling with sculpture and ablaze with different coloured marble, make its interior magnificently overwhelming. Illusionistic works – 18th century frescos by Filippo Randazzo on the nave ceiling and Vito d'Anna in the dome – heighten the senses while the colours and textures cavorting around the walls extort an emotional response to the ritual at the altar.

Perhaps the most magnificent elements of this interior are the inlaid, mixed marbles. Examine them in detail – start perhaps with the panel depicting the story of Jonah on the first pillar on the right of the nave. Here the whale is orange, and Jonah, before his meeting with fate, is yellow. Notice that the rigging of the ship is actually made from little pieces of wire. The scene on the next pillar depicts the Sacrifice of Isaac, equally worth a close look.

The choir and the Chapel of St Catherine in the left-hand transept are both also particularly fine: the former is the work of Giacomo Amato (1643–1732, see Appendix II), as is the altar with its tabernacle of amethyst; the latter was designed by Andrea Palma (1664–1730, see Appendix II). Filled with different marbles, it provides a lavish showcase for Antonello Gagini's (see Appendix II) statue of St Catherine (1534). The richness is kept just short of vulgarity by its astonishing versatility.

Backing on to the Piazza Pretoria is the **Piazza Bellini (7)**, containing an extraordinary conglomeration of buildings in which the layers of Palermo's history are visible piled one on top of another. Apart from the **Teatro Bellini (8)**, now an excellent pizzeria, the most conspicuous buildings are the churches of the **Martorana (9)** and **San Cataldo (10)**, which sit side by side on a raised platform (part of the Roman walls). San Cataldo sports little flat-topped red domes. Both are among the earliest surviving buildings in the city.

The Martorana, the real name of which is Santa Maria dell'Ammiraglio and which was named after its founder, Roger II's Admiral, George of Antioch, was consecrated in 1143 during the reign of that great Norman king. It was in this church in 1295 that the Sicilian nobles met to decide, in the wake of the Sicilian Vespers, to offer the crown of Sicily to Frederick of Aragon. Eloisa Martorana founded in 1193 the now vanished convent to which the church was presented in the 15th century. The nuns were once famous for their marzipan fruit which the Palermitani still call *frutta di Martorana*. So skilled were they, the story has it, that the different marzipan fruits they hung from trees in their garden deceived a visiting archbishop.

The Martorana church offers the satisfying challenge of unravelling the layers of its past. The original plan of the building (which includes the bulk of the present nave) derives from the tradition of mosque building, and the craftsmen responsible for it here were probably Islamic. All the mosaics are Norman and are roughly contemporary with those in the Cappella Reale (see Chapter 4). The church was renovated in 1588, enlarged in 1683, fell victim to the earthquake of 1726 (when the campanile collapsed), and was restored by Giuseppe Patricolo in the 19th century.

After the king himself George of Antioch was the most powerful man in Sicily – he had the rank Emir of Emirs and Admiral of Admirals. He was also an orthodox Greek Christian. This is the context in which you have to read the mosaic decorations. The craftsmen who made them were probably Greek, heirs to the Byzantine tradition which, under Arab domination of Sicily, had not been entirely lost. In the dome is a mosaic depicting Christ Enthroned; between the dome and the altar is the Annunciation and the Presentation in the Temple; in the left apse is St Joseph, in the right one St Anna – they, the Virgin's parents, probably originally flanked an image of the Virgin herself in the main apse (now gone); in the vaults down the side are the Apostles; near the left pier the Nativity and near the right pier is the Dormition of the Virgin – you find these facing each other just before you look up into the dome. Most interesting is the mosaic in the right-hand aisle, of King Roger receiving the Imperial Diadem from Christ. The political implications of this would not have been lost on the congregation: Roger modelled his concept of royal authority on that of Justinian, the illusion being that the king's authority came from God alone. In a corner of the left-side aisle is an image of George of Antioch himself.

If you go to this church early in the morning, when it first opens, you will have it to yourself: the shadowy Norman structure and the staring eyes of the mosaic figures impart a sense of mystery which somehow becomes elusive if the building is filled with people – which it generally is. No external feature of the Martorana is preparation for the controlled richness within.

San Cataldo (10) is quite different. Its brooding, shadowy interior is practically devoid of decoration and the 'sculpted' masses of the three domes, the squinches and the columns that support them are the chief visual interest. Its style is more obviously Muslim than the Martorana's. Founded in 1154 by William I's chancellor, Maio of Bari, in 1182 it became the chapel of the Benedictines and so remained until it was transformed into a post office in 1787. This church also was restored by Patricolo in the 19th century.

Continue down the Via Maqueda, which crosses the southern end of the Piazza Bellini. The **Via Calderai (11)** branches off to the left: this street was the traditional haunt of Palermo's iron- and copper-smiths. Each artisan had his own forge and workshop here and until the end of the 1960s you could still bring things for repair. Everyone – even people from the outlying villages – knew about the Via Calderai, which sold everything from nails to farming implements.

Continue down the Via Maqueda to the 17th century church of **San Nicolò da Tolentino (12)**, contained within the walls of the former synagogue in the centre of what had been, from the 9th century until the end of the 15th century, Palermo's Jewish quarter. In Muslim Palermo this was the Harat-al-Yahud and its synagogue was called the Meschita, commemorated today by the Piazzetta Meschita directly behind San Nicolò (go down the Via Giardiniaccio, a little further down the Via Maqueda, and turn left).

Back in the Via Maqueda, between the Piazza Nicolò Scalzi and the Via Santa Rosalia, is the façade of the **Palazzo Santa Croce-Sant'Elia (13)**. This massive palace, one of the most impressive baroque buildings in Palermo, was constructed in the middle of the 18th century for Tomaso Celestri e Grimaldi, Marquis of Santa Croce. Although the name of its architect is not known for certain, it is thought that Giovanni Battista Vaccarini (1702–68, see Catania, Chapter 13, also Appendix II) may have had something to do with it. It has been closed for forty years, since it was sold for a conversion to flats that never happened, and if you wander through the vast ancestral entrance portal which opens on to an inner courtyard, and which takes up one of the building's fifteen bays, you will notice that everything is in an advanced state of dilapidation. A variety of ornate urns, allegorical figures of Plenty and Justice and a copy of the Farnese Hercules all cling desperately to the remnants of niches built there to house them, and boarded up windows partially obscured by bedraggled creepers present a miserable spectacle. Notice though the alternating window pediment designs on the street front. Together with the ornately bulbous wrought-iron balconies at *piano nobile* and mezzanine level, they were designed to keep the façade from monotony. Above the entrance are Tommaso Ferriolo's stucco putti unveiling the owner's heraldic device.

This building raises beguiling questions; there are few records of what it looks like inside. Is it furnished? And why, from time to time, have bits of internal stucco work been found scattered about the Via Maqueda? Fulco Verdura remembers being there in his youth (his book *Happy Summer Days* describes his childhood in Palermo), and mentions 'the ... twin staircases and lugubrious, very high-ceilinged rooms'.

Beyond the Palazzo Santa Croce-Sant'Elia, go left into the Via Santa Rosalia (taking a look as you go at the haphazard rear of the palace) and continue down to the Via Roma. Turn left and, keeping to the opposite side of the road, make for the Via Sant'Anna which opens into the Piazza Sant'Anna. There are two important things to see here: the church of Sant'Anna (14), 1606–32, and the Palazzo Gangi. The billowing serpentine façade of the former, built by Giovanni Biagio Amico (1685–1754, see Appendix II) around 1736 (see San Lorenzo at Trapani, his other great building), is a particularly dramatic example of Palermitan baroque. The external statues are by Giacomo Pennino and Lorenzo Marabitti (after designs by Giacomo Serpotta) but, apart from Vito d'Anna's *Ascension* in the left-hand transept, and the 17th century fresco of Santa Rosalia with its view of Palermo, in the fourth chapel on the right, the interior is not very remarkable.

Without a map or a guide, you will undoubtedly have great difficulty finding the Palazzo Gangi (15). Sometimes it is known as the Palazzo Valguarnera-Ganci, and at other times as the Palazzo San Vincenzo. It depends on which branch of the family owns it at the time, and you can bet your last lira that the locals – even the man in the kiosk on the corner – will have never heard of it; they will enthusiastically misdirect you to some quite different place. But, for the informed, this palace opens on to the Piazza Croce dei Vespri which is adjacent to Piazza Sant'Anna. It is the one with the large Alsatian guarding its courtyard and is the piazza's only building in good condition. It is highly unlikely that you will be able to get inside unless you go there to a wedding (the owners no longer live in it but hire out some of its rooms for parties), bribe the porter, or know a friend of the presiding princess. But, should you be lucky, you will see beyond the external 18th century staircase designed by an unknown architect into a cavernous entrance hall hung with painted leather. Beyond this, at the end of a suite of *salone* hung with old damask and cluttered with porcelain and paintings, is the legendary Galleria degli Specchi, the palace ballroom, about which a visiting French author remarked 'Versailles n'a rien de plus'.

Dating from the first half of the 18th century (and possibly the work of Filippo Juvarra), this room is the most remarkable excercise in unrestrained adornment to have survived in any domestic building in the city. Not only are the walls caked with filigreed, gilded rococo panelling, old dappled looking-glasses in gilt frames, and delicate painted swirls, but the ceiling has two levels, the lower of which is pierced to reveal a higher coved area painted with frescos of allegorical subjects (the work of Gaspare Serenario). The gilding and the encrustation ripples around the room, piles high above the looking-glasses, then leaps up to the ceiling in a flurry of illusionistic architectural devices, putti, swags and clouds. The floor is of ancient majolica depicting patterns and animals, including leopards. This remarkable room is still furnished with its original, and rather unyielding, gilded sofas and stools, and there are huge velvet covered banquettes, great rococo candle sconces attached to the walls, and vast, low-flying chandeliers in Murano glass hanging from the upper ceiling.

If you cannot gain entry, then go and see Visconti's film of Giuseppe di Lampedusa's book *The Leopard*. He uses the magnificent Galleria degli Specchi for the Ponteleone Ball. In the book, the scene is set in the ballroom of the Palazzo Monteleone, which faces the Piazza San Domenico. But that room no longer exists and of all Palermitan palaces with ballrooms still intact, the Palazzo Gangi, which would have been 'old fashioned' to the books characters, was the best for Visconti's purposes.

Facing the Palazzo Gangi in the Piazza Croce dei Vespri, are the remains of the Franciscan **Convent of Sant'Anna (16)**, now a car park and general all-purpose tip. Its colonnaded cloister, which can be seen from the street through a rather mannered early 17th century portal, is surrounded by dilapidated conventual buildings. They replace a palace built on the site by Jean de Saint-Remy, Charles of Anjou's Prefect of Palermo. During the Sicilian Vespers in 1282, the Sicilian Palermitans, responding to the cry, '*moranu li Franchiski*' – 'death to the French', murdered with few exceptions every French man, woman and child they could find. Nearly 2000 corpses from the palace were buried in this piazza. The column on the corner of the square is a commemorative one erected in the 19th century.

The south-east corner of the Piazza Croce dei Vespri (go past the column) leads to the Piazza D'Aragona situated in the heart of the Lattarini quarter and home to shops traditionally selling hemp and textiles. In the days of the Arabs it was the spice market called the Souk-el-altarin.

One of Palermo's most distinguished old streets leads out of the Piazza D'Aragona: the **Via Alloro (17)**. Although it does not form a part of the itinerary, for reasons which will become obvious if you walk only two thirds of the way down it, it was once favoured by the medieval aristocracy who lined it with their palaces. A great many survived in altered, renovated or rebuilt form until the Second World War, but with one or two unremarkable exceptions they have now gone and the street is mostly derelict. Halfway along, on the right-hand side (at No 54), are the pitiful remains of the Palazzo Bonagia which had what Anthony Blunt calls the most spectacular of all Palermitan staircases. Attributed to Andrea Giganti of Trapani (1731–87, see Appendix II), it was a late baroque master-piece of inventive genius: the staircase acted as a bridge between two opposite wings of the same building. Its architectonic elements were picked out in different coloured stone – either tufa or marble. Sadly the palace was hit by a bomb during the last war but remarkably the stair survived unscathed. It was, though, allowed to succumb to absolute dereliction thereafter. If you squeeze through the tin hoarding surrounding this aristocratic skeleton, you will see Giganti's masterpiece lying about in heaps, awaiting, we are told, eventual reconstruction.

Further along, on the opposite side of the road and just by the Vicolo Palagonia all'Alloro, was the Palazzo Palagonia where Nelson and Lady Hamilton lived when the Neapolitan Court was here in exile. It made a suitable embassy because its *salone* (some of them decorated in the Chinoiserie style) were so magnificent. Well, these are now only a memory preserved in diaries and letters of the period; the palace itself is a pile of rubble in a huge hole.

Retrace your steps up the Via Alloro and turn left just before the Piazza D'Aragona into the **Piazza Rivoluzione (18)**. This is the ancient Fiera Vecchia, the site of the old market, chosen because so many of the old routes coming in and out of the city passed this way via the old Porta Termini, the city's east gate which was situated at the end of the Via Garibaldi. That gracious old street leads out beneath the washing lines from the south side. At the centre of Piazza is the **Fontana di Panormus (19)**, a fountain also known as the

Genius of Palermo, which was erected here in 1684 as a symbol of municipal majesty. At its centre is a statue of a bearded old man sitting on a pile of stones, a crown on his head and a snake in his hand.

In 1820 a revolt against the Bourbons began in this piazza, as did another led by Giuseppe La Masa as part of the abortive revolt of 1848 (a wall plaque commemorates six patriots who were shot here in 1850). And on 27 May, 1860, it was the triumphant scene of Garibaldi's entry into Palermo. Immediately after having broken into the city from the outlying countryside via the Porta Termini (now the Porta Garibaldi) and the long straight Strada di Porta Termini (the Via Garibaldi), he rushed into the piazza yelling '*Avanti! Avanti! Entrate nel centro!*'. Christopher Hibbert writes in *Garibaldi and his Enemies* that 'the Sicilian *picciotti* [Garibaldi's men] had now come up to the cross-roads by . . . the Porta Termini; but the cross-fire was still strong here and they dared not cross the road . . . it was not until a young Genoese placed a chair in the middle of the road and calmly sat down on it with his legs crossed, under a tri-colour flag, that the *picciotti* were prepared to believe that they might survive the crossing. And then. . . they dashed across the road . . . towards the Fiera Vecchia. Here Garibaldi, astride his horse . . . [was] now the centre of a wildly excited, cheering crowd.'

Overlooking the Fiera Vecchia, on the south-east corner of the square, is the **Palazzo Scavuzzo (20)**, built in the 16th century for the family of the same name. It is also sometimes known as the Palazzo Trigona. Apart from being architecturally interesting – an impressive Renaissance palace with anachronistic Gothic archivolts and a simple, almost medieval, entrance portal with sculpted imposts – it was the home of the Trigona family, one of whose members was the ill-fated Giulia, Countess Trigona of Sant'Elia, lady-in-waiting to Queen Elena at the Quirinale Palace in Rome, and aunt of Giuseppe di Lampedusa. Giulia was the central figure in a notorious scandal that rocked Palermitan society in the 1890s. She fell in love with a notorious gambler, Baron Vincenzo Paternò del Cugno, though his passion only lasted as long as she agreed to pay his debts. Then, when eventually her husband agreed to a separation with a financial settlement in 1911, del Cugno demanded that she give him a share of it. The Countess refused, and ended up with her throat slit and back stabbed in a sleazy hotel near the station in Rome to which her lover had lured her. Del Cugno tried to shoot himself but was unsuccessful and in 1912 was sentenced to life imprisonment. In 1942, however, he was freed by Mussolini. Trigonas still live in a part of the palace, though presumably Giulia's payments to her lover depleted the family fortune because it is a shadow of its former self.

One façade of the building faces on to the Via Garibaldi. This at one time was one of Palermo's finest streets, and still is in a way, but its elegance is now smudged by grime and obscured by electric cables and washing lines laden with drying sheets. On the left-hand side, beyond the Palazzo Scavuzzo, is the **Palazzo Aiutamicristo (21)**, built in 1490 by Matteo Carnilivari for the Baron of Calatafimi and Misilmeri, Guglielmo Aiutamicristo. It sits serenely amidst a scene of urban chaos, sporting on its street façade Catalan-Gothic details which you can see quite clearly if you unpick in your mind's eye the baroque encrustations on top of them. In the main courtyard the original detailing is finer and more distinct, and here you get a clearer impression of the building's great age. Amongst its more illustrious visitors was Charles V who stayed here on his way back from Tunis in 1535.

Beyond, in the Via delle Magione, is the church of the **Magione (22)**. This was founded in 1150 by Matteo D'Aiello, chancellor to King Roger II, and given to the Cistercian Order. Although it is one of the great local Norman buildings, it tends to be eclipsed by the others because of the damage it suffered during the last war. But now a gargantuan restoration programme has revealed the building's ancient structure and its monumental gravity. If you walk around to the back, you will see the the original interlaced blind arcading, while inside there are ogive arches on great solid piers. Inside it is plain and mostly unadorned, except for the original painted wooden ceiling, some tombs of Teutonic knights and a late 15th century stucco relief of the Pietà from the workshop of the Gagini (see Appendix II).

Cross the bombed-out Piazza Magione behind the building, then turn right into the Via Rao and continue until you reach the Via Abramo Lincoln. Turn left. The Via Lincoln leads down to the sea, passing on the way the **Orto Botanico Tropicale (23)**, the Botanic Gardens, and the lush Villa Giulia, a formal garden laid out in the 18th century on the edge of the Marina.

The Botanic Gardens were founded in 1785 and today they contain some magnificent specimens of palm and *ficus magnoliodes*. At their centre is the so-called Gymnasium which houses the library and the Herbarium and which is flanked by Venanzio Marvuglia's Calidarium and Tepidarium. The handsome neo-classical Gymnasium was designed between 1785 and 1795 by Léon Dufourny, a French architect and archaeologist who came to Sicily to study the Doric elements of classical architecture. Having examined the temples at Agrigento, he produced this massive building with an interior dominated by a central domed circular hall. The stucco decoration is by Gaspare Ferriolo, who also did the statues of the four seasons on top of the portico facing on to the gardens. The building is a fairly free interpretation of the Doric style, and is thought to be the very earliest attempt in Sicily to revive it; it set 19th century architects off in a search for 'national' styles of architecture from Doric to Arab-Norman.

Next door is the **Villa Giulia (24)**, the very first gardens laid out outside the city walls (1777-8). They were designed by Nicolò Palma at the instigation of the Viceroy Prince Colonna di Stigliano, after whose wife they were named. The Marquis Villabianca in the 18th century called them '*villa delle delizie*', gardens of delight, a description that Goethe himself might have used. He thought them 'the most wonderful spot on earth' and found that they could easily transport 'one back into the antique world'.

They were, and still are, laid out formally with parterres, arbours and fountains, and there are formal avenues, statues and classical-style pavilions dotted about amongst the undergrowth. But while they still contain some splendid specimens of local flora, they have gone the way of most public gardens and are now a bit dog-eared and frayed around the edges. If you do not have much time, make straight for the very centre and sit on one of the marble benches whose seats are supported by, instead of legs, carved stone volutes. Their 'squashed' appearance gives the illusion that they are giving beneath your weight. Behind the seats are the frescoed exedrae, four faintly Pompeian pavilions designed by Giuseppe Damiani Almeyda in 1866. In the very centre of this arena is a fountain that supports a late 18th century sundial showing the hours of the day. It is by a mathematician, Lorenzo Federici. There are other interesting locations scattered about the gardens. To the west is a second fountain named the Genius of Palermo, the allegorical figures on it were sculpted by Ignazio Marabitti late in the 18th century. The niche figures originally adorned a fountain once in the Piazza Sant' Anna, but now lost, and are by Lorenzo Marabitti. They date from 1735. To the south is a mangy lion in a cage – perhaps a latent remnant of the Sicilian love of exotic wild animals – even Frederick II had an elephant. According to Fulco Verdura there was once also an orangutan called Bernando, who lived next door to the lion.

Verdura, as a child, despised the city's public gardens filled with 'pallid children making little sandheaps'. Quite other feelings were invoked in the Prince of Paternò who in the 18th century was so excited by the idea of these pleasure grounds that he donated a large sum in gold to be spent in perpetuity on musical entertainment. As a result there is still music in the Villa Giulia from 1 April – 30 September, for part of the day and also for some of the night.

Across the road from the gardens is the Kalsa quarter, with its chaotic architectural environment, narrow streets and, sadly, large areas of wartime dereliction. Among its most venerated relics are the remains of the church of the **Spasimo (25)**, founded in 1508, which you enter from the Piazza Spasimo. The history of this building has never been happy: abandoned for several years, it was last used after the Second World War as a depository for archaeological and artistic material taken from a variety of destroyed and partially destroyed buildings around the city. Now it is a ruin, though extensive restoration is planned. Raphael's '*Spasimo di Sicilia*' was commissioned for this church in 1517 but when the Olivetan fathers sold the building and its convent to the Senate in 1573 they transferred the painting to Santo Spirito, outside Palermo's walls. In 1661 it was given to the Viceroy D'Aya, who gave it to Phillip IV of Spain, which is why it is in the Prado today.

Bearing north-west from the Piazza Spasimo, you will find yourself in the Piazza dei Bianchi overlooking which are the remains of the Oratorio dei Bianchi. This was the headquarters of a guild founded in 1550 to pray for the souls of condemned prisoners. 'White Brothers' would trail behind a victim on his way to the scaffold, urging him to confess in return for the Church's pardon.

Back in the Piazza Spasimo, turn towards the sea, going down the Via Santa Teresa to the Piazza della Kalsa, stopping in at the church of **Santa Teresa (26)** on the way. The façade of this imposing baroque monument dates from 1686 and it was built for the Barefoot Carmelites by Giacomo Amato, one of Palermo's most important early baroque architects. Its façade has a lively, loose design though it is less moulded than say Sant' Anna, built a few years later. Amato used as his model Carlo Rainaldi's Santa Maria in Campitelli (begun in 1663) which he had seen in Rome.

Inside is a rare surviving example of Amato's interior decoration,

enriched with a glorious array of stuccos, statues, altars and paintings (in particular you should see Santa Teresa by the Flemish
painter Borremans in the second chapel on the left, and the Holy
Family attributed to Vito d'Anna in the first chapel on the right).
The stuccos in the nave and on the vault were made by Giuseppe
and Procopio Serpotta in 1702 (see Appendix II); in fact their statues
of Santa Teresa and Sant' Anna (on either side of the altar) are the
church's best pieces. See also Ignazio Marabitti's marble group in
the second chapel on the right.

On the seaward side of the Piazza della Kalsa is the eccentric
Arab-Norman looking **Palazzo Forcella (27)**, built in the 19th century for the Marquis of Forcella on the ruins of an old city gate called
the Porta dei Greci. Having been a private palace it then became a
nightclub and is now a rather sorry ruin. The Via Torremuzza leads
north-west out of the piazza, cutting across the bottom of the Via
Alloro. At the crossroads is the church of the Madonna della Pietà,
next door to which is the Palazzo Abbatellis and the Church of
Santa Maria degli Angeli. Going the other way out of the Piazza
della Kalsa, to the right, the Via Cervello leads to the Villa Giulia
and the Porta Reale (1784), a magnificent gateway with two out-
stretched 'arms'.

But back to the Via Torremuzza: notice the façade of the Palazzo
Torremuzza, just to the right of the Santa Teresa. Opposite is the
church of San Mattia with its monastery of the Holy Cross, both
designed by Giacomo Amato in 1686. The church has a bold façade
notable now mainly for its supremely derelict state. It is flanked to
the north-west by the 18th century Palazzo Petrulla.

On the corner of the Via Alloro and the Via Torremuzza is the
church of the **Madonna della Pietà (28)**, another magnificent early
baroque building by Giacomo Amato dating from 1689. It is more
fluid and more boldly articulated than Santa Teresa, though it owes
as much to Rainaldi. Inside, the key thing to see is the vault of the
nave, where Procopio Serpotta's rich and varied stucco frames surround Antonio Grano's illusionistic *Glory of the Dominican Order*.
See the gilded wood and stucco frame to Vincenzo da Pavia's 16th
century Pietà in the third chapel on the right – a decorative project
of Amato's. Pietro dell'Aquila designed the mythical men and
beasts who hold up the musicians' galleries nearest the altar. The
eclectic decoration of this interior is a foretaste of things to come in
Palermo.

Going up the Via Alloro, behind the church of the Madonna

della Pietà is the vast and ancient 15th century palace of Francesco Abbatellis (or Patella), called the **Palazzo Abbatellis (29)**. The work of Matteo Carnelivari, it is particularly memorable for its portal on to Via Alloro, a bizarre rendition of several architectural styles skilfully entangled which, if unravelled, reveals principally florid Catalan-Gothic and early Renaissance forms. The struggle of these two styles for supremacy creates a tension which gives the Palermitan architecture of that period its vigour. The building was badly damaged in the Second World War but was restored and adapted by Carlo Scarpa for use as the Galleria Nazionale della Sicilia. Here you can follow the development of Sicilian painting from its Byzantine origins. In particular you should look for the mid 15th century fresco *The Triumph of Death*, originally painted for the Palazzo Sclafani in the Piazza della Vittoria. The skeletal archer on his scrawny horse of death, pushing through crowds who surrender to oblivion under his arrows, is an image that stays in the memory. There is also an Annunciation by Antonello da Messina and the full gamut of local baroque: Pietro Novelli (1603–47, see Appendix II), Vito d'Anna, Borremans, Martorana and others. Francesco Laurana's (1430–1502, see Appendix II) exquisitely sculpted head of Eleanora of Aragon is kept here and there is a whole host of works by Giacomo Serpotta, Palermo's baroque master *stuccatore* (1656–1732, see Appendix II).

Flanking the Palazzo Abbatellis is **Santa Maria degli Angeli (30)**, also known as La Gancia, which contains almost as many venerable works of art as the gallery next door. A few highlights are the stuccos by Giacomo Serpotta in the chapel of the Sposalizio immediately to the left of the high altar (the paintings are by Vincenzo da Pavia) and in the corresponding chapel of the Madonna of Guadalupa to the right of the altar. And there are some (rather doubtful) illustrious attributions – for instance the painting of St Michael in the 7th chapel on the left is 'thought' to be by Antonello da Messina.

Hidden away is the building's least known treasure: if you can get in, go to the Oratorio dei Pescatori, now used as the reading room of the adjacent Archivio di Stato – just within the cloister of La Gancia. Its interior is covered in stuccos and frescos of the life of St Peter and, on the vault, of St Francis. The names of the *stuccatori* involved are unknown, but their work is clearly of the 18th century, and is fantastic even by Palermo's standards.

As you pass back down the Via Alloro, you will see what is called the Salvation window in the flank of La Gancia. During the 1860 anti-Bourbon revolt, two revolutionaries hid amongst the corpses in La Gancia's crypt. Knowing that they would inevitably be discovered and shot (if they didn't die of hunger first), they escaped out of this hold to freedom while local women diverted the Bourbon soldiers' attention by causing a commotion in the street outside.

Turn left into the Via Butera. The first thing you will notice as you walk along it, dodging children, Vespas, emaciated cats and laundry plunging from washing lines above, is that there is only one building in it in excellent condition. This is the **Casa Lampedusa (31)**, purchased after the war by the Prince of Lampedusa, who wrote *The Leopard*, to replace the destroyed Palazzo Lampedusa (Chapter 3). Here the author lived out the last ten years of his life. By palazzo standards it is fairly small. The 18th century façade overlooking the Marina is its most splendid aspect: this is one of the most scenic stretches of Palermo with views extending out to the bay.

The **Hotel Trinacria (32)** also has Lampedusa associations. Here *The Leopard's* Don Fabrizio, Prince of Salina, dies. From his little room overlooking the sea he could (allowing for just a little bit of artistic licence) 'turn his head to the left; beside Monte Pellegrino could be seen a cleft in the circle of hills and, beyond, two hillocks at whose feet lay his home' [the Villa Lampedusa].

For years the Trinacria was just a dirty tenement. But after the restoration now in progress it will take its place alongside other Palermitan curiosities. It first became a hotel in 1844, after conversion from a private theatre, and its first illustrious guests were the King of Bavaria and his suite. But its moment of glory came during the days of the 1000, when wounded and ravenous Garibaldini were housed by the long suffering patron Salvatore Ragusa. Later that century, still run by the attentive Ragusa, it seems to have attracted Anglo-Saxons and it had an enviable reputation: 'one of the best . . . south of the Alps', said the John Murray Handbook of 1892. It closed in 1911.

The Via Butera's most impressive building is without doubt the **Palazzo Butera (33)**. Until recently the north-western end of this huge palace was a gaping hole, wrenched open by a stray Allied bomb. This end of it was once called the Palazzo Benso and here Goethe stayed. The Prince of Butera, the richest man in Sicily (in the 19th century he had an annual income of £60,000) bought it in 1801 and incorporated it into his palace.

The 17th century Palazzo Butera is almost as magnificent now as it was in the past. Still private, it easily equals the grandest European

palaces, its 'interminable vista of rooms' (Fulco Verdura) filled with
baroque and Louis XV furniture beneath 18th century frescos by
Gioacchino Martorana. Even its tapestries were embroidered with
pearls and at the end of the 19th century the household footmen
wore silver mitres and had the family crest emblazoned on their
stockings. In fact, so rich was the livery worn by the staff that at the
frequent fancy dress balls it was nearly impossible to tell who was in
disguise and who was not.

The magnificence of this establishment was matched by its illustrious occupants, the Branciforte and the Lanza, two of the great
families of Palermo. The family who have the house today are the
descendants of the 'grandest woman in Sicily' (according to Raleigh
Trevelyan), Stefania Branciforte e Branciforte, Princess of Butera,
Scordia, Pietrapertosa, Leonforte, Campofiorito di Catena, Radali,
Countess of Mazzarino and so on, who married, some time at the
end of the 18th century, Giuseppe Lanza, Prince of Trabia. She gave
one of her titles, that of Radali, to her lover, and her various
descendants shared out what was left on her death. The labyrinthine
ramifications of who is related to whom in Palermitan high society
today are extremely puzzling as a result.

It is hard to imagine life inside a palace as vast as this. At a party in
1799 some 300 guests were served dinner and supper which included
such copious supplies of ice cream, says Mary Taylor Simeti in
Sicilian Food, that 11,000 lbs of snow were consumed in its preparation. 'Pleasant indeed it must have been to stroll between one
quadrille and another upon the terrace . . . and to look out across
the waterfront to the sea and savour the cool sweetness of a *granita di
limone* or a cinnamon sorbet.' In its heyday the palace was filled with
retainers and hangers-on, and was run like a small village. Giovanni
Verga in his book *Maestro Don Gesualdo* (set in the first half of the
19th century) captures a sense of the scale of living and of domestic
ritual in an aristocratic household. Don Gesualdo stays in his daughter's house in Palermo: 'a great palace so vast that you lost yourself inside it. Everywhere curtains and carpets till you didn't know
where to put your foot'. It had 'an army of . . . lackeys and chamber-
men . . . Everything regulated by a bell ringing, with as much
ceremony as high mass – to get a glass of water, or to go to your
daughter's room. And the duke dressing himself up at meal-times
as if he was going to his wedding'.

At the turn of the century, Palermo became the theatre in which
southern Europe's version of the Belle Epoque ran its course; this

was the last enchanted moment in Sicily's history and the Palazzo Butera was centre stage. Lavish receptions were held on a regular basis on its terrace overlooking the Marina, and what better excuse to entertain than when some foreign royal was passing by? The balustraded terrace is still there as magnificent as ever with its majolica tiling, vaguely chinoiserie wrought-iron gazebos and exotic smelling jasmine. But the most you are likely to see of the palazzo now, unless you hire the ballroom for a wedding or a private party, is the inner atrium which is guarded, like the Palazzo Gangi, by a large ferocious hound chained to the wall. And if you did get inside, you would not see very much of the famous Butera furniture: that has been removed to the family villa at Bagheria – the Villa Trabia (see Chapter 8).

Beyond the Palazzo Butera, the Porta Felice opens on to the **Marina (34)**, a large open space once the pride of the city. Nowadays it is mostly taken up by a large highway which leads out of town via Romagnolo and the coastal suburbs to Bagheria.

Both Goethe and Brydone were enchanted with this spot. Brydone found the Porta Felice the 'handsomest of all [the city gates]', opening to the 'Marino – a delightful walk which constitutes one of the great pleasures of the nobility of Palermo . . . it is bounded on one side by the wall of the city, and on the other by the sea, from whence, even at this scorching season, there is always an agreeable breeze. In the centre of the Marino they have lately erected an elegant kind of temple, which, during the summer months, is made use of as an orchestra for music . . . the concert does not begin till the clock strikes midnight, which is the signal for the symphony to strike up: at that time the walk is crowded with carriages and people on foot . . .'. The scene is quite different today. Although the usual Italian *passeggiata* still takes place here in the evenings, Brydone's elegant temple has been replaced by a Luna Park festooned with gaudy lights. To reach it you risk being flattened by traffic driven at a speed more suitable for Le Mans.

It is hard to imagine the Prince of Lampedusa in the early 19th century driving his carriage, as he did, naked along the Marina. This offence had him banished for a period to his country estate at Santa Margherita di Belice. No doubt the noble prince's exhibitionism had something to do with the Marina's reputation as a louche point of rendezvous. Certain bars, beaches and pavements inexplicably become pick-up places, and so did the Marina for the Palermitan upper classes. 'The better to savour pleasure and intrigue,' Brydone continues, 'there is an order, that no person, of whatever quality, shall presume to carry a light with him [on the Marina]. The flambeaux are extinguished at the Porta Felice, where the servants wait for the return of the carriages; and the company generally continue an hour or two in utter darkness; except when the intruding moon, with her horns and her chastity comes to disturb them. The concert finishes about two in the morning, when, for the most part, every husband goes home to his own wife. This is an admirable institution, and never produces any scandal: no husband is so scandalous as to deny his wife the Marino; and the ladies . . . very often put on masks.' Indeed Brydone also noted that 'the ladies are very prolific'. He had recently been to yet another 'lying-in' of a pregnant princess and found that there were 'for the most part three or four of these assemblies going on in the city at the same time'. 'Possibly the Marino may not a little contribute towards [these],' he thought.

Well, the Palermitans will not have changed their habits all that much though the venue for illicit liaisons these days seems to be the Villa Giulia just across the way – and why wait for darkness to obscure the view?

The Marina, once one of the most beautiful waterfronts in Europe, is now one of the tragedies of contemporary Palermo, though if you wander along it in the spring when the eritrina trees are in blossom, closing your mind to the traffic and the funfair opposite, the atmosphere can be as charmed as it was in the past. It is still flanked by an early wall of the city, although nothing like as formidable as it once was. The terrace of the Palazzo Butera and the gardens of the Casa Lampedusa back on to the Cattive, a walkway on top of the wall which was opened after 1823 and to which access is via a flight of steps just behind the Porta Felice. Cattive translates as 'bad-tempered', a name it acquired because widows and spinsters used to sit here and glower at the goings-on below. For years the Cattive was closed, but a recent imaginative decision by the *comune* has reopened this walk, one of the most pleasant in the city if you do not mind stepping over the broken majolica tiles of its pavement. It is lined with stone benches resting on slowly squashing volutes – like those in the Villa Giulia – and with busts of unknown deities and tufa herms by Girolamo Bagnasco. Just behind you are tantalizing glimpses of the gilded *piano nobile* of the Palazzo Butera.

The **Piazza Marina (35)** is the first stop on the way up the Corso

Vittorio Emanuele from the Piazza Butera. This vast piazza has had a varied history: at one time it was a part of the Cala, the 'Allhaven' of antiquity, but it began to silt up in the days of Arab Palermo and by the 16th century was completely covered over. It became a popular venue for local fairs, feasts, tournaments, markets and other public celebrations, and was immensely popular as the place of public execution. The grander citizens were allowed the dignity of a quick death by guillotine while other, lesser, mortals were first pilloried then dispatched more slowly. Under the Spanish Inquisitors many a heretic met his end here. The condemned were kept ready and waiting in two nearby prisons – in that of the Spanish Inquisition in the Palazzo Chiaramonte (the Steri) in the south-east corner of the square, and in the Vicaria, Palermo's jail, which stood in the north-western corner where the Palazzo delle Finanze is now. The Corso Vittorio Emanuele, where it cuts the piazza at its northern end, was known when it was first opened as the Via Cassaro Morto.

As you enter the piazza from the Corso, you see on the left the little 16th century church of **Santa Maria della Catena (36)**. Ever since the Norman period there has been a church on this spot, which marks the anchorage point of a great chain – *catena* – closing off the harbour. In this church you see again the tension between Gothic (in this case Catalan-Gothic) and Renaissance styles. Inside, for example, the columns have fine composite capitals but stand on Gothic bases and carry Gothic ribbed vaulting.

Diagonally across the Corso from Santa Maria della Catena is the much plundered church of **San Giovanni dei Napolitani (37)**, built between 1526 and 1617. If you can get into it, you will find that practically the only art works to have survived are Raffaele La Valle's (1543–1621) organ and the late 16th century ceiling painting of St John the Baptist by Giuseppe Salerno (1570–1632, see Appendix II).

Opposite is the **Zecca (38)**, the old mint, rebuilt at the end of the 19th century, next door to which is the fortress-like **Palazzo Chiaramonte (39)**. This illustrious building, dating from 1307, was built by the Chiaramonte family, whose power came to a sudden end when in 1392 Andrea Chiaramonte was beheaded in the piazza in front of his palace. Andrea had in fact more power than sense: Manfredi II Chiaramonte had been Great Judge of Palermo (1342) and Manfredi III Great Admiral. Meanwhile, Andrea, the latter's son, set himself up in opposition to the Aragonese king Martin I, thus inviting his own demise. Later the palace became the seat of the Spanish viceroys and in the 17th century was used by the Inquisition as their headquarters and court. Prisons were installed beneath it and the Inquisitors tortured their victims with an appalling array of devices some of which can still be seen in the basement along with the graffiti of the frightened inmates. The building is closed to the public and to visit it special permission must be obtained from the university Rector's office inside. Within is an arcaded courtyard decorated in what became known as the 'Chiaramonte style', a very ornamental version of Arab-Norman as it developed in the 14th century when the Chiaramonte family were at the height of their power (see also Chapter 14). And there is the great Sala Magna, a magnificent early chamber which, if you cannot get into it, you can at least see from the piazza. The painted wooden ceiling, 1377–80, by Cecco di Naro, Simone da Carleone and Dareno da Palermo, is a fairly late – and rare – survival of the Mudejar style (a style of architecture deriving from the Christianized Moors in medieval Spain).

In the western corner of the piazza, at No 18, is the **Palazzo Fatta (40)** which contains the Museo Internazionale delle Marionette, the puppet museum, and a puppet theatre. Puppets are an essential part of the lore of Sicily. Giuseppe Pitré, Sicily's principal writer about folklore, said: 'In Sicily the past is not dead, but rather accompanies one from the cradle to the grave, in festivals and games, in spectacles and in church, in rites and traditions; everywhere it lives and speaks.' Folklore reveals the soul of the Sicilian people. It is traditionally depicted on the elaborately painted carts of the peasants which show in great detail the battles fought between Christian and Saracen knights. The puppet dramas are an essential part of this as well: these re-enact the same old tales of knights and chivalry, of Orlando, Astolfo and Angelica. In reality they are characters drawn from everyday life, thinly disguised, and they reflect contemporary Sicilian ways and thought. This is why the puppet theatre – which you should go and see if you possibly can – has survived for so long. It took hold in the 18th and 19th centuries, during which time it was a rare and highly prized form of entertainment for the peasants. It was carried on through the influence of ballad singers and the skilled craftsmen who made the puppet figures. The collection on display in the Palazzo Fatta examines the Sicilian puppet theatre tradition in a series of magnificent rooms decorated in 1771 in a French rococo manner.

From the piazza the Via Lungarini struggles south-west past ranks of derelict palaces. It soon branches into the Via Merlo in which is situated the **Palazzo Mirto (41)**. Though as I write the authorities have closed this for restoration it is normally open to the public, and that is rare for palaces. The Mirto was given to Palermo by Prince Stefano Filangeri complete with its collection of furniture, painting, textiles and ceramics. While the building itself, 17th century with 18th century modifications, is not particularly remarkable, the collection inside certainly is, if only because it is still intact. Chief among its treasures is the Salottino Cinese, a small chinoiserie chamber complete with furnishings and textiles which reflect the vogue for the Chinese taste that swept 18th century Europe. Of still greater intrinsic interest perhaps are the scenes from Chinese life in the vaults and on the walls. These are the Sicilian painters' own version of the calligraphic style of the Chinese. Pagoda style seats covered in painted leather, lacquered cabinets and oriental porcelain complete the picture. Beyond the Throne Room, and the drawing rooms of various colours, is a tiny internal courtyard with an elaborate baroque fountain encrusted with shells, stucco and tufa. At receptions, wine flowed from it into a huge scallop shell at its base.

The Via Merlo ends in the Piazza San Francesco on the east side of which is **San Francesco (42)** itself, one of the most interesting churches in the city. With its adjacent convent, it was the Franciscans headquarters. In early days the teachings of St Francis were not what the authorities wanted the masses, repressed by feudalism and poverty, to hear, and the papal support they enjoyed was on more than one occasion enough to get them packed off to the mainland by Frederick II, who spent his life engaged in battles with the Pope.

Inside the church, look out for the first chapel in the left-hand aisle, and the chapel of the Madonna della Neve, where Domenico Gagini (1463?–92, see Appendix II) designed the doorways, the statues of the Virgin and Child and of St John the Baptist on its altar, and also the right hand figure of the Virgin. Francesco Laurana's Chapel of Mastrantonio, of 1468 (fourth on the left), is one of the very first Renaissance monuments introduced into Sicily. In the presbytery are two of Giacomo Serpotta's works – Victory and Chastity – and in the nave are others of which Theology, on the pier to the left of the main entrance to the church, and Modesty, on the great left-hand pier halfway down the nave, are the best, the one for its daring drapery (which, according to Donald Garstang, author of *Giacomo Serpotta*, would be even more wonderful had it still been covered with the patina of marble dust intended to deepen the chiaroscuro), the other for its delightful attitude of disdain. Eight statues by Giambattista Ragusa (d. 1727, see Appendix II) were erected in 1772 in the Chapel of the Immaculate Conception to the right of the main altar, and the display of polychromatic marble surrounding them is one of the most impressive in Palermo.

Across the piazza from the church is the Via Paternostro, an ancient street once the haunt of the saddle-makers and called Via dei Cintinai; it is even now dotted with makers of belts and suitcases. Just a short distance away down on the left is the entrance to the massive **Palazzo Cattolica (43)**. The most remarkable thing about this building, built in about 1720 by Giacomo Amato, is its internal courtyard divided into three separate parts by two transverse porticoes. The grandeur of the building's exterior once reflected an extremely lavish lifestyle within. Michele Palmieri di Miccichè in *Pensées et Souvenirs*, described a ball given by the Prince of Cattolica some time before 1830: 'Immense salons, their walls covered from top to bottom with mirrors, were masked by trees that had been uprooted whole from the earth and were festooned with fruit. The spaces between the foliage and the mirrors gave the idea of another world existing on the other side of the passage: the illusion was complete. We danced English quadrilles along trellised aisles from which ripe bunches of exquisite grapes dangled, and French country dances in tree-ringed squares disposed about a pool in which a graceful jet of water played. At the very back, in the last salon, a delightful little hill rose up, this too covered with trees, and in the middle a path leading to its summit, bordered on each side by a great abundance of sweets and cakes of every variety.'

The real jewel of this area is the **Oratorio di San Lorenzo (44)** in the Via Immacolatella which runs west just on from San Francesco. In it is one of the most remarkable examples of the art of the *stuccatore* anywhere, and a masterpiece of Giacomo Serpotta, executed between 1699 and 1706. To get into this building, which was begun in the second half of the 16th century for the Compagnia di San Francesco, then transformed after 1699 by Serpotta and Giacomo Amato, you have to ring a bell at No 5 Via Immacolatella. A small round custodian will lead the way to the little oratory hidden behind the undergrowth at the back of a tiny inner courtyard.

Barely any wall surface is without stucco decoration: while most of the scenes, the *teatrini*, represent episodes from the lives of St Francis and St Lorenzo, there are also allegorical figures and flirtatious, jovial putti bouncing about all over walls. At one time the whole chapel was dominated by Caravaggio's *Nativity with St Francis and St Lorenzo*, painted during his stay in Palermo in 1609, but that was stolen in 1969. As Donald Garstang explains, all of the stucco figures, the architectural settings of the *teatrini*, are remarkable not just for their attention to detail, their range of facial expression and the attitudes of their bodies, but for the virtuosity their creator exhibits in the handling of his medium. The allegorical figures are each linked to an adjacent scene: they give each a moral significance and take an active part in the acting out of the conceit. For example, to the right of the chancel arch, the figures of Penitence and Constancy are linked to the Temptation of St Francis while next to them Humility is linked to the scene of St Francis Clothing the Beggar. This sequence is followed right around the nave, and while the St Francis story culminates in his apotheosis, on the chancel arch, the story of San Lorenzo comes to its glorious and tragic end in the martyrdom scene on the end wall of the nave.

From the Piazza San Francesco, the Via Paternostro, going right, leads back to the Corso Vittorio Emanuele which in turn leads back up to the Quattro Canti.

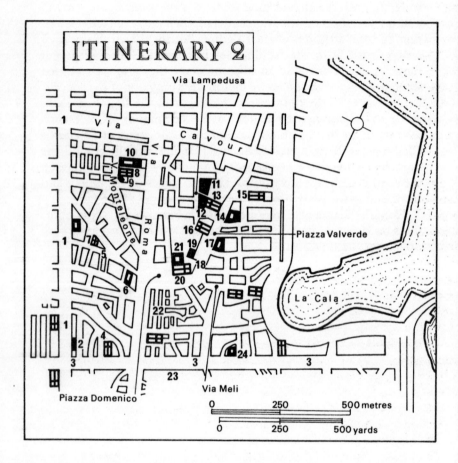

ITINERARY 2

Itinerary Two
The Northern Quarter

The Olivella, Loggia and Castellammare regions: Via Maqueda, Palazzo Merendino-Costantino, Corso Vittorio Emanuele, San Matteo, Via Bandiera, Palazzo Termini-Pietratagliata, San Gioacchino, Sant'Ignazio all'Olivella, Oratorio di Santa Caterina d'Alessandria, Museo Nazionale Archeologico, Palazzo Lampedusa, Oratorio di Santa Zita, Santa Zita, Conservatorio di Musica, San Giorgio dei Genovesi, Santa Maria Valverde, Palazzo Niscemi, Via Bambinai, Oratorio di San Domenico, San Domenico, Museum of the Risorgimento, Vucciria, Via Argentaria Nuova, Palazzo Rocella

The **Via Maqueda** (1), running north from the Quattro Canti to the Piazza Verdi, is rather forbidding, dark and filled with traffic. The pavements are narrow and the shops along them either empty or uninteresting. Lining the street too are palaces blackened by exhaust fumes. At night, their cavernous openings to the street are uninviting holes. In fact, though, there are interesting architectural details and a range of magnificent baroque portals.

Just by the Quattro Canti, on the right hand side, is Venanzio Marvuglia's **Palazzo Merendino-Costantino** (2) (1785–8). It has a magnificent courtyard beyond a gigantic portal and, although its exterior is now a bit forbidding despite its wrought-iron balconies, there are magnificent salons on the *piano nobile* which were frescoed by Gioacchino Martorana in the 18th century.

Double back to Quattro Canti and proceed down the **Corso Vittorio Emanuele** (3) towards the sea and the early baroque church of **San Matteo al Cassaro** (4) a couple of blocks down on the left hand side. A crisp sculpted façade of 1662 terminates in a triple

53

belfry – a peculiarly Sicilian feature. The interior is mostly 18th
century. Entering from the street you will need a few moments to
adjust to the gloom, from which will emerge orange and yellow faux
marbling, gilded stucco and some fine statues by Giacomo Serpotta
who is also buried here. These statues are dotted about the church:
above the entrance portal is a relief of Christ ministering to the souls
in purgatory; against the piers nearest the chancel are two allegorical
figures of Justice and Faith; on the chancel arch are angels with a
banner.

The decoration of the vaults – the frescos (the main one the
Apotheosis of San Matteo) and the stucco – are the work of Vito
d'Anna and Bartolomeo Sanseverino respectively, working to the
designs of Francesco Ferrigno (1754) by whose time rococo elements
had begun to creep into the building. Severino's vault stuccos are
the rather restrained evidence of this. In the chapel in the left
transept is a painting of the Mass of San Gregorio by Giuseppe
Salerno.

Continue down the Corso to its junction with the Via Roma.
Turn left on to it and continue until, on the left, the **Via Bandiera**
(5) turns into the Olivella region. Here a daily market rambles
through the whole block to the Via Maqueda: banks of pirate
cassettes and videos flank bloody innards of massacred beasts, and
huge dead fish jostle piles of plastic boots and nylon underwear. On
a hot summer's day the smell is vile and you will need a peg for your
nose. Making your escape, you will all too easily knock into a large
oozing cheese or a mound of sticky boiled sweets made for some
long past feast day. But as you splash through the blood, smelly fish
water and melting ice-cream, and avoid the half-starved cats with
tails macerated in fights or car doors, remember such markets represent one of the few unbroken links with Palermo's past.

On the corner of the Via Roma and the Via Bandiera is the
Palazzo Termini-Pietratagliata (6) (1573), a relic of early Spanish
influence on the island's architecture. Opposite, the road branches:
take the Via Basilio, turning right into the Via Patania, passing on
the way the church of **San Gioacchino (7)** built to Paolo Amato's
designs in 1727. Inside, the stucco decoration is by Procopio
Serpotta, who draws heavily on his father Giacomo's work elsewhere.

At the end of the Via Patania is the Piazza Olivella, a quiet backwater dominated by the magnificent church of **Sant'Ignazio all'**
Olivella (8) and its adjacent Oratorio dell' Olivella. Though the
church was founded in the late 16th century, the five stars awarded

it in the annals of Palermitan architecture are due to the 18th century decorative schemes of its vaults and to the little oratory next door, both designed by Venanzio Marvuglia in the neo-classical style. His work here inspired and served as the model for other churches well into the 19th century.

In 1722 Giacomo Serpotta undertook to execute the stuccos in the Chapel of St Philip Neri (for the canonization of whom the church was originally opened in 1622). What he produced was swept away in 1823, and in this chapel (fifth on the left-hand side of the nave just before the transept) remains an extraordinary soup of polychromatic marbles and semi-precious stones with, on the altar, a painting of the saint by Sebastiano Conca (1740). See also the statues of St Joseph and St Jacob by Ragusa. Even more overwhelming is the third chapel on the left (1630) which is awash with lapis, agate, jasper, and topped by Pietro Novelli's vault fresco of the Pietà. The statues of SS Peter and Paul in the choir are by Ignazio Marabitti, and the painting of the Virgin in the fourth chapel on the right by Borremans.

While in ecclesiastical mode, there is another oratory nearby. This is the **Oratorio di Santa Caterina d'Alessandria (9)**, in the Via Monteleone, generally recognised as Procopio Serpotta's masterpiece (1719–26). While Giacomo Serpotta might have been the more brilliant of the two, Procopio's work is none the less charming and elegant. It tells the story of the saint's life and what it lacks in technical mastery and that rubber-like flexibility so typical of his father's work is made up for in the fascinating wealth of detail – hairstyles, clothing, furniture, perspective, expressions and so on. On the altar is *The Martyrdom of Saint Catherine* by Giuseppe Salerno.

On the other side of the Sant'Ignazio is the **Museo Nazionale Archeologico (10)** housed in what was once the Phillipine monastery attached to Sant'Ignazio. Here, beyond the lovely Tuscan-looking courtyard is one of Sicily's great collections of sculpture and artefacts (vases, glass, terracotta figures, jewellery and tools) taken from the sites of the Sicilian cities of Magna Graecia (Tyndaris, Termini Imerese, Agrigento, Syracuse – see the famous bronze ram that once decorated the Castello di Maniace), the Phoenician colonies (Motya) and the Roman Empire. Chief among the collections on display are the metope sculptures from Selinunte, the quality of which ranks easily with what was being produced in other parts of the Greek Empire and in Greece itself.

Down the side of the museum, the Via Bara all'Olivella leads to the Via Roma, crosses it, and plunges right down into the densely packed Castellammare region of the city (noted by Giuseppe di Lampedusa as 'crawling with hovels and squalor . . . with a stench of horrors and filth to traverse'), an area which, until the Second World War, was packed with palaces, convents and churches. Here too was the **Palazzo Lampedusa (11)**, the remains of which line the Via Lampedusa at the very bottom of Via Bara all'Olivella. Sadly an Allied bomb in 1943 savaged the building ('My beloved . . . which bombs . . . searched . . . out and destroyed' – Giuseppe di Lampedusa), signalling the end of what must have been a glorious monument to the Lampedusa family.

There is just a hole there now, and some bits of old wall. In the 1980s David Gilmour, biographer of Lampedusa, found himself courteously restrained from photographing this wall by three *carabinieri*: 'As I retreated along the Via Lampedusa, I noticed a loose plank in the padlocked gates of the palace. The next day was Sunday and I rose before dawn, reached the building in the grey half light, and squeezed through the gap in the gate. The front court-yard was full of rubble but I remembered the layout of the palace from Lampedusa's memoirs and knew which way to climb. As the light improved I could recognize some of the rooms: his mother's boudoir with its domed ceiling in gold and shades of blue, her dressing room overlooking the Oratory of Santa Zita, the place of Giuseppe's earliest childhood memory. Perhaps the most pathetic sight in the place was the wreck of the old library . . . Underneath the rubble, scattered pages of Lampedusa's favourite authors mixed with the remains of his library catalogue, burnt and insect eaten cards bearing the names of Shakespeare, Dickens and others. Buried among them, I found a number of more personal documents: pho-tographs, ancestral correspondence, papers in his own handwriting, letters from his mother which testified to the closeness of their rela-tionship'. (*The Last Leopard: A Life of Giuseppe di Lampedusa*). The Lampedusas decided not to rebuild after the war, moving instead to the Casa Lampedusa in the Via Butera, taking with them what was left of the original furnishings. There these remain to this day.

In *A Tale and Two Memories* Lampedusa remembers looking out over his mother's balcony from her boudoir (decorated in a design 'gentle and corporeal as a piece of music by Mozart') and being able to see the back wall of the **Oratorio di Santa Zita (12)**. Sheer luck kept this fragile building just out of range of the bombers; happily, because it houses some of the most magnificent stucco decoration in Sicily – the work of Giacomo Serpotta (after 1688).

The oratory is dedicated to the Rosary; it takes its theme from the miraculous intervention of the Virgin of the Rosary at the Battle of Lepanto, a stucco relief illustration of which is embedded in a great wall of stucco drapery at its rear. Around the walls are small panels representing the fifteen Mysteries of the Rosary, stucco allegorical figures and putti.

This interior is a landmark in Serpotta's career as a *stuccatore*, and Donald Garstang in *Giacomo Serpotta* says: 'from this moment onwards, there was to be nothing he could not do with his chosen material'. The stucco figures seem almost real; perhaps some thunderbolt turned them temporarily into stucco. You can nearly hear the chortling, farting and giggling of the putti, the rustling of undergrowth, the crack of a bottom slapped, the clank of armour and the swish of drapery. The putti flap about with excited abandon, sitting on or half falling off window ledges, their stomachs rolling about, their buttocks wobbling. Like miniature adults they have muscles and seem to be completely devoid of normal childish innocence. You can also imagine the scent of the allegorical 'ladies', two of whom, Esther and Judith, are dressed more as elegant courtiers than biblical matriarchs. Look at Judith's head dress and at her foot poised to deliver a sharp kick to Holofernese's head.

The oratory overlooks a little courtyard which leads into the 16th century church of **Santa Zita (13)**. This is filled with the works of Antonello Gagini from an earlier building on the site. Miraculously, they have been very well preserved. There is a great sculpted triumphal arch in the apse behind the main altar (his triumphal arches have a classical composure which will have been absorbed from the art of Renaissance Florence), the sarcophagus of Antonio Scirotta (*c*. 1627) in the second chapel on the left of the choir, and another sculpted arch, a monument to the Platamone family, in the second chapel on the right of the choir. Antonello Gagini was the brightest star in the family constellation, setting the scene stylistically for more or less the next century.

Directly opposite Santa Zita in the Via Squarcialupo, is a 14th century doorway from the ancient church of the Annunciation which was hit by a bomb. It is now the entrance to the **Conservatorio di Musica (14)**, whose presence is clear from the unharmonious clangour of clumsily played scales coming from the upper windows.

Just to the left is the unhappy wasteland of the Castellammare region. Not much survives here except, miraculously, the church of **San Giorgio dei Genovesi (15)** built in 1576 by Giorgio di Faccio for the Genoese merchant community. Today, deconsecrated, it is kept permanently locked. Currently in the process of being restored, it contains (or contained) a wide variety of paintings collected by wealthy Genoese merchants. Of these, two attributions are the most interesting: *the Virgin of the Rosary* attributed to Luca Giordano in the first chapel on the right and the Annunciation in the third chapel to left attributed to Jacopo Palma who is also thought to have painted the Baptism in the third chapel on the right.

From the Via Squarcialupo, continue into the Piazza Valverde (going right from Santa Zita) and you will come to the entrance to **Santa Maria Valverde (16)** on the right, and on the left, the Palazzo Niscemi. Santa Maria Valverde, designed in the 1630s by Mariano Smiriglio (b. 1561, see Appendix II), has a splendid polychromatic interior of the late 17th century designed by Paolo Amato and completed after his death by Andrea Palma. The interior is quite extraordinary. Heaven only knows whether the devout were able to surface above the luxurious colours and textures of the coloured marbles swilling about the nave and side chapels and catch a glimpse of the Almighty. This church has over the years been severely vandalised, the altarpieces stolen except for Pietro Novelli's *Virgin of the Carmelo* (1641) which is now in the Museo Diocesano.

The **Palazzo Niscemi (17)** is a rather bedraggled, mostly 18th century palace with a very fine 16th century first floor loggia in its courtyard. Here lived Lampedusa's relatives, the Niscemi family, whose most illustrious member was Corrado Valguarnera, Prince of Niscemi (see the Villa Niscemi, below), who had been one of Garibaldi's Thousand, and whose wife Maria Favara was the model for Angelica in *The Leopard*. Less distinguished perhaps, but far more interesting – and certainly more decorative – was Corrado Valguarnera's grandson Fulco Santostefano della Cerda, Duke of Verdura, who lived in this house from time to time as a youth. Fulco (1899–1978) was one of this century's most original designers of jewellery, and produced opulent pieces for a long list of glittering clients. In the words of one writer, 'Verdura was to jewellery what Chanel was to clothes and Fabergé to eggs'.

From the Piazza Valverde, continue into the **Via Bambinai (18)**, the former doll-makers' street once filled with shops selling wax votive figures, limbs and crib figures. One shop survives and here you can buy breasts (singly or in pairs), limbs, the odd finger, noses, eyes – votives to draw an infliction to the attention of an intermediary saint. You will see them nailed to the wall in the chapels of countless Sicilian churches. A few doors beyond this shop is the **Oratorio del Rosario di San Domenico (19)**, yet another masterpiece to become acquainted with amongst the works of Giacomo Serpotta. To enter, ask for the key in the little waxwork shop.

It is difficult to decide which is the best of the Serpotta oratories. This is the latest. The art treatises list each of their various plus points in terms of technical virtuosity, versatility, imagination and so on. Perhaps for sheer sensory indulgence, this is the one that stands out above the others. Serpotta ravishes the viewer with delightful, whimsical fantasies in gilded and plain white stucco, and there are additional enrichments such as mahogany furniture (sometimes delicately inlaid with mother of pearl) and great religious paintings of subjects with titles like the *Flagellation*, the *Crowning with Thorns* and the *Crucifixion*. The idea of pain and suffering – especially when it takes on brutish reality under the brushes of a range of 17th century Neapolitan and Flemish painters – must have induced a fervent religious response from the devotees of this particular establishment.

From ceiling to floor the room is magnificently overwrought. Angels scramble over the chancel arch and putti abound. Groups of them play at the foot of the large wall medallions containing scenes in high relief taken from the Book of the Revelation. On the tier below, beneath the windows, allegorical figures in niches alternate with the paintings. Some of these figures are extravagantly attired in exotic, almost theatrical costumes – the reason being that the more opulent the adornment, the more exalted the figure's prestige. Donald Garstang notes that the figures of Divine Providence and of Grace (just beside the altarpiece) were 'sources of infinite riches [that] could not be represented with less ostentation in a society in which understatement played no part'.

Unusually, this oratory still has its paintings of which the *Madonna of the Rosary* altarpiece is by Van Dyck (1624–8). Commissioned in Palermo, completed in Genoa, then sent back to Sicily, it was painted when Palermo was in the throes of plague, which is why the figure of Santa Rosalia was hurriedly included in one corner. As patroness of Palermo she alone had the power to intercede on behalf of the city and avert disaster (see Chapter 1). Other paintings are by Borremans, Stomer, Luca Giordano (*The*

Agony in the Garden, first painting on the right in the nave, the *Resurrection*, on the entrance wall, and the *Assumption*, also on the entrance wall) and Novelli (for the latter's work see the ceiling fresco of the *Coronation of the Virgin* and the *Doctors in the Temple*, the last painting in the nave just to the left of the altar).

Next door to the oratory is the vast church of **San Domenico (20)**. It flanks Piazza Meli at the bottom of the Via Bambinai and opens on to the Piazza San Domenico around the other side. As you enter the Piazza Meli, look back through the Piazza San Giacomo and the Via Meli at the church of Santa Maria la Nuova, an extremely fine 16th century building with clashing Gothic and Renaissance elements in the portico: see the capitals which are a strange mixture of Gothic and Gaginiesque elements.

At the other end of the Via Meli, beyond Santa Maria la Nuova, is the church of San Sebastiano the façade of which is dominated by a lovely portal executed in the manner of the Gagini. Inside, in the choir, are some stuccos thought to be by Giacomo Serpotta (1692).

The façade of San Domenico, one of the grander expressions of Palermitan baroque, seems only to be an excuse to provide a back-drop for the Piazza San Domenico, one of the first planned urban spaces in old Palermo (1724). The façade's main concern seems to be display: its great columns, its towers (one of which is by Napoli), statues and stuccos (by Giovan Maria Serpotta, grandson of Giacomo) are the chief visual interest. The architect responsible for church façade and square was Tommaso Maria Napoli, one of Sicily's principal baroque architects who in the early 1720s was sent to Vienna to ask permission from the Habsburg ruler of Sicily, Emperor Charles VI, to re-order the square. It is often surmised that while he was there he met, and sought the advice of, the Imperial Architect Johann Bernhard Fischer von Erlach. The square, originally enclosed, was opened up when the Via Roma marched across its western end in the 19th century. In its original form the contrast between it and its surroundings – mostly undistinguished and filled with much smaller buildings riven with warrens of passages and alleys – must have been extraordinary. Napoli also began the column at the centre of the square. This was rebuilt in part by Giovanni Amico in 1726. Today it is topped by Giambattista Ragusa's figure of the Virgin.

By comparison with such external display, the interior of San Domenico is rather uninteresting. A quick look at the Giacomo Serpottas on Paolo Amato's Ramondetta monument, and Antonello

Gagini's Santa Caterina in the third chapel in the left-hand aisle is all that is needed before paying a visit to the cloisters to the left of the church. This is the best place to cool down on a baking day. They belonged to the original monastery which was constructed along with the very first church on the site, San Domenico's predecessor of about 1300. Nowadays the **Museum of the Risorgimento (21)** is housed here on the first floor.

To get some idea of what the area now occupied by the Piazza San Domenico must have looked like before it was opened up, you have to go deep into the **Vucciria (22)** market either down the Via Maccheronai or the Via Coltellieri. You cannot miss either of these; the noise fills the air and an endless stream of shoppers spews out from it in every direction. Nowhere in Palermo do memories of the old souks survive with such intensity; this was the most disorderly, ramshackle and chaotic of places even in Arabic days. Merchants, hawkers, bootleggers and artisans of every description still cluster here. This is the market where you are as likely to bump into a duchess buying a huge fish for the family dinner as you are an urchin offloading boxes of illicitly acquired cigarettes. Sawdust mingles with blood, lettuce with fishscales and flies with everything; the Vucciria market is also the best advertisement for the traditional fecundity of Sicily.

At the centre of the market is the Piazza Caracciolo off which, leading east, is the **Via Argentiera Nuova (23)**, once the haunt of silversmiths and their workshops. These were very profitable businesses in the 17th and 18th centuries when the nobility were busy spending to maximize personal display. Wedged in behind the vast palaces on the Corso, the barbers and wool merchants were here too. Even the Gagini had their workshop here. In the Via Cassari and the Via Chiavettieri were the key makers and in the Vicolo Tintori the dyers. This area today is silent, closed and largely deserted. Street patterns are as they always were and, cheek by jowl, ancient crumbling doorways, little forgotten churches and derelict courtyards cling together in an effort to remain upright.

Between the Via Argentiera Nuova and the Via Cassari is the Piazza Garraffello, from which the Via Loggia (named after the market loggias that once filled the area) leads to the Corso Vittorio Emanuele which here is lined with heavy palace façades, most of them savaged by modern shopfronts. Here and there you will see interesting portals that lead to once magnificent palace courtyards, for instance the Mannerist **Palazzo Rocella (24)** at No 137.

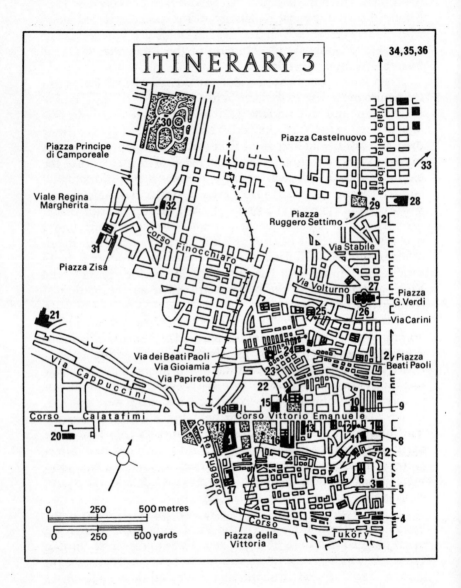

ITINERARY 3

34, 35, 36

Piazza Castelnuovo

Piazza Principe
di Camporeale

33

Viale della Libertà

Viale Regina
Margherita

32

29

28

Corso Finocchiaro

Piazza
Ruggero Settimo

2

31

Via Stabile

Piazza Zisa

Via Volturno

27

Piazza
G. Verdi

21

25

26

Via Carini

Via Cappuccini

Via dei Beati Paoli

24

2

Piazza
Beati Paoli

Via Gioiamia

23

Via Papireto

22

Corso   Calatafimi

19

15

14

10

9

9

20

Corso Vittorio Emanuele

8

1

16

13

12

11

8

Co Re Ruggero

17

6

3

5

Corso

4

Piazza della
Vittoria

Tukóry

0   250   500 metres

0   250   500 yards

Itinerary Three
The Southern and Western
Quarters

San Giuseppe dei Teatini, Via Maqueda, Palazzo Comitini,
Palazzo Cutò, Via del Bosco, Casa Professa, Palazzo Speciale,
Piazza Bologni, Palazzo Belmonte-Riso, Palazzo Geraci,
Palazzo Ugo, Palazzo Villafranca, Palazzo Castrone-Santa
Ninfa, Cathedral, Palazzo Arcivescovile (and Museo Dio-
cesano), Palazzo Sclafani, San Giovanni degli Eremiti, Palazzo
Reale (and the Cappella Reale), Porta Nuova, Cuba, Convento
dei Cappuccini, Loggia and Cappella degli Incoronati, Piazza
Papireto, Santa Maria di Gesù, L'Immacolata Concezione,
Teatro Massimo, Chiosco Ribaudo and Chiosco Vicari,
Politeama, Chiosco Ribaudo, Villa Malfitano, Zisa, Villino
Florio, Villa Igiea, Palazzina Cinese, Villa Niscemi, Piana dei
Colli (and its villas)

The southern corner of the Quattro Canti has been sculpted from
the flank of the huge Theatine church of **San Giuseppe (1)**, begun
in 1612. The church's entrance in the Corso round the corner seems
insignificant compared to the massive theatricality of the curved
'screen' of the crossroads. In fact standing at the Quattro Canti you
do not even notice how vast is the bulk of the church. But inside,
where stucco is piled on top of polychromatic marble and overladen
with gilding and frescos, the impression is quite different. It lives
up to all expectations of baroque display. Not that it ravishes the
senses with an otherworldly beauty. Clumsily heavy-handed, it
bludgeons them with the sheer activity of its various elements,
which for the most part are not very beautiful at all. The architectural

history books do not speak very highly of this interior, except to point out the quite magnificent mid 18th-century altar frontal in the sacristy. Decorated with inlaid marbles, it looks like a stage set. The altar in the left transept chapel, by Andrea Palma, is a more elaborate and even more beautiful exercise in the same technique. The painting of San Gaetano in the left transept chapel is by Pietro Novelli, and the dome fresco, *The Triumph of Sant'Andrea Avellino* (1724), by Willem Borremans. In the chapel to the right of the main altar is a crucifix by Fra Umile da Petralia, a 17th century naturalistic work at odds with the overblown decoration of the rest of the interior.

Moving south down the **Via Maqueda (2)** from the Quattro Canti, following the direction of San Giuseppe's nave, you soon come to the Via del Bosco (about halfway along the Via Maqueda). At the junction of the two is the Prefettura, housed in the former **Palazzo Comitini (3)**. Now a sickening shade of orange, the Comitini is the work of Nicolo Palma, and was built for Michele Gravina, Prince of Comitini, between 1766 and 1771. The exterior is fairly lighthearted with fanciful, billowing wrought-iron balconies. Unusually in the Via Maqueda, this building is in good condition and gives some idea of the street's former grandeur. It is possible to get inside it (enquire at the tourist office in Piazza Castelnuova); much of the internal decoration has survived on the *piano nobile* which is still recognisably 18th century. Much else is 19th century. The marble floors are intact, and in some instances so are the stucco ornamentations around the doors and on the wall panelling and ceiling. Two rooms in particular are worth a look: the princess's boudoir (which opens off a large decorated chamber possibly once the princess's bedroom but now an office), and the Sala Martorana. The panelling of the former was decorated at the end of the 18th century or early in the 19th century with little glazed terracotta roundels of landscapes set into gilded rococo stucco frames. At intervals tiny wooden shelves support oriental porcelain which the Prefettura (in a brave attempt at authenticity) have reinstated. The Sala Martorana, now the council chamber, was frescoed in the 18th century by Giuseppe Martorana and is one of the more splendid rooms of the period to have survived in Palermo. The frescos, with names like *The Triumph of Real Love*, are intact, as are the multi-tiered Murano glass chandeliers. Two other nearby rooms are filled with painted panels from other Palermitan palaces; most are *fetes galantes*, and amongst the collections are panels by Elia

Interguglielmi (late 18th century) who was responsible for some of the decoration of the Palazzo Gangi.

Further on, at No 26, is the **Palazzo Cutò (4)**, built in the 1720s to the designs of Giacomo Amato for the Filangieri, Princes of Cutò. Its façade is rather bland but none the less represents an important milestone in the development of Palermitan palace design. The position of the main staircase is considered the principal innovation: positioned directly opposite the main Via Maqueda entrance, it divides the building's internal courtyard into two, with a front colonnaded section and a plainer one behind the stair. Lying on the main axis the stair is more prominent than any predating it, even on the Italian mainland. Halfway up it are two magnificent, enormous stucco volutes which serve as balustrades. Far, far larger than life, these are wilfully outrageous. Not much of the palace's internal decoration has survived, though if you stay in the *pensione* on the *piano nobile* it is highly likely your bedroom ceiling will be decorated with the very last remnants of a period fresco, and some old gilded panelling might be glimpsed behind a wardrobe.

Retrace your steps down the Via Maqueda as far as the **Via del Bosco (5)**. In many ways this street is like the Via Alloro (see Chapter 2); it retains its medieval irregularities as it straggles into the heart of the Albergheria quarter. And, like the Via Alloro, it is lined with ancient palaces, or rather the remains of ancient palaces, since some are now nothing more than elaborate entrance portals leading nowhere. At No 2 is the Palazzo Filangeri di Santa Flavia almost opposite which is the Palazzo Gravina di Palagonia, the house in which lived the Prince of Palagonia renowned for the peculiarities he inflicted on his villa at Bagheria (see Chapter 8).

This was the man who gave his huge fortune away to the poor, an eccentric thing to have done in those days, especially in Palermo. Goethe saw him collecting money for charity: "The shopkeeper . . . pointed . . . to a tall, thin gentleman, dressed in the height of fashion, who was walking down the middle of the street through all the dung and dirt with an air of imperturbable dignity. In a freshly curled and powdered wig, carrying his hat under his arm and wearing a silk coat, a sword and neat shoes with jewelled buckles, the elderly gentleman walked solemnly on, ignoring all the eyes that were turned in his direction. 'That is the Prince of Palagonia,' said the shopkeeper. 'From time to time he walks through the city collecting ransome money for the slaves who have been captured by Barbary pirates.' . . . 'If,' I [Goethe] said, 'instead of spending vast sums on follies for his villa, he had used them for this cause, no prince in the world would have accomplished more.' My shopkeeper disagreed: 'Aren't we all like that? We pay gladly for our follies but we expect others to pay for our virtues.' '' Nowadays his villa is more of a monument to him than this sorry place.

Behind the Via del Bosco is the church of the Gesù or the **Casa Professa (6)** (go into the Piazza Ballaro, then the Via Casa Professa), the massive church of the Jesuits and its adjacent convent and library. This magnificent building was badly damaged during the Second World War but has since been very well restored.

Dating from the 17th and 18th centuries, the interior is one of the masterpieces of persuasive religious decoration. Even though large areas of what you see there are restorations, the original intentions of the Sicilian craftsmen and the Jesuit fathers are not all lost. The marble decoration enlivens the severity of the architectural forms; it is a seething mass of marble or stucco putti, herms, animals and assorted undergrowth. But if these figures could speak it would not be in the dulcet, clear harmonies of the celestial choir but the raucous, vulgar discords of the nearby fishmarket. And as the tritons wrestle on some pillar, or across an arch, with dolphins and sea-snakes, surely they swear in pure Sicilian?

From the Piazza Casa Professa, go west along the Via Rimpetto Casa Professa and the Via Raffadali until the junction with the Via G.M. Puglia on the left, and the Via D'Alessi which leads to the Piazza Bologni on the right. In the Via G.M. Puglia is the **Palazzo Speciale (7)**, an elaborate late Gothic style palace erected in the 15th century by Pietro Speciale, Judge of the City Court of Palermo. It survives much altered though Speciale's building is easily recognizable. At the top of the courtyard stair is a marble bust in a niche of the building's founder, thought by some to be the work of Domenico Gagini and by others, Francesco Laurana.

Going the other way, the **Piazza Bologni (8)**, filled with palaces, is one of Palermo's most gracious squares. As you enter from the narrow medieval warren of alleys and streets that surround Speciale's building, the immediate vista is filled with Venanzio Marvuglia's façade of the **Palazzo Belmonte-Riso (9)**. Miraculously the building still stands though it was the victim of an Allied bomb in 1943. Nothing has ever been done to restore the damage beyond erecting a tin fence to save intruders from being hit on the head by chunks of falling masonry. The building is a good example of the stylistic mixture that characterized much of Marvuglia's work: while all the architectural details are severely classical, there none the less remains a sense of baroque drama. The classical elements are more visible nowadays than the baroque ones, and before the Second World War, had you been able to go beyond its entrance portal, you would have seen a double arcaded courtyard, much like that of the Palazzo Cattolica (see Chapter 2).

The Belmonte-Riso neatly fills the western end of the piazza; physically it seems slightly divorced from the space because it is cut off by the Corso rushing past its doors. Aligned directly with its entrance portal is a statue of Charles V erected in 1631 – one of the few royal monuments to have survived the ravages of a population not inclined to revere monuments to foreign overlords.

Next door is Marvuglia's ruined **Palazzo Geraci (10)** and, facing the Palazzo Belmonte-Riso on the other side of the square, is the 18th century **Palazzo Ugo (11)** at right angles to which, on the western side of the square, is the **Palazzo Villafranca (12)** belonging to the Alliata family. Reconstructed in the middle of the 18th century by Giovanni Battista Vaccarini (see Catania, Chapter 13), this palace contains some of Palermo's most magnificent stuccoed rococo *salone*, of 'unparalleled splendour' and characterized by an 'elegance and light fantasy that have few rivals during this period' (Donald Garstang). Some idea of what exists there may gleaned from a visit to the Palazzo Fatta down near the Piazza Marina (see Chapter 2) to examine the decoration of the great *salone* there, substituting stucco medallion-relief panels for the painted scenes in the cove of its ceiling.

Moving to the Corso Vittorio Emanuele, not far beyond the Piazza Bologni on the upper right-hand side, is the Via Montevergine, a narrow street in which, had you come before the Second World War, you would have seen the ancient Palazzo Verdura in which the writer Fulco Verdura's family once lived. 'More like a Kasbah than a palace', it was impossibly old, a 'rambling conglomeration of buildings . . . filled with a musty, dusty smell' and ancestral bric and brac. Not a stone of this old pile exists any longer and nobody seems to remember it. The street is sad and empty, even the numerous churches along it are boarded up. So prolifically endowed with convents and churches was this particular neighbourhood that the constant din of the bells irritated one of Fulco's ancestors to the point where one day he took his gun and shot the local bellringer – who happened to be a nun. That earned him a brief sojourn in a country jail (*Happy Summer Days*).

Further on up the Corso, on the left-hand side of the street at No 452, is the **Palazzo Castrone-Santa Ninfa (13)**, a fantastical 16th century palace built in a peculiar Mannerist style – see the exuberant, massively rusticated entrance portal opening on to an inner courtyard. In the courtyard itself is a fountain representing Perseus and Andromeda thought to be the work of Mariano Smiriglio and his circle of sculptors. Opposite the palace, on the right hand side of the Corso, is the **Cathedral (14)** which displays as many architectural styles as there have been rulers of Sicily since the advent of the Normans in the 11th century.

The cathedral was founded in 1184 by the Archbishop of Palermo, Walter of the Mill, known to the locals as Gualtiero Offamilio because they could not pronounce his English name. (He was a boy when Henry II of England sent him to Sicily as tutor to William the Good whom the king wished to marry to his daughter Joanna.) Dedicated to Santa Maria dell'Assunta, the Cathedral is far more magnificent outside than in. If you walk around the apse end, facing the Piazza Settangeli, and then down the Via dell'Incoronazione on the building's west side, you can see much of the 12th century work unaltered: the sturdy Norman construction is easily visible, overlaid with strangely alien decoration deriving from Palermo's Islamic heritage. The lower zones of the two towers are Norman, as are those at the building's entrance front. The building took so long to complete that you can see an almost continuous development of the Gothic style from the 13th century to the 14th century. The main door is mid 14th century.

The entrance front is connected to a tower on the other side of the Via Bonello by a strange arched bridge which is more than just a buttress. One of its arms contains a secret passageway, an escape route from the Cathedral to the Palazzo Reale. In fact the whole of the roof structure as well as some of the massive walls are riddled with narrow passageways; in its early days the building was as much a fortress as the castle itself, and a speedy exit route was a grim necessity.

Although the main entrance to the Cathedral is in the Via Bonello, you enter the building nowadays via the porch on the south side which faces into the Piazza della Cattedrale. Dating from 1453 it is considered a masterpiece of the Catalan style. Dotted about it is an eclectic array of sculptures and fragments of earlier buildings: the left hand column for example is thought to be a lone survivor of the Great Mosque once on this site. On it are inscribed some lines from the Koran. Above the main door from the porch into the church is a ruined Byzantine mosaic of the Virgin and Child about which not much is known. Could this have come from the basilica that occupied the site before the Great Mosque?

Inside, the Cathedral is rather bland following a radical remodelling in 1781. At this time the dome was built. The most interesting things in it are undoubtedly the royal tombs clustered together in an enclosure on the south side of the nave, just to the left of the south porch entrance. They represent Sicily's short-lived independence from the Arab period to the Spanish domination of the island. In the 18th century they were squeezed together out of sight in this ignoble spot, once having magnificently graced the south transept.

In the Cathedral's earliest days the tombs must have overwhelmed with their splendour. Most are made of porphyry, and resemble the tombs of classical antiquity. If you stand facing the enclosure you can see, on the left-hand side placed against the wall, the tomb of William, Duke of Athens and son of Emperor Frederick II (d. 1338). The arms are those of the Aragon and Hohenstaufen families. Facing it, at the front of the enclosure, is the tomb of Frederick II himself (d. 1250). It was made for Roger II, and is the one that Frederick stole from the Cathedral at Cefalù (see Chapter 8). It is the most magnificent tomb in the collection. The Emperor rather oddly shares it with Peter II of Aragon. Behind it, placed so that you can hardly see it, is the tomb of Roger II (d. 1154), a far less grand affair than the one for which his corpse was originally intended. On the far right-hand side, against the wall, is the tomb of Queen Constance (d. 1222), the first wife of Emperor Frederick II. It is in fact a re-used antique tomb. Facing it is the tomb of Henry VI (d. 1187), the father of Frederick II, and husband of the occupant of the tomb just behind it, Queen Constance, daughter of Roger II and mother of Frederick. In the Cathedral treasury you can see the crown of Frederick II's wife Constance which was found in her sepulchre; this was the imperial diadem of the Norman Kingdom.

The rest of the building is studded with works by the Gagini family of whom Antonello is the most prolific representative. From him was commissioned a magnificent retable for the main altar which included forty-two statues and a series of reliefs. This no longer survives in its original position (it was broken up in the 18th century) and its various parts are scattered around the building. On the main altar is the Resurrection and there are statues from it on the nave pillars. The second chapel in the left aisle has three bas reliefs, and there is a magnificent array of statues in the right transept chapel.

On a different note, the chapel on the right of the main altar is dedicated to Santa Rosalia (see Chapter 1). The silver urn contains her remains (or what are thought to be her remains). In the chapel to the left of the main altar is a magnificent 17th century lapis lazuli tabernacle, the work of Cosimo Fonsaga.

Just across the road from the Cathedral is the **Palazzo Arcivesco-vile (15)** which contains the Museo Diocesano. Facing the Piazza della Cattedrale, the palace itself was begun by the Archbishop Simone di Bologna in 1460. The portal of its main entrance from the street is thought to be the work of Domenico Gagini; if it is, then it must be one of the very earliest examples of his work in Palermo, having been executed very soon after his arrival. In general it is typically Catalonian, although it has a broad band of classical-style acanthus leaves carved in shallow relief running around its arch. Whether or not it is by Gagini we will probably never know; suffice it to say that it is typical of the manner in which the old (Catalonian) and the new (Renaissance style with the acanthus deco-ration) were often juxtaposed in Sicilian architecture of the late 15th and 16th centuries.

The museum within contains a great many splendid works of art from Palermo's destroyed or derelict churches but maddeningly it is closed indefinitely.

Continuing up the Corso from the Cathedral and the Palazzo Arcivescovile, immediately ahead is the massive bulk of the Palazzo Reale flanked by the Porta Nuova. In front of both of these is the Piazza della Vittoria at the centre of which is a rather scrawny public garden called the Villa Bonanno. Here were found the remains of some patrician Roman villas, the surviving contents of which are now housed in Palermo's archaeological museum (see Chapter 3). At the eastern corner of the Piazza is the **Palazzo Sclafani (16)**, the magnificent residence built in 1330 for Matteo Sclafani. Most of this illustrious building has been rebuilt following the decline of the family in the 15th century but the façade is still adorned with inter-esting versions of Norman decorative motifs. The entrance portal has survived, a delightful geometric display of curves and right angles. From this building came the strange fresco *The Triumph of Death* which is now housed in the city's art gallery.

Before entering the Palazzo Reale, the Piazza's principal

monument and another of Palermo's earliest buildings, the church of **San Giovanni degli Eremiti (17)**, deserves a visit. This church was built in 1141 in the grounds of a mosque, the fragmentary remains of which still survive hidden among the undergrowth of an exotic garden. It was also partially incorporated into the church building itself (see the rectangular room to the right of the main altar). These are among only a handful of such survivals anywhere in Sicily, (along with the fragments on the Cathedral and the Loggia degli Incoronati – see below) and their existence points to the hallowed tradition of the site. This church itself reflects certain Islamic architectural traditions with its flattish domes, their squinches and its filigreed windows. In its ramshackle dotage, shorn of painted and sculpted adornments, it relies for visual interest on the simple abstracted shapes of its bare bones.

Come to this spot early in the morning if possible; it is so much more peaceful and mysterious without troupes of tourists getting in the way. Between the church and the ruins of the mosque are the remains of a cloister which is all that is left of a former Benedictine monastery. Reconstructed in the 19th century, it creates a picturesque display in the garden.

From this wonderful place go back to the **Palazzo Reale (18)**. Remember that you cannot enter from the Villa Bonanno side, but must go round to the back and enter from the Piazza Indipendenza via a ramped walk up through a garden. It is impossible to visit the palace itself without special permission. All that the ordinary tourist is allowed to see is the magnificent Cappella Reale which overlooks the palace's great central courtyard.

The Cappella Reale, the Royal Chapel, was built by Roger II between 1132 and 1140 on a surprisingly modest scale to a plan that is a simple aisled basilica (here the nave is flanked by two raised aisles) with a raised choir. It was decorated in two phases: the choir and the nave belong to the 1140s while the aisles were decorated some time soon after 1154. The interior is one of the most magnificent spectacles in Sicily principally because it is lavishly adorned with brilliant polychromatic mosaics. Just about every surface is ornamented: there is a Cosmati work pulpit and the marble floor, Cosmatiesque as well, is inlaid with gold and multicoloured tesserae. (Cosmati was the name given to the workers who carved pulpits, pavements, tombs and so on in a type of marble inlaid with coloured stones, mosaic, glass and gilding, very popular particularly in the 12th–14th centuries in Rome and Naples.) The capitals of the columns too are intricately carved with acanthus leaves, and some of the marble columns are striated or polished so that their veins gleam from within the stone.

The vaults and the dome of the chapel must be one of the most extraordinary coverings to any Christian place of worship anywhere. There is an Islamic-style stalactite ceiling, of wood, intricately decorated with the earliest datable group of Arabic paintings in existence. The craftsmanship here is without parallel in the Islamic world even today. The graphic decoration running at eye level around the walls is also Islamic in origin, while the language of the mosaics is mostly Byzantine. This strange mixture is a reflection of the hybrid nature of the Norman Kingdom. Even the inscription on one of the columns facing the chapel's entrance – referring to a water-clock that Roger had constructed – is in three languages, Latin, Greek and Arabic.

The Palazzo Reale, with its many rebuildings and its restorations, may not look very interesting from the exterior but it has a number of elaborate rooms in its royal apartments that are far from dull. These lie above the Cappella Reale and the most interesting one is the Sala di Re Ruggero, a magnificent mosaic ornamented chamber decorated for Roger II. The motifs expressed around the walls and in the vaults are simpler than those in the chapel and you can see clearly the influence of oriental imperial art, the peacocks and the love of ornamental foliage of trees and flowering plants. The walls are clad in marble, in the manner of palaces of both Greek and Roman antiquity.

Recent excavations in the basement (which is still closed to the public) have revealed parts of the Phoenician fortifications of the site, and way below the Cappella Reale in a labyrinth of black, damp passageways and forgotten, vaulted chambers grafitti presumed to be the work of Norman soldiers clearly shows the arrival in Sicily of Norman ships. Perhaps these depict the Norman conquest of the island.

It is a silent ageless world down there, light years removed from the squalid traffic thundering into the city beneath the rusticated sweep of the arch of the **Porta Nuova** (19) and the gaze of the eight great Moors (four on either side) which hold up its first storey. This gateway at the head of the Corso is a magnificent structure. It has a fantastically eclectic array of ornament and architectonic devices slightly Mannerist in style and was built to celebrate Charles V's victorious campaign in Tunisia in 1535, replacing a more modest structure. It was itself reconstructed after being damaged by lightning in 1667.

From the Porta Nuova, the long, straight Corso Calatifimi runs west and out of the city to Monreale. A short distance down it (take a taxi) is the **Cuba (20)**, a Norman hulk which is all that remains of one of the summer palaces – or pavilions – used by William II. Built in 1180 in the royal park that surrounded the city, it was the setting for the Sixth Story, Day Five, in Boccaccio's *Decameron*. One of his main protagonists was 'lodged with a retinue in a sumptious villa in one of his gardens, known as La Cuba'. Sadly, however, it is now a roofless ruin, and is missing its filigreed windows and its marble cladding and mosaics. Moreover, it is closed to the public.

Not far from the Cuba (in the Via dei Cipressi) is the **Convento dei Cappuccini (21)** and its well-known subterranean catacombs crammed with 8000 skeletons and mummified corpses which have filled with horrible fascination and morbid curiosity the minds of thousands of tourists over the centuries. It was last used in 1881; many of the inmates are dressed in period clothing, which is perhaps the single most fascinating thing about this macabre place. In the church of the Cappuccini (a Norman church rebuilt at the beginning of the 16th century, and again in 1934) is the sumptuous baroque funeral monument (fifth chapel to the left) of Francesco Ferdinando Gravina, Prince of Palagonia, builder of the Villa Palagonia at Bagheria (see Chapter 8).

Returning to the Porta Nuova, go back down the Corso in the direction of the Cathedral and turn left into the Via Bonello, passing the Palazzo Arcivescovile (that is, the archbishop's palace) on your left, the Cathedral on your right. Just beyond the latter is the **Loggia** and the **Cappella degli Incoronati (22)**, the former containing some surviving fragments of the original Muslim mosque (9th century), the latter founded around 1184 and possibly nothing more than a modification of the former mosque.

The Via Bonello runs into the **Piazza Papireto (23)**, a ramshackle place half sunk into the ground and dominated by a small flea market (good for ancient terracotta floor tiles) and the façade of the Palazzo dei Principi di Santa Rosalia opposite. Probably built in the last decades of the 16th century, this building has a heavily rusticated entrance portal and some rather bizarre ornamentation of Mannerist inspiration.

This piazza is part of the Capo region, a noisy, anarchic area where once slave traders lived. It is a fairly squalid, poor district, one

into which you should never venture unaccompanied. The Capo has
always been rather cut off from the rest of the city; its reputation saw
to that and, even now, the city's traffic is routed around and not
through it. If you study a map of the city you will see that the heart
of the Capo is still a tightly knit warren of alleys and passages.

From the Piazza Papireto, take the Via Gioamia which exits
northwards from its eastern corner, and go on to the Piazza dei Beati
Paoli in which is the little church of **Santa Maria di Gesù (24)** with its
lovely late 17th century Spanish-looking portal framed by barley-
sugar columns. Via Beati Paoli leaves the piazza going north and
then becomes the Via Porta Carini. On the corner of the latter and
Via Pagano, is the 17th century **L'Immacolata Concezione (25)**, just
opposite Sant'Ippolito. This church, says Giuseppe Bellafiore in
his book *Palermo*, mirrors the epoch in which it was built. In an area
of excruciating poverty, here was an interior awash with marble,
frescos, wrought-iron and stucco, in which 'the overwhelming
colours, the light, all made them [the local poor] kneel in front of
God, in front of the authorities . . . it left them speechless, made
them pray for happiness beyond, while they did not dare to try to
alter their miserable situation on earth. The florid Baroque signifies
the triumph of the Feudal and Baronial system . . .'. This church is
particularly important because everything you see in it – and principally the inlaid marble decoration – is, unlike the celebrated interior of the Casa Professa, original.

Continue along the Via Porta Carini turning right at the Via
Volturno. Ahead the way is blocked by the massive lumpen bulk of
the **Teatro Massimo (26)** which is one of the biggest theatres in
Europe. Designed by G.B. Basile and erected in 1874, it is also one
of the ugliest: it seems top-heavy while its body is too low slung and
its weight seems to push it into the ground. Impressive none the
less, it shows none of the romantic inclinations of the buildings of
Basile's son Ernesto (1857–1932, see Appendix II). This theatre
recently saw a great deal of activity as one of the settings for Francis
Ford Coppola's *Godfather III*.

Far more exotic are the little newspaper kiosks, the **Chiosco
Ribaudo** and the **Chiosco Vicari (27)**, also in the Piazza Verdi (also
called the Piazza Massimo), situated along the edge of the Via
Maqueda. These were designed by Ernesto Basile and each is a
delightful example of the local Art Nouveau ('Liberty') style,
though the florid embellishments could also point to an Islamic
provenance (Basile was particularly concious of Sicily's architectural

heritage). Painted wood, stained glass, wrought-iron and filigree window surrounds complete the idyll.

Continue along the Via Maqueda from the Piazza Verdi. It soon becomes the Via Ruggero Settimo which vanishes into a long narrow piazza called the Piazza Castelnuovo. Like the Piazza Massimo, this too is dominated by a theatre, called the **Politeama Garibaldi (28)**, a much more elegant building than the Teatro Massimo, designed by Giuseppe Damiani Almeyda in 1874. Facing it on the other side of the square is a little neo-classical music pavilion designed by Salvatore Valenti. For years it fell quietly to bits, but this is one of the few works in Palermo that have successfully been restored. Salvare Palermo was the motivation behind the project (see Chapter 1). In the piazza is another of Ernesto Basile's Art Nouveau newspaper kiosks, also called the **Chiosco Ribaudo (29)**.

Basile was largely responsible for helping to make Palermo, in Leonardo Sciascia's words, a 'little capital of art nouveau'; in fact the journal *The Studio* described him as 'the centre and leader of the art movement in Sicily . . . inexhaustibly inventive', an architect responsible for translating 'Sicilian medieval tendencies into forms suited to modern requirements'. The kiosks in the Piazza G. Verdi are the most accessible examples of his work and as well as showing a certain lighthearted romantic tendency in their designer, they prove his interest in the local traditional crafts of stone carving and wrought-iron work, both of which were important channels for the diffusion of the florid Art Nouveau style throughout Sicily. And, with his preference for the cultural idioms of the 15th century and their links to Sicily's Arabic and medieval, pre-Renaissance heritage, Basile was able to graft his 'floreale' style on to the island's own traditional styles, so that eventually it became one with them. Ernesto Basile is without doubt the greatest architect produced by Sicily in the last 150 years, and one with truly international standing. Sadly, even these (relatively minor) instances of his work are rare survivals, since like most things in Palermo a great many of his works have been neglected or destroyed.

Not far from the Piazza Castelnuovo is the **Villa Malfitano (30)**, a huge 19th century mansion set within a walled park. This was the home of the richest branch of the Whitaker family, makers of Marsala wine (see Chapter 7). To get to it, take the Via Dante from the Piazza Castelnuovo, go under the railway line and continue until your reach Olivuzza. Turn right into Via Francesco Spalita, and you will know which is the Villa Malfitano by the high perimeter wall and thick jungle of palm trees, yuccas and magnolias glimpsed beyond the main gate.

The Whitakers lived here in great style, periodically entertaining visiting monarchs (including George V and Queen Mary in 1925), who were passing by on their yachts. Joseph 'Pip' Whitaker, his wife Tina and their two daughters Delia and Norina epitomized bourgeois social success in an effete aristocratic world that worshipped money and the power it brought. And the Whitakers were very rich, as the contents of the Villa Malfitano testify even to this day. The last member of this family, Delia, died in 1971, leaving Malfitano and the family island of Motya (see Chapter 7) to a non-profit making organization which she called the 'Joseph Whitaker Foundation' (after her father) whose main aim was the 'promotion of the study and knowledge of Punic-Phoenician culture in the Mediterranean'. The Villa Malfitano would be its headquarters and in accordance with her will its interior would remain as little changed as possible.

The contents of this magnificent house are still intact and it can be visited upon application to the Foundation. Its chief treasures are the collections of sculpted coral from Trapani (see Chapter 6), a series of Gobelin tapestries from the Palazzo Colonna in Rome, and a collection of Louis XV furniture in the Louis XV Drawing Room. Fitted up like an English country house, including a billiards room and a series of comfortless bedrooms with brass beds and faded chintz curtains, it is rather incongruous in the middle of the Mediterranean.

In the Olivuzza area there are two other lesser-known landmarks to be seen. The first is the Zisa palace of the Norman kings, the other is the little Art Nouveau garden villa of the Florios, the Villino Florio. The Zisa (31) is in the Piazza Zisa not very far from the Villa Malfitano. It is a strange building constructed during the reign of William I and completed by William II. While it has the verticality you might expect from a Norman structure, it lacks solidity. It is atypically fragile and delicate looking, and was used as a pleasure palace. Certain elements of its design are distinctly Arabic: the very narrow lancet windows set within heavy niches, for example. Early descriptions tell of an artifical lake in front of it and the idyllic style of life led there. There is also a stucco inscription inside which, written in Arabic, glorifies William II and praises the building's delightful situation.

The passing of time has not been very kind to the Zisa; it has been

derelict for many years, though a much needed restoration programme is currently under way. If you can get inside notice, in the
great hall, the lovely fountain decorated with mosaics of peacocks
and hunters.

The **Villino Floria (32)** in the Viale Regina Margherita which
opens out of the Via Dante just beyond the Via Francesco Spalita is
among the very best of Ernesto Basile's works (1899). It is a delightful folly in which he displays his most artful games in the 'floreale'
style. The house has little corner turrets, Art Nouveau doors and
pointed roofs, and until fairly recently was still furnished with pieces
from the Basile era, if not designed by the architect himself. A
mysterious fire recently ruined the interior, though the exterior
remained unscathed. Local rumour has it that the fire was no accident. One can only speculate on the value of a plot such as this to
local property developers.

While on the subject of Ernesto Basile, the **Villa Igiea (33)** should
also be mentioned. It is not very conveniently situated for easy access
from the Olivuzza region (so at this point hop into a taxi) but lies on
the other side of the city by the sea on the lower slopes of Monte
Pellegrino, just above Acquasanta. This was once the seaside home
of the Florio family (see also Chapter 6).

Basile rearranged an existing building to make the Villa Igiea
into a large and luxurious summer villa. Today only one really
magnificent period room survives (it is now one of Palermo's
grandest hotels): a dining room which, says Gianni Pirrone in
Palermo Liberty, with its 'remarkable unity of space and colour, its
intimate fusion of structural and ornamental elements, is sufficient
by itself to remind us today of one of the happiest moments in the
evolution of modern art in Europe'. The Art Nouveau wall decorations are by Ettore da Maria and the furniture was made for the
room by Ducrot who, in collaboration with Basile, represented
Sicily in the field of furnishing and cabinet-making. An exact contemporary of William Morris, his methods were none the less the
antithesis of arts and crafts. Pirrone says he had a 'dialogue with the
machine'; and between them Basile and Ducrot were responsible
for Palermo's short-lived reputation as 'one of the testing grounds
of the modern movement in Italy', along with Milan and Turin.
The dining room at the Villa Igiea is one of their most prominent
surviving collaborations.

If you have time, cross the road from the Villa Igiea. Up on the
hillside is Venanzio Marvuglia's neo-classical Villa Belmonte built

in 1801 for the Princes of Belmonte. Crumbling in its park is a
classical rotunda, possibly also the work of Marvuglia, and close in
spirit to the 18th century English tradition of garden architecture.
The road up past the temple continues on to the Sanctuary of Santa
Rosalia on Monte Pellegrino.

On the landward side of Monte Pellegrino is the Parco Favorita,
(get back into a taxi), at the centre of which is the strange chinoiserie
palace the **Palazzina Cinese (34)**. The Favorita park was laid out in
1799 by the Bourbon King Ferdinand IV who, after the French invasion of his kingdom in 1798, somewhat ingloriously fled Naples
aboard the *Vanguard*, with Admiral Nelson's help. He regained his
kingdom in September 1799, again with Nelson's help, for which
the latter was awarded the Dukedom of Bronte (see also Chapter 13).
The palace is thought to have been started a year later by Giuseppe
Marvuglia on the orders of the king's temperamental wife Maria
Carolina (Marie Antoinette's sister) who saw it as a kind of Petit
Trianon. Here, in preference to the drafty Palazzo Reale in Palermo
and the vast and sepulchral palace at Caserta, court was held on a
small and intimate scale.

What an extraordinary place it is. If only you could get inside it
you would see half the building decorated with the most exquisite
gilded chinoiserie interiors and the other half painted to imitate the
interior of a Pompeian villa. The Chinese rooms, one after another,
are laden with delicate gilded filigree woodwork, and in most of the
rooms the original furniture survives. Wall textiles, frescos of exotic
Chinese scenes, stucco tracery and faux marble and turquoise act as
backdrops.

And of the Pompeian rooms, perhaps the most amazing is the
vaulted chamber painted as though it were itself a ruin in Pompei,
seen by a visitor to the city in the 18th century. Other rooms are
equally deftly painted: the king's bedchamber is decorated in what
seems to be Pompeian chinoiserie; 'in altogether novel taste' in the
opinion of one 19th century guide to the city. And there is a Turkish
parlour, and a Pompeian parlour decorated with painted scenes said
to represent Emma Hamilton in a variety of 'attitudes'.

A private dining room is equally extraordinary: 'In the supper
room, by means of ingenious devices [a sort of winch system], the
table already laden with the repast rises from the kitchen coming
to rest in the midst of the seated diners; who, without the assis-
tance and ministration of domestics, but calling for their needs
with the aid of convenient ropes corresponding to divers bells

artfully disposed to carry their sound into the lower room, are served with plates, glasses, and what else they may require, the whole being raised up by a skilful arrangement of springs'. This extraordinary contraption still survives but in such dilapidated condition you would be hard-pressed to find anything to say in its praise.

The exterior conforms to what was supposed at that period to represent Chinese architecture, and it is to Palermo what the Brighton Pavilion is to Brighton. It is a fantasy place that muddles the Gothic with the oriental; to give a more authentically Chinese appearance the architrave of the two entrance porticoes have Chinese inscriptions on them. Next door to the little palace are the stables and the royal chapel, also decorated in a Chinese style. These now house the Museo Pitré, an excellent museum of Sicilian folklore.

Next door to the Palazzina Cinese is the **Villa Niscemi (35)**, once the home of Fulco Verdura (see also Chapter 3). It is a big 18th century mansion with one or two interesting rooms filled with pieces of furniture on which Verdura himself used to bounce as a child. In 1986 it was sold by one of his relations, Maria Immacolata Valguarnera, the present Princess of Niscemi, to the city of Palermo. Both the villa and its furnishings are in an excellent state of repair (and open to the public); one hopes that it does not go the same way as the Palazzina Cinese. The sale to the state ended a long period of ownership by a family who came to Sicily in 1282, and who acquired this estate at the end of the 17th century.

The chief interest of the place is the *piano nobile* with its Kings of Sicily Gallery (so called because of the dubious portraits of all of Sicily's kings from the Hautevilles to the Bourbons on the walls), the Santa Rosalia Drawing Room (the *Apotheosis of the Saint* adorns the ceiling), the Four Seasons Room (on whose walls the personifications of the seasons are flanked by mirrors), the Green Room (which despite its name is mostly red) and Tobias' Room (so called because of the fresco of *Tobias and the Angel* on the ceiling).

The Villa Niscemi is just one of the many villas in this area which is called the **Piana dei Colli (36)**. Like Bagheria (see Chapter 8), it was a favoured summer retreat for the nobility in the 18th century and its beauty contributed no small part to the Conca d'Oro's reputation as a gloriously fertile place filled with fruit trees, oleanders, bougainvilleas and other flowering plants. The villas in the Colli, although mostly begun about the same time as those at Bagheria, are, according to Anthony Blunt, less mature than those at the latter.

That is to say the Bagheria villas 'are more ambitious . . . and incorporate ideas which seem to have been tried out in simple form in the smaller villas of the Colli'.

There are a great many villas scattered around the Colli, most conforming to a distinct type with an outside 'horse-shoe' stair in a variety of forms climbing up to the *piano nobile* where the main rooms lay. Villa Niscemi is unusual in that it does not have the stair addition; one was planned but never built.

Most of the villas are slowly crumbling and their parks are destroyed; but among those which are still recognizable as villas is the Villa Boscogrande in Via San Lorenzo, an 18th century building now used mostly for weddings. Further along the same road, at No 78, is the lovely and mysterious early 18th century Villa Cordova. Nothing seems to be known about this place: who commissioned it, who lives there or who the bell amongst the creepers by the gate will summon if you ring it. But it is one of the best villas in the district. And nearby, in the Via dei Quartieri which opens out of the Piazza Niscemi (in front of the Villa Niscemi), is the 18th century Villa Lampedusa, a pleasing one-storey building fading to a gentle saffron colour, very dilapidated and now surrounded by cows and old bath tubs. It has an ingeniously designed outer staircase. The villa was a property of the Prince of Lampedusa (see also Chapters 2 & 3) and one of the settings featured in *The Leopard*. There are other villas to see if you have the time; you should spend time driving slowly around the area, stopping wherever you see one. There is the Villa Resuttana (dating from about 1700) at No 364 Via Resuttana which opens off Piazza Leoni, and the Villa Spina (early 18th century) almost buried by bougainvillea directly opposite the Palazzina Cinese on the other side of the Viale Duca.

PART TWO

WESTERN SICILY

5

Palermo to Alcamo

Monreale, San Martino delle Scale, Carini, Montelepre, Piana degli Albanesi, Bosco della Ficuzza, Corleone, Alcamo

Going west from Palermo, the A29 is the most efficient escape from the confines of the Conca d'Oro. Monte Pellegrino and Monte Gallo in the north and Monte Castellacio in the south-west squeeze the road seawards. Thereafter, it hugs the coast of the Golfo di Castellammare for about 50 km, then loops inland not far from Alcamo, before crossing the empty heartlands of the Val di Mazara for 61 km until it reaches Mazara del Vallo on the south coast. A branch of it, the A29 *dir* diverges just west of Alcamo and heads for Trapani, 41 km to the west, sweeping dramatically through a range of mountains and wide, open plateaux. These, in summer, are Carlo Levi's 'stubble-covered expanses of the feudal lands' in which the 'light multiplies itself . . . and seems to open up and reveal the fantastic shapes of the mountains and to make sky, earth and sea compact and hard as steel . . .' (*The Words are Stones*).

There are alternatives to quitting the capital westwards along the coast. One of these is the SS186 that leads to Monreale and the Monastery of San Martino delle Scale on the slopes of Monte Gibilmesi.

Monreale is home to a great Norman cathedral magnificently endowed with rich architectural ornamentation and six acres of spectacular 12th century mosaics. It towers over a valley stretching away to the Conca d'Oro and the sea; as you approach through the orange groves from Palermo, you can set it in your sights and watch it loom larger and larger. The cathedral is the most conspicuous part of a complex which includes a Benedictine convent and the archbishop's palace. The whole project was instigated by William the Good in an effort to rival the power of the archbishop of Palermo, Walter of the Mill.

Walk slowly around the building both inside and out and

examine its multiplicity of stylistic components. The architects were Muslims and the mosaic decoration was the work of mostly Byzantine artists; but it is also known that among the highly specialized craftsmen seconded to the project were Romans, Venetians, Campanians, Provençals, Apulians and Pisans.

The original plan envisaged a royal palace to one side and the archbishop's palace and the convent to the other. With the cathedral to the Normans what Hagia Sophia was for Constantinople, and with its palace attached, the complex was to be an expression of equilibrium between the spiritual and the secular poles of power. But only the façade of the royal palace remains visible on the north side of the cathedral's apse. The archbishop's palace remains, though in a much reconstructed form, and the convent is merely a magnificently ornamented cloister.

The cathedral is still more or less in its original form though the porch at the front is an 18th century addition. It is very similar to the other great cathedrals of Norman Sicily and was among the last to have been built (1174–1176). Only the cathedral of Palermo (1184–85) postdated it and it is stylistically and functionally the fruit of much experience. Like Cefalù (see Chapter 8), and later Palermo (see Chapter 4), it was to serve as a royal sepulchre, and in the right aisle of the sanctuary is the mausoleum of King William I and II, the latter in the white marble sarcophagus, the former in an original work in porphyry of the 12th century.

Although Monreale seems massively solid, the interior structure is extremely delicate. This effect is increased by the dazzling mosaic which lines every inch of wall space above the marble dado. A single idea unifies the entire mosaic cycle – 'a majestic pageant', says Vincent Cronin – which is narrated to the most ordinary of the faithful in a simple, comprehensible language. The mosaics express the triumph of Christianity through the prophecies, the Redemption and the Triumph of the Church.

The mosaic cycle comprises three separate phases: in the nave are the facts in the Bible before the Incarnation of the Word, for example the Creation and the Flood, and other stories from the Old Testament; in the aisles, the sanctuary, the choir and the transepts is the Incarnation of the Word: episodes from the Gospels and the teachings of SS Peter and Paul (see the large figures of each in the transept apses); events after the Incarnation of the Word occupy the three main apses, the walls of the main porch and the embrasures of the windows and include more episodes from the Gospels, the

Acts of the Apostles, events from the Lives of Saints, popes, martyrs and so on (notice the very first portrait of St Thomas à Becket in the central apse; the image was executed ten years after his murder, and his inclusion here is not odd when you think that William II was son-in-law of Henry II of England). This magnificent spectacle culminates in the great figure of Christ Pantocrator in the act of benediction, with beneath him the Virgin, the archangels, seraphim and cherubim.

The mosaics show a vigorous attention to detail and a freedom and liveliness of form. In this sense they are different from their predecessors at Cefalù and in the Cappella Reale (see Chapter 4) in Palermo, and they have a lot in common with Byzantine pictorial art of the later Commeni period. This is often taken to mean that the artists were culled directly from Byzantium.

The origins of other elements of the interior are equally interesting: the stars on the beams of the aisles' roofs for instance are clearly Islamic, as are the stalactite elements of the transept ceiling. Look at the royal throne up near the main altar: many of its adornments – like the forward facing marble lions and the mosaic lions in the tympanum – are of oriental inspiration. So are the porphyry, serpentine and jasper star-filled polygon floor patterns of the presbytery which is the only part of the Norman floor ever to have been completed. Its design matches the wooden ceiling of the choir. The puzzles of this building's decoration are exciting to unravel.

One clear survival in the Sicilian artistic tradition, of Arab origin, is the seething, over-ebullient ornamentation that erupts from the flat wall surfaces. Compare the 17th century Chapel of the Crucifix (to the left of the left hand apse) with any bay of the Norman nave or aisles. The exuberant richness of the baroque decoration, with its carved, coloured and inlaid marbles and the voluptuous hysteria of its tone, meets its match in the work the consortium of Islamic, Byzantine and other craftsmen of Monreale's Norman period had produced so long before.

Monreale's cloisters are scarcely less embellished. There is a wealth and complexity of detail on their columns: some carved, some plain and others inlaid with richly lustred tesserae. All have sculpted capitals. This wonderful architectural complex is predominantly Muslim in style: see the double-arched lintels of the pointed cloister arches, each one framed by bands of mosaics in fanciful geometric designs. The cloister's sumptuous ornamentation provides a glimpse of the kind of backdrop against which King

William the Good, who liked luxury, would have lived in the royal palace at Palermo with his eunuchs, concubines and Negro guards.

Magnificent, but for different reasons, is the great Benedictine abbey at nearby **San Martino delle Scale**, founded, say the legends, by Gregory the Great in the 6th century. If you are in a hurry, confine your visit to the building's massive main staircase, designed by Venanzio Marvuglia in the middle of the 18th century. It leads out of the entrance vestibule past a huge marble group of St Martin and the Beggar by Marabitti. Much of the rest of this inspired building is also Marvuglia's. His mastery of its dramatic site would be more obvious had today's visitor been allowed to approach the vast bulk of the monastery (twenty-three bays long) by the road, which runs in a straight line up the hill towards it. Happily you can at least walk along this road, though it is now overgrown and throttled by weeds.

Monreale and San Martino delle Scale overlook Goethe's 'fertile plain', where the lemon and orange groves are now threatened by development creeping out from the suburbs of Palermo. Further west, the road climbs up the side of the mountain and creeps over to Partinico. It is a slow, arduous climb and extremely scenic, a great favourite with farmers and Sunday drivers.

Up here is beautiful and mountainous countryside, deserted except for the occasional huddle of a township pressed against some inhospitable crag with the skeleton of an antique feudal castle on its top. For the purposes of this itinerary though, the gateway to this area is Via Carini and is approached from the north, the sea and the coastal A29 from Palermo.

As you draw closer to **Carini**, the great iron-grey cliff of Monte Saraceno looms up behind the town and the deadened spirit of the area begins to creep into your consciousness. This is Danilo Dolci country and also the 'gloomy realm of [Salvatore] Giuliano' (Carlo Levi, *The Words are Stones*): Dolci was a campaigner, Sicily's Gandhi who, in the 1950s, drew attention to the plight of the peasants of western Sicily, Giuliano a Robin Hood of this oppressed class. Giuliano started out as a reforming outlaw at war with the landowners but he was transformed into a monster by the devious manipulations of state, police and *mafiosi*, and ended as the Mafia's 'marionette with a machine-gun, who killed mindlessly, and strictly to order' (Norman Lewis, *The Honoured Society*). Dolci and

Giuliano personify two very different responses to the problems facing Sicily in the postwar period, yet both chose to fight their campaigns in the heartland of the great hereditary and once repressive feudal estates – the *latifondi* – of western Sicily.

Well into the 20th century, the *latifondi* in these remote country areas remained almost unaltered from their medieval scale and form. While the despotic power of the owners of the feudal estates had waned in most other parts of Sicily after the Risorgimento and the unification of Italy, here in the west it lingered on. Horror stories about the plight of the Sicilian peasants are legion, and nowhere more potent than in Dolci's own books.

Beyond Carini, the principal towns are Montelepre, Partinico, San Giuseppe Jato, Piana degli Albanesi and Corleone, 'names that by their very sound awaken an echo of memories, even in those who do not recall the detailed story of an ambush and slaughter, in the same way (though by different means) as places of mythological or heroic fame' (Levi). It is against a background of banditry, violence and hopeless poverty that you must view this mountainous enclave and its towns and villages. Passing through, homing in on a café on a hot summer day to down an espresso or an icecream, exclaiming at the remarkable views and the antiquity of the town centres, it is none the less hard to forget that rivers of blood were shed here by the local people.

The John Murray *Handbook for Southern Italy and Sicily* (1892) calls Carini one of the most attractive towns in Sicily. Modern travellers might not be so effusive with their praise. It is dominated by a crumbling 12th century castle and its only real attractions are Giuseppe Salerno's painting of the Flagellation in the church of the Cappuccini, Alessandro Allori's *Adoration of the Shepherds* (1578) in the Duomo (fourth chapel on the left), and Vincenzo Messina's (see Appendix II) magnificent stucco work from the (first quarter of the 18th century) in the little Oratorio del Sacramento in the Piazza Duomo. Almost the entire wall and ceiling surface of the Oratoria is covered in stucco putti, angels, shells, flowers and garlands in the manner of the Serpotta. This should not be missed.

Carini is more memorable as the scene of 'The Baroness of Carini', an epic poem that relates one of the island's grim legends. It tells of the doomed love of two members of the La Grua family (the coat of arms of which can be seen on the castle's inner gate). The story goes that there was once a 'lovely Baroness', Caterina Talemanca La Grua, who fell hopelessly in love with her cousin

Vincenzo Vernagallo, the poem's '*bellu Cavaleri*', who, by way of courting her, took to riding around the castle singing. A 'great fire' had melted Donna Caterina's heart and she and her rustic lordling were drawn together 'like a magnet'. Her father the Baron disapproved. He rushed back to Carini from Palermo at the goading of the local friar, who had been spying on the lovers' illicit goings on, and murdered his daughter. In 1563 a woman called Donna Caterina La Grua was indeed murdered in Carini but she was the wife and not the daughter of her assailant.

Donna Caterina is not the only local female to have carved a niche for Carini in the annals of local history. Centuries before she ever dallied on the ramparts of the castle, Carini was famous as the birthplace of the lovely 5th century BC courtesan Lais. At the time it was known as Hyccara, and in 415 BC was at war with nearby Segesta. During the course of this event, Lais was snatched from her home by the Athenians, Segesta's allies, who were sailing along this coast, and sent into slavery in Corinth. Contrary perhaps even to her own expectations, she never looked back; in fact she became highly sought after in her new home both for her beauty and for her favours. The former was sought after by the painters of the day, the latter by her lovers' including Diogenes. Both were very costly.

About 12 km away, on the other side of Monte Saraceno, is **Montelepre**, which has always been famous – or infamous – for poverty. It was the base of Salvatore Giuliano during his lifetime, a wretched place with nothing to offer. Pressed against the side of the mountain and surrounded by deadbeat, scrawny cacti and inhospitable rocky mounds, it still looks wearily out over the great plain of Partinico. In the 15th century it was the *feudo* of the Archbishopric of Monreale, and at that time a smallish fort was built in the centre of the town. Its four-square silhouette dominates the place even now. And at one enlightened moment in its dreary history someone commissioned an *Adoration of the Magi* from Giuseppe Salerno; this can still be admired in the church of Sant' Antonio.

For anyone who has read *The Honoured Society*, Montelepre will be a source of ghoulish fascination. At the age of 21, Giuliano was known as its king. Norman Lewis says that he appointed himself arbiter of the town's morals, setting about his task with brute force. But like all the members of his band, he was forced into banditry by the hopeless poverty he was born into. Says Aldous Huxley, introducing the English translation of Danilo Dolci's *To Feed the Hun-*

gry: 'For a large body of men there was simply nothing to do. They had no reason, as far as society was concerned, for their existence. Banditry was a solution . . .'. And the terrible irony of Giuliano's life was that in the end he was forced into working for the very people against whom he was fighting to protect the Monteleprese.

During his short life, whose final few years were spent living amongst the crevices and gulleys of the mountains surrounding Montelepre, he was fêted by the press: he murdered, he was daring, he was courteous, he was romantic, his story sold newspapers. But he was used, first by the Sicilian separatists and then by the Mafia. Some of the former (most of them from the nobility), seeing a chance to prevent the inevitable upheaval should the island's uncultivated estates be handed over to the peasants, were in favour of a Sicily ruled by an absolutist king without a parliament, while others (including the Mafia) saw Sicily as America's 53rd state, or at the very least a British colony. Since the latter looked after the landed interests of a great many of the former, effectively becoming the 'feudal' overlords of Sicily, their interests interlocked. Giuliano was appointed the commander of their guerilla forces in western Sicily: marauding bands of lawless bandits were just what the separatists needed to harry the forces of the Italian State.

Yet when it became clear that this army was an uncontrollable rabble and that the separatist cause was a dead duck, Giuliano's backers dumped him. Now he was taken up by a new alliance of Mafia with, suggests Norman Lewis, members of the elected powers and those who feared the spread of communism, already strong in northern Italy. The appalling results of Giuliano's misguided attempt to aid this alliance in the defense of feudalism were tragically realized on May Day 1947.

It was a local feast day and the neighbouring towns of San Giuseppe Jato and Piana degli Albanesi had arranged celebrations and speeches to take place on the nearby grassy plateau of Portella della Ginestra. While the townsfolk were settling down, Giuliano and his band watched, hidden behind the rocks of Monte Pizzuta. At a given moment they opened fire, killing eleven people and wounding fifty-five others (some of whom died soon afterwards). These events so horrified the world that they ended Giuliano's usefulness. He was murdered three years later in Castelvetrano.

Not far from this tragic spot is **Piana degli Albanesi**, on a lesser road south-east of the Monreale-Partinico SS186. It is a bright little place, one of eight in Sicily peopled by the descendants of refugees from the Turkish invasion of Albania in the 16th century.

The Balkan heritage is very much in evidence: signboards in the main street are in both Italian and the local dialect and if you happen on Piana degli Albanesi during a festival, you will find yourself engulfed by high kicking folk dancers in traditional hand-me-down costume, swirling about to the sound of wild piped music outside the Bar Shjperia. Easter Week is the best: Palermitans flock to Piana for the festivities, which include the playing of spine-tingling funeral dirges and a procession in which the bishop plods through the town on Palm Sunday on a donkey. The rites of this Rava e Madhe, the 'Great Week', are generally Byzantine and are peculiar to this place which the rest of Sicily, confused, insists on calling Piana dei Greci.

The importance of this festival in the civic and ecclesiastical calendars is matched by the richness of the heavy costumes which are hauled out of mothballs in its honour. Clad in a *ntsilona* (a gold embroidered skirt) with a *keza* head-dress and decked in fine *domanti* and *pindjets* (varieties of jewellery) with a *brezi* (a heavy metal belt incorporating the figure of St George) to match, the women of Piana degli Albanesi are easily the most exotic of the Sicilian Easter Week.

A small country road straggles to the south out of Piana degli Albanesi and is immediately consumed by vast open prairies which in summer turn the colour of sand. Nothing but a distant flock of sheep and a lone shepherd leaning on a stick breaks the monotony of the dusty vista until, after about 18 km, an obelisk divides the road in two. One branch leads to **Bosco della Ficuzza**, the other to Corleone.

Ficuzza itself is a tiny hamlet dominated by a large classical hunting lodge built by Venanzio Marvuglia for Ferdinand III in 1805. Up in the hills behind it are the remnants of the king's hunting preserve, the Bosco della Ficuzza, at one time filled with boar and still brimming with chestnuts and old oaks. Much fought over, this *bosco* is one of the last tracts of wild woodland left in Sicily, the rest of the island having been stripped of trees almost unremittingly since the days of the Normans.

Locked into the forest to the south is the Rocca Busambra, a small mountain whose great cliff-face menaces Ficuzza. There is a magnificent gloom about this place, which is also known as the 'cemetery' of the Mafia. Scores of their victims were disposed of here, their corpses dropped into seemingly bottomless crevasses, where their bones lay undiscovered, sometimes for years.

Perhaps the most famous corpse to be dumped in this way was that of Placido Rizzotto, an idealistic young trades unionist from nearby Corleone. He whipped up support for a move to have the local feudal estate expropriated and the land redistributed amongst the local peasantry. He was killed by the Mafia in 1948 on a lonely slope outside the town. Norman Lewis writes: 'It happened on a fine evening of early spring at about nine o'clock – a time when the Via Bentivegna and the Piazza Garibaldi were crowded with people out for an after-supper stroll before going to bed. Everyone knew what was happening, saw the pointed guns, knew that Placido was being lead away like an animal to the slaughter house. What took place was a sad Gethsemane sequence of averted eyes and abandonment, of doors quickly closed and lights quickly put out. Within minutes the streets and the square of Corleone were empty, and Placido walked alone with his captors towards the crevice on the mountainside . . .'.

Corleone, on the other side of the Rocca Busambra from Ficuzza, lies beneath a craggy rock formation prickly with cacti and dominated by what was once the town's gaol. Of all the towns in this part of Sicily, Corleone has the most violent history of interfamilial feuding and Mafia intrigue. Danilo Dolci was told 'they shoot people everywhere, wherever they happen to be. There's not a corner of the town where some incident has not occurred.'

All this was happening in spite of the venerable Chiesa Madre (begun 1382) with its *Madonna of Help*, (school of Domenico Gagini) and the town's respectability in the days of the Norman Count Roger. Its murderous traditions began in the 13th century, when during the Sicilian Vespers, the people of Corleone enthusiastically murdered more Angevins than did any other town in the vicinity.

After returning to the SS186, it is a short run to Partinico and the SS113, which crosses the Plain of Partinico to **Alcamo**. From afar Alcamo is just an innocent sprinkling of bleached houses on the flank of Monte Bonifato. Those who know it, however, are aware that in the 1950s and '60s it was the lair of the notorious *mafioso* Vincenzo Rimi. He was head of a dynasty linked with the American Cosa Nostra, which commanded an important drug trafficking

route from Sicily to America and whose activities were screened by
political protection. Gaia Servadio in *To a Different World*,
describes him as a thug, a much convicted criminal, and a 'man of
respect' who established himself and his 'family's' supremacy in
Alcamo by sheer violence. Such was his corrupt power that he was
able to have men of his clan elected to parliament: his lawyer,
Giovanni Leone, an important Christian Democrat minister, eventually became President of the Italian Republic, 1971–8.

Rimi recruited couriers from Alcamo and Castellammare to work
on the principal drug route from North Africa to America via Sicily.
Drugs and other contraband arrived and left the country undetected
via the remote coast of nearby San Vito lo Capo. Some drugs entered
the USA secreted into cavities gouged out of slabs of marble
quarried from the foot of Alcamo's hill: 'Of course the quarries also
belonged to the Mafia . . .' (Servadio).

Over the years Rimi's activities have become a part of Alcamo's
folklore, and wary foreigners skirt the town transfixed by the pos-
sibility that they might acquire a new pair of concrete boots and a
permanent home under the waves of the Golfo di Castellammare.
But Rimi died in 1975 – go and examine his absurd marble sepulchre in the town's cemetery (ironically he was to die peacefully in
his bed) – and in any case, the Mafia rarely concerns itself with
outsiders.

Alcamo is on the way to the glories of the temple at nearby
Segesta, and the unspoilt coves and mountain slopes of Capo San
Vito. Most visitors rush by. Even Goethe gave Alcamo only a cursory
glance, merely recording, rather prissily, that the town was a clean
one. It was though a fairly large one at the time, wealthy, fortified
(with a vast castle built by the Counts of Modica in the 14th century)
and enviably placed at the crossing of two main routes – one from
the Port of Alcamo (now Castellammare del Golfo) to the island's
interior, the other from Trapani to Palermo. This position ensured
that it was always moderately rich and even in the 12th century it
had beautiful mosques and thriving markets. Inevitably its wealth
led to the construction of ornate palaces in the centre of town, as
well as a great many churches, some of which were decorated by the
Gagini and the illustrious Giacomo Serpotta.

Alcamo is still filled with churches. They dominate the open
spaces and the narrow side streets. There is the vast hulk of the
Collegiata which stands squarely at one end of Alcamo's main
square, the long thin Piazza Ciullo. Memorable only for its scale, it

none the less looks insignificant beside the 17th century church of SS Paolo e Bartolomeo and the early 18th century SS Cosma e Damiano, both at opposite ends of the Corso VI Aprile.

The walls of the interior of SS Paolo e Bartolomeo positively squirm with 18th century stucco putti, angels, cornucopie and floral tributes. There are lumpen angels hoisting themselves up the back of the altar and someone (God?) seems to have tipped some putti upside down out of a sack above the transept altars. One is falling on his head and is only a hair's breadth from cracking his skull on a triumphal arch. Best are the gossiping female deities sitting swinging their legs over the edge of the cornice at the junction of transept with nave, waving their arms and gossiping. They could have been modelled on the modern Alcamese on the beach at Alcamo Marina oiling their bodies in the sun, nattering and sharing intimate secrets of the previous night's encounter. And when the *stuccatore*, Vincenzo Messina (see Appendix II), his son Gabriele, and Antonio Vultagio, were not slapping the putti into shape and arranging the plaster bouquets, Antonino Grano was busy, also during the 18th century, covering nearly all the wall and ceiling space with frescos. All this is very provincial, wonderfully spirited and immensely decorative. Whether the Alcamese ever found God amongst it all is a point open to question.

Serpotta's allegorical figures in the Badia Nuova take life more seriously; they have names like Purity, Peace, Fortitude and Meekness. In addition to these there are figures on the altar of SS Crocifisso of the Addolorata and St John the Evangelist, and in the chancel large figures of SS Peter and Paul which are supposed to be among the finest from the *stuccatore's* later years. Nearly as good are Charity and Fortitude (1722) leaning up against the pilasters of the chancel arch of SS Cosma e Damiano, a Borrominiesque sort of place built on a centralized plan. One quite unusual point to notice about these Alcamese Serpottas is the fact that, unlike their Palermitan counterparts, they still have their surface sheen of marble dust. This removes the deathly pallor from their flesh and enlivens their drapery, giving it the effect of satin.

Alcamo is also prolifically endowed with a whole range of Gagini sculptures. The vast barn that calls itself Santa Maria Assunta is littered with them. There is a particularly lovely Mary Magdalen in the church of San Francesco.

The church of Santa Oliva too has some magnificent pieces. There is an *Annunciation* by Antonino and Giacomo Gagini (1545), and Sant'Oliva herself was sculpted for the fourth chapel on the right by Antonello Gagini. This particular church you will notice is quite unlike any other in the town: it has some of the most splendid late 18th century decoration in Sicily. There is something very sophisticated about its interior and something very north European and rococo about Francesco and Giuseppe Rosso's decoration of the vault. While the ceiling is animated by the elegant swirls of the frames surrounding the fresco *Glory of the Mystic Triangle*, the nave ripples with the undulations of the piers and the cornices. This is Giacomo Amato's work and it dates from 1723.

6

Alcamo to Trapani, The Egadi Islands and Pantelleria

Scopello, Capo San Vito (Castelluzzo, San Vito lo Capo, Scurati), Segesta, Calatafimi, Salemi, Trapani, Egadi Islands (Favignana, Levanzo, Marettimo), Erice, Pantelleria

Not far from Alcamo are two of western Sicily's chief attractions. One is the peninsula of **Capo San Vito**, a uniquely (for Sicily) protected area. The other is the temple of Segesta, one of the best preserved 'Greek' temples in Italy. The *capo*, a great chunk of land part of which has been preserved as the Riserva Naturale dello Zingaro, is horn shaped with San Vito lo Capo at its tip and Trapani and Castellammare del Golfo on either side of its neck. The peninsula is accessible just as easily from either of these towns, though the roads tend to be small and winding.

Before the existence of the Zingaro Reserve, this area was unviolable because of the Mafia activities which took place among its creeks, rocky coves and sheltered hideaways. Any attempt at road or villa building was discouraged, much to the region's advantage. It is ironic that in the heartland of the Mafia a very large tract of natural landscape should be protected from development when there are other, perhaps even more beautiful, parts of Sicily equally under pressure which receive no protection at all. You cannot even take a car into the Reserve, which means a good hard slog on foot to its remoter beaches.

To get to San Vito lo Capo from Alcamo, you have to skirt Castellammare del Golfo on the coast, one of the prettiest of Sicily's small fishing ports. The sleepy idyll that presents itself down among the smell of fish, the piles of old nets and the upturned boats belies a past almost as rough as Alcamo's. In the late 1950s it was amongst Sicily's poorest towns, with a quarter of its families officially classed as destitute. The sparks ignited by poverty and crime were fanned into a raging fire by the Mafia, and it has been estimated that in the late 1950s eighty percent of the town's male population had seen the inside of a gaol. Castellammare was the main embarkation point for Sicilian emigrants to America and in the 1930s it gave its name to the bloody Mafia war in which the 'Cosa Nostra' (as the Mafia prefer to call their organisation) struggled to find a leader, a struggle that provided the background to Mario Puzo's *The Godfather*.

Rising above Castellammare in the west is Monte Inici up which a winding, climbing SS187 leads to pleasant unspoilt countryside beyond, and to **Scopello**, the first stop on the way to San Vito lo Capo. Actually there are two Scopellos – Scopello Tonnara and Scopello di Sopra.

Scopello Tonnara is a tunny fish trap operated by a force of fishermen-butchers from March to June every year. It is an ancient Sicilian *tonnare*, though not the most antique of all or by any means the biggest. But is must be among the most idyllically situated and is still in excellent condition; most of the others scattered around the west coast of Sicily are falling into disrepair due to the increasing centralization of the industry. At one time tunny fishing was one of the most profitable livelihoods on the island and great 19th century fortunes were founded on it.

This *tonnara* was in existence in the 14th century, and above the present buildings are two so-called Saracen towers, one ruined, the other restored. They seem to protect the huddle of *tonnara* buildings: the owner's bleached pink palazzo, the storerooms, the chapel and the barracks where the *sciurma* (crew) live during the season. Out of season these buildings are almost monastically calm. Gavin Maxwell, who came here in 1953, wrote of his experiences in *Ten Pains of Death*. He was told by an old crone who lived in the complex and whose husband had been one of the *tonnaroti* (tunny fishermen), that in a terrific storm one year the arched bridge that had once joined the towers had come crashing down, bringing with it piles of ancient human skulls hidden inside it, each one with a spike driven through it from front to back.

The traditional tunny fish catch is an extraordinary spectacle. From March to June the huge fish are returning to their breeding grounds through Sicilian waters. The fishermen lie in wait in broad wooden boats. At a given moment they trap the fish in an elaborately prepared series of nets and then hack them to death in a ritual that has its origins in the island's Arabic past. One end of the system of nets is tied fast to the shore – this is the mouth of the trap – and the other end of it is anchored out at sea. The fish are funnelled into a succession of net 'chambers' which get stronger and stronger the deeper the fish penetrate the trap, until finally they are in the 'death chamber' from which they cannot escape. Once there, its floor is raised and the fish are forced to rise to the surface. Then the slaughter begins. This is the *mattanza* – from the Spanish for slaughteryard – and as many fish die by thrashing against each other (some weigh as much as 1000lbs) in the struggle to get out as do by harpoon. It is an uncontrollably violent scene, fuelled by the steady background rhythm of a chant called the *cialoma* and the yelling of the crew. The sea turns the colour of blood as the huge fish churning about in the foam slowly die.

The hunt has its own lore and language which derive, according to Mary Taylor Simetti (*On Persephone's Island*), directly from its Arabic origins. The captain is called a *rais* (which in Arabic actually means captain), and the *cialoma* (which is thought to be a Middle Eastern word in the same vein as 'salaam' or 'shalom' – 'greetings'), begins and ends with the cry 'aimola! aimola!' which might possibly derive from 'Allah! Che Muoia!' – Allah! May it die!'

Scopello di Sopra, on the hill above the *tonnara*, is a tiny village with a single pot-holed, semi-cobbled street and a large archway into the vast courtyard of the Baglio Ispano. In the Middle Ages Scopello di Sopra grew and developed away from the sea (even though its inhabitants were *tonnaroti*) because of the menace of piracy. Nothing as exciting as that ever happens here nowadays, and the nearest you will get to a Saracen marauder is the enduring legacy of his cuisine which is often dished up in one of the little *trattorie* or cafés in the Baglio: couscous with meat, north-African style. Up here the homes of a population now mostly emigrated to America have been turned into simple *pensioni* and bars. When people left, they just closed and locked their front doors, hoping one day to return with their fortunes made. Many of these old houses are now being allowed to crumble slowly away.

The road continues northwards along the coast from Scopello towards the Riserva Naturale dello Zingaro, where it peters out. To reach San Vito lo Capo and its promontory from Scopello, you have to go west, skirting the base of Monte Speziale which lies between the two. The road is not difficult to find: it straggles over the seaward flank of Monte Sparigio, passing on the way the gaunt remains of the Castello di Baida. This old castle, actually more of a small fortified village (known as a *borgo*), which is slowly slipping down the hill, once functioned as the centre of the estate of the Taralus family and was later much frequented by that old hunting enthusiast King Ferdinand III (1759–1825). Of the original building, all that survives apart from a baronial gateway emblazoned with a coat of arms, are the fragments of fortified walls, a chapel, and a huddle of cottages where once the castle stood.

The road continues on to the tiny hamlet of Luppino then, branching right, leads to Castelluzzo and San Vito lo Capo. The peninsula from Castelluzzo to San Vito is rather a peculiar place. The great inhospitable mounds of rock, like Monte Cofano which faces Castelluzzo from the west, create a sense of primeval remoteness. Monte Cofano, which juts out of the sea like a huge tooth, separates two very different worlds: while Castelluzzo and the little towns leading up to Capo San Vito are like places time forgot, the towns to the south – Erice, Trapani and Marsala – are the hub of modern-day western Sicily.

Castelluzzo was laid out in the 18th century and looks very much a one horse town you might have found in the Mexican outback in the last century. The odd chicken scratches the dust by a doorway, and lying in the sun there may be an exhausted dog that lifts its head as a car passes by, then sinks back into dreamy oblivion. Castelluzzo has a wide main street lined with low, boxy houses. It leads to Macari, a hamlet sunken into what looks from afar like a peat bog. All around it are old dry-stone walls crumbling in the wind. At Macari an antique watchtower on a jagged cliff of rock surveys the unusual rock formations which bring geologists with their hammers and sample jars. Here too were the coral beds that provided Trapani with its most well known decorative craft, sculpted coral (see the Museo Pepoli, Trapani, mentioned below).

From Macari the road skirts a wild shoreline on its way to the little town of **San Vito lo Capo** nearly on the tip of the promontory of Capo San Vito. The country road sweeps into town in a single extravagant gesture and expectations are high as you read in the guide books about its 'dense ranks of trattorias, hotels and bars' and about the finest sandy beaches on the island which line the coast in its vicinity. The reality is more modest. There is a little bit of everything, but though the beaches are magnificent, it is not very sophisticated. There are some palm trees in pots in the piazza and a huge castellated church which glowers over the main street. If you want to follow up the primeval theme of the surrounding landscape, west of the town is the Grotta Cala Mancino whose walls are covered with rare Paleolithic incision drawings of deer and humans.

This area has played an active part in the life of the island since time immemorial. Apart from the caves, there is evidence that the Phoenicians set up a victualling post for their ships here on their way from the Egadi Islands to Palermo. The Greeks were here, so were the Romans (outside San Vito lo Capo are the excavated remains of their *tonnara*) and the remains of both can be seen in the Museo Pepoli in Trapani.

On the Trapani-Erice flank of Monte Cofano is a vast cave at whose mouth is the tiny hamlet of **Scurati**, a group of single-storied medieval cottages that were occupied until very recently. A nearby cave, the Grotta della Misericordia, contains wall paintings by Sicily's earliest Christians, who took refuge here from persecution. Another cave, the Grotta Mangiapane, about ½ km from Scurati, is named after the family who lived in it until fairly recently. It was excavated in the 1920s by Vaufrey who found traces of Paleolithic occupation, which again are housed in the Trapani museum.

Another of western Sicily's greatest sights, **Segesta**, is reached by taking either the SS113 or the A29 *dir* from Alcamo going west. The temple stands at the top of a well trodden path beneath Monte Bernardo. Even that old misery Cardinal Newman, who went there in the 19th century, forgot all about the recurring aches and pains of his recent illness and his possible next one, and went into raptures when he saw it in the distance: 'Oh that I could tell you one quarter what I have to say about it! . . . oh wonderful sight! – full of the most strange pleasure. Strange from the position of the town, its awful desolateness, the beauty of the scenery . . . its historical recollections . . . it has been a day in my life to have seen Egesta.'

Goethe grudgingly admired the temple and its natural surroundings, leaving his complaints for the rest of the ruins, the theatre and the remains of the city. He saw no pleasure in visiting those because he had already been wearied by his walk to the temple. He must have had a terrible time in this particular part of the world for he ends his diary entry for that day on a very low note: 'there are some insects about . . . The leeches, lizards and snails here are no more beautiful in colour than ours; indeed, all those I saw were grey'. There are some more effusive late 19th century descriptions of trips to this venerable old site which convey the sheer delight of discovering so sublime a spectacle in the lonely remoteness of the Sicilian hinterland, even though (or perhaps because) the trip by either mule or mule-pulled cart was fraught with danger of attacks by bandits and highwaymen. One wonders what Brydone would have said about Segesta. Unfortunately he never got there.

Like all ancient sites, Segesta has a history laden with legends and invention. It is accepted though that the very earliest occupation of the site was by the Elymian people who came to Sicily from the east in about the 12th century BC, settling on the borders of Sicanian territory and founding the towns of Eryx (Erice) and Egesta (Segesta). They professed to have originated in Troy, though these days such a claim is not held to indicate a reliable connection with any known city or land.

Theocritus says that Segesta was founded by Agestus, son of the water nymph Egesta and the legendary dog Crinisios. After the latter had had his evil way with the nymph, she turned him into a stream (the Fiume Freddo which flows down through Castellammare del Golfo to the sea). Virgil has Acestes (the Roman name for Egestus) going off to defend Troy and, having no luck, returning to Sicily with refugees from that city who then become the town's first occupants. At the same time he has Aeneas founding the temple to his mother Venus at Eryx.

Hence this illustrious connection with the Trojans may have a kernel of truth in it. Certainly the Greeks and the Elymian people occupying this city state hated each other; might this be an ancient legacy of the old enmity between the Trojans and their neighbours? The Trojan connection seems to have been exploited by later Segestans; it impressed the Romans who themselves were always on the look-out for more illustrious antecedents for their own city. When they marched into Sicily they freed Egesta from tax, though they suggested a change of name to today's Segesta.

The first occupants spoke a mysterious language. Fragments of pottery found amongst the ruins of the old city on the flank of Monte Barbaro, the low hill just to the left of the temple, are covered in Greek lettering, but the language is not Greek and still incomprehensible today. This mystery aside, we know quite a lot about Segesta from Diodorus and from Cicero, who between them illuminate various aspects of the real history of the city, most of which remains unexcavated.

Segesta was best known for the devious nature of its people who had a hand in the destruction of nearby Selinus (Selinunte) in 409 BC. Earlier, in 415 BC, Athens had been duped into signing a treaty of friendship with the Segestans who needed help against the threat of attack from Selinus, on their borders to the south and at the time a far more powerful city state. Athenian officials were sent out from Greece to inspect the Segestans' claim to great wealth and military expertise. They were taken to Eryx's famous Temple of Venus and led to believe that the silver-gilt vessels on display were of solid gold, and the property of Segesta (in fact most belonged to Eryx). Impressed, the Athenians returned home thinking that Segesta was formidably wealthy, and the treaty of friendship was duly signed.

Not until about thirty-five years later, when the Segestans were having problems with their neighbours at Selinus, was the treaty with Athens invoked. An expedition duly set out from Athens, only to be thwarted by the Syracusans, Selinus's allies. The way was thus clear for an open attack on Segesta. The wily Segestans, however, had also applied to the Carthaginians for support and an attack was mounted on Selinus by Hannibal, their general, which lead to the eventual slaughter of its people and the total devastation of the city in 409 BC. Selinus never recovered and its gigantic temples still lie in ruins, some destroyed by the Carthaginians, others toppled by natural forces. The builders of those still incomplete were murdered, or fled.

Less than 100 years later the tyrant Agathocles razed Segesta and murdered 10,000 of its inhabitants, sending the rest into slavery. The brutality with which this was carried out was unmatched, says Diodorus, by any other tyrant: the citizens were tortured, slaughtered, then flung into the river Skamandos (now identified with the river Gaggera nearby). Segesta recovered however, to be repopulated by Agathocles, who renamed it Dikaeopolis.

For now, the tangible reminders of the antiquity of this site are the temple and the theatre. The temple is roofless, and there is no cella (the main body of a temple – distinct from the portico – which contains the religious image) inside it; in fact it was never finished. Not much is known about the building, though it is thought to have been built about the time of Athens' alliance with Segesta – somewhere between 426 and 416 BC. Basically it is a Doric building, though the six massive columns along the front and the twelve down either side have none of the characteristic fluting. Bernard Berenson came here in 1953 and muttered that the columns did not even have the usual entasis either, concluding that, unlike the Parthenon, this temple was a far from perfect Doric building.

The general haziness about the temple's origins has led to speculation about its exact purpose. Some think it was built as a massive 'stage set', a prop in the elaborate plan to dupe the Athenians in the 5th century BC. Perhaps its builders simply lost interest, or maybe in its 'unfinished' state it constituted the setting for a religious ritual about which we know nothing. Indeed Biagio Pace, an eminent Italian archaeologist, suggests that the rites practised in this building did not require a temple in the normal Greek mould – which would explain the absence of a roof and a cella – but this theory is countered by the stones found inside which probably came from the base of the cella. They were later removed.

In fact building work was surely abandoned around the time of the tussle with Selinus. Nowadays, Segesta is thought of as a good example of 'work in progress'; the architrave has no holes for the insertion of roof beams. The floor is rough and, as Goethe noticed, the temple steps have 'peglike projections to which ropes were attached when the blocks were transported to the site'. These ought to have been sawn off – and would have been had the building been completed. There would no doubt also have been other refinements such as dressed surfaces and fluting for the columns.

Yet in spite of its raw state, this building is a sophisticated example of its genre and it has a certain *genius loci*. Its squatness and ponderous solidity seem to reflect a finely tuned sensitivity to the rugged, mountainous setting.

Segesta's theatre, which dates from the end of the 3rd century BC, was also designed with an awareness of the grandeur of the landscape. Unusually, it faces north, possibly so that the audience had a better view out beyond the stage to the wide plateau, the mountains and the sea in the far distance. This must be one of the most spectacular settings for an open-air theatre anywhere.

A few kilometres away is **Calatafimi**, where Cardinal Newman stopped on his way to Segesta 'to have an egg or two.' Most travellers in the past used Calatafimi as their base and were horrified by it. The Cardinal, not usually one to mince words, said: 'The towns of Partinico and Alcamo are masses of filth; the street is a pool; but Calatafimi, where we slept! – I dare not mention facts'.

An exception however, was Samuel Butler, author of *Erewon* as well as of the fantastical thesis that the author of the Odyssey was a woman and the original Ithaca, home of Odysseus, was one of the Egadi Islands off Trapani, called Marettimo. He chose to make it his home at the turn of the century. Butler's Calatafimi was swept clean away however, in the Terremoto di Belice, the earthquake of 1968. Even the Castello – in the 15th century an important and strategic fortification of the Aragonese rulers of Sicily – is now a pathetic ruin held together by a kind of strap in an effort to preserve some sense of civic dignity. In view of this, it would be best to make quickly for the war memorial on the Piante di Romano just outside the town to the south-west.

The memorial, an obelisk designed by Ernesto Basile in 1892, commemorates the Battle of Calatafimi fought on the site on 15 May 1860. Here Garibaldi and his band of just over 1,000 volunteers won their first victory over the Neapolitan armies of the Bourbons; its successful outcome left open the way to Palermo.

The Garibaldini had arrived in Sicily (at Marsala) only four days previously. They had then marched through the parched, dusty summer landscape via Rampingallotto and Salemi to Calatafimi where they found the Neapolitans waiting for them on the rocky summit of Pianta di Romano. 'Here we shall make Italy – or die!', Garibaldi yelled. The Neapolitans outnumbered the Garibaldini by nearly three to one and they had more efficient weapons. Garibaldi's motley array of men and boys seemed no match for the formidable, uniformed force they faced. But in fact it was doddering old General Landi, of the Neapolitan forces, who was outmatched.

Garibaldi spent the night before the battle at **Salemi**, a hilltown just 12 km south of Calatafimi. It is one of the oldest towns in the area, but much altered since the damage it sustained in the Terremoto di Belice. The makeshift prefab shelters put up to house the inhabitants still stand, while what is left of old Salemi rises like a skeleton from the rocky hill, surrounded by olive groves, orchards of lemon trees and the ubiquitous prickly pears. Salemi is an ancient town whose site has been in continuous occupation since the days of the Siculians. It has a 13th century castle built by Frederick II on the foundations of a much earlier construction and, restored after the tremors, this now houses the Museum of the Risorgimento. Here Garibaldi slept after the battle.

A small but interesting art collection survived the earthquake of 1968. Works of art from collapsed local churches were placed in the former Collegio dei Gesuiti (1652), which was adapted to become Salemi's Civic Museum. It contains works by Domenico and Antonello Gagini, two statues attributed to Francesco Laurana, and a Madonna with angels by Mariano Smiriglio brought from the Duomo. Smiriglio supervised the construction of the Duomo from 1615 and its loss is particularly tragic. Its functions have been taken over by the Chiesa del Collegio, a 17th century building enlarged and partly rebuilt in the 18th century.

From Salemi, it is easy to reach the coast along the so-called Strada di Salemi, the one Garibaldi used and which runs around the base of the Gibellina mountains directly to Marsala. But for the purposes of this itinerary, go back to Calatafimi and continue either on the country highway the SS113 or on the *autostrada* A29. Both lead directly to Erice and Trapani, the latter sweeping into town via a series of flyovers, counter-flyovers and sliproads, the former coming to a more dignified halt outside **Trapani**, beneath Monte San Giuliano and its hilltown **Erice**.

People come to the west of Sicily more for the attractions of Erice the hilltown (see below) than for those of Trapani the gutsy port. Carlo Levi called Erice 'the Assisi of the south, full of churches and convents and silent streets and of extraordinary accumulation of mythological memories'. Trapani by contrast tends to be a side attraction, its salty vigour eclipsed by the quaint beauty of Erice with its winding cobbled alleys and tiny provincial palaces ebulliently decorated.

If you decide to visit both, pick a hotel in Erice and visit Trapani during the day. The heart of Trapani is a crooked peninsula that pokes into the sea towards the Egadi Islands. The town is narrow and labyrinthine and cut down the middle by the Corso Vittorio Emanuele. Modern Trapani is filled with concrete apartment blocks and wide, uninteresting streets; but by contrast, the old heart of the city, confined to the peninsula, is lively and crammed with old palaces and churches.

Churches in fact dominate old Trapani. Some are virtuoso exercises in the baroque manipulation of masonry. The cathedral of San Lorenzo for example, in the Corso, is a memorable performance of unrestrained twisting, bullying and massaging of stone. Its massive (and in contrast to the rich undulations of the exterior angular) classical entrance portico, designed in 1740 by Giovanni Biagio Amico, dominates the street.

In the Corso, going further east, is another baroque façade belonging to the Jesuit Noviciate. This was designed by Natale Masuccio early in the 17th century, and is one of his first (and finest) surviving works (see Messina, Chapter 11). Its significance lies in the striking contrast between the robust carved caryatids and grotesque figures and the rigid, classical pilasters, columns and capitals. This rather curious combination is very typical of west Sicilian architecture.

Adjacent to the Jesuit church, and facing the full run of the Corso from the east, is the magnificent Municipio, built in 1696. From the west end of the Corso it provides an imposing visual finale to the street, an effect which sadly has been spoilt by a vulgar modern stump of a building which the *comune* has allowed to be constructed behind it.

Other places to look out for in Trapani are the late 15th century Palazzo della Giudecca, the church of Santa Maria del Gesù, and the Sanctuary and Convent of the Annunziata, the last housing the Pepoli Museum. The Palazzo della Giudecca is a very curious building with an 'egg-box' façade. It can be found in the Via Giudecca at the heart of the old Jewish quarter developed in 1363. Santa Maria del Gesu, in the Via San Pietro, has a traditional 16th century exterior and within there is a lovely full-size Andrea della Robbia *Madonna* in a niche adorned with angels, fruit and flowers. There is also a *baldachino* by Antonello Gagini (1531). At the bottom of the Via San Pietro is the much bashed about Templar church of Sant'Agostino, whose dramatically sawn-off façade is decorated with a rose window and entrance portal both of which date from the 14th century.

It is the Pepoli Museum, adjacent to the Sanctuary of the Madonna of Trapani, that is perhaps Trapani's greatest curiosity. Some way out of the centre of the old town, in the Via Giovan Battista Fardella, the museum contains a very large collection of decorative art from the city and its outlying provincial centres.

Trapani in former days had a reputation for very high calibre decorative art of which the most conspicuously ornate pieces were made of coral. Great fields of coral lay off the coast of the city and the peninsula of Capo San Vito. These were harvested and turned into jewellery, church ornaments and devotional objects, the best of them made in the 17th century. So sought after were these objects that coral has now vanished almost entirely from Trapani's shores and the only evidence of its existence lies in glass cases in museums like this one.

The museum's history begins with Count Agostino Pepoli who in the 19th century spent a great deal of time seeking out and gathering up the best of the province's artistic treasures. His collection ended up in this converted Carmelite convent which was taken over by the state in 1925. Later it was augmented by local collections of paintings, books, ceramics, jewellery, silverwork, coral, furniture, paintings and archaeological fragments, all unvisited, forgotten and in danger of dispersal. Pepoli's quest was made all the more urgent by the fact that so much of the artistic patrimony of the province – for instance the coral works – was extremely fragile.

A bewhiskered bust of the count stands guard at the museum entrance. Beyond him is a vast cloister scattered with bits of classical statue, chunks of defunct baroque church and the battered tombstones of unknown Spanish aristocrats. The cloister leads to the entrance hall just inside which is a remarkable early 17th century staircase made from different kinds of marble; it is decorated with marble intaglio and designed with an elaborate series of landings and half landings so that the ascent is gradual. It is a wonderful example of the intaglio technique (which the Sicilians were inordinately good at), and its design is far in advance of any contemporary stair built on the mainland. It leads past a rogues' gallery of Gagini sculptures, a vast and ungainly gilded carriage, and up to the huge halls of the convent, where Pepoli's eclectic collections are displayed.

If you are short of time, then make for the coral sculptures. The most lavish object is a lamp made in 1633 by Matteo Bavera for the church of San Francesco at Trapani. It is 1½ m tall, and it marries salmon-coloured coral with gilded bronze. But it is eclipsed by the sheer vulgarity of Bavera's crucifix: the figure of Christ is fashioned from coral, the cross from ebony and the whole ensemble layered with a variety of details in tortoiseshell and mother of pearl. Also collected from local church treasures are chalices, reliquaries and devotional plaques depicting saints at the centre of florid bowers, all in coral (some even more remarkable pieces are in Palermo's Villa Malfitano collection – see Chapter 4).

Pepoli filled other parts of his collection with miniature 17th and 18th century figures once used to people Nativity scenes in

Christmas cribs. These cribs – *presepi* – are still seen in a great many Sicilian and Neapolitan churches. The figures were of paste, wax or ceramic, and generally dressed up in the costume of the period. The king figures from the 18th century *presepi*, for example, are dressed as fashionable gentlemen; miniature clothes are richly worked with embroidery and there are tiny covered buttons and real leather boots. Even the goats and the sheep have real hair. One particularly beautiful crib, made by Andrea Tipa in the 18th century, uses shells and coral and is peopled with gilded figures. There is even a marble city in the background whose architectural details are picked out in gold leaf. If you go out into the Corso in Trapani you can buy the modern equivalent of these *presepi* though nowadays the figures are carved out of wood and then painted.

Having waded through the silver collections, studied the uniform of the Garibaldino killed in battle, gorged yourself in the painting gallery on the resurrections, depositions and martyrdoms (each one bloodier than the next), and seen Titian's *Saint Francis receiving the Stigmata*, there is still the Sanctuary of the Annunziata next door awaiting a visit.

Here a warren of little shrines compete for the attentions of pilgrims, the biggest is that of the Madonna of Trapani, a pious lady of uncertain origin and the subject of rapt devotion for several centuries. It is said to be by Nino Pisano (*c*. 1315–*c*. 1368), son of the great Andrea (famed for the bronze doors on Florence's Bapistry), and there is a very curious legend which details the statue's arrival in Trapani.

On its way back from a crusade, a Pisan ship put in at Trapani during a storm. When a sealed crate was offloaded from its hold and set on the quay, a cripple sat on it and immediately felt a strange tingling in his legs. Finding that he was able to walk, he threw away his crutches and ran home. Astonished observers hacked opened the case and found a marble statue of the Virgin and Child. At once, anyone and everyone with a deformity or a disease, or those simply down on their luck, rushed to the quay hoping for a reprieve from their misery; many, says the legend, were miraculously healed.

At first the statue was placed in a church near the site of the present sanctuary. But the Pisans naturally wanted it back and threatened war if it was not returned. The city fathers decided that the Madonna herself should decide where her final resting place was to be. So she was loaded on to an ox drawn cart: if the oxen moved readily portwards, the Pisans would have their statue back; but if, on the other hand, they went in the opposite direction, the Madonna would remain in Trapani.

Well, she is still in Trapani today, housed in an ornate wrought-iron cage whose marble frame is the work of both Antonino and Giacomo Gagini (1537). She is very much venerated even now, particularly by fishermen and sailors; you can hardly ever approach her for a closer look, so busy is her little chapel, thronged with old widows in black bobbing up and down in genuflection. This reaches a peak on 16 August, her feast day.

In an adjacent series of chambers there are five other sanctuaries. One is dedicated to Sant'Alberto, founder of the Carmelites and patron saint of Trapani, Messina and Erice (while Trapani and Erice have rival claims to being his birthplace, he actually died in Messina in 1307). His bones are kept in Trapani and here you can see his likeness clad in silver and enshrined in a marble tabernacle with numerous porcine putti. You should also visit the Beato Luigi Rabata, born in Erice in 1443, who stands in his own little chapel, an arrow clean through his head. In a Gothic-style case you can see his mouldering jawbone and its two remaining teeth resting on a dusty pink silk cushion.

Perhaps the Beata Maria Vergine, with her felt handbag, may better answer your prayers, or the statue of the Sacred Heart fronted by a row of electric candles that flash on and of. In another nearby shrine St Joseph and a rather fat Christ child are going shopping, the latter swinging a wicker basket by his side. The two repose on a sea of putti who smile out at the devotees from behind a thick hedge of gladioli. Without these no Sicilian shrine is complete.

Perhaps the best time to visit Trapani is Easter when everybody assembles in the city to celebrate the Procession of the Easter Mysteries. Continuing from Good Friday afternoon through the night until early the following morning, twenty-one groups of life-size wooden statues (called the *Misteri*), each tableau of a different event in the Passion of Christ, are carried through the town in musical procession by members of the local guilds.

The event has an air of carnival about it and falls way short of portraying the mystery of Easter, yet the statues are worth seeing. Carved mostly in the 18th century (some by Andrea Tipa) they tend to favour realism: muscular, flesh coloured soldiers, harrowing facial expressions and rivers of painted blood flowing from Christ's wounds. The Madonna Addolorata has a real lace handkerchief in her hand.

The tableaux are carried around the town on pallets heavy with flowers piled up against the statues, and a band leads the way beneath canopies of foliage. Solemn, sweaty and progressively more drunk, the carriers speed up and slow down at intervals along a pre-ordained route. In centuries past, townspeople from the various guilds took the place of the statues – live actors who were followed by *Scuriate* who in the name of Christ flagellated themselves with leather whips. Very Sicilian, but too emotive, and these were soon replaced by the *Misteri* which you can inspect out of season in the church of the Purgatorio in the Via San Francesco d'Assisi.

This is one of Sicily's most popular Easter festivals and hence you can guarantee all the town's churches, some of which are generally locked, will be open for visits.

From the port of Trapani there are regular ferry and hydrofoil services to the **Egadi Islands** of Favignana, Levanzo and Marettimo. Much further away is Pantelleria, also accessible by ferry from Trapani, though it would be quicker to fly either from Trapani or Palermo. From Pantelleria, the ferries continue on to the Pelagic Islands, although the quicker route is from Porto Empedocle, just outside Agrigento.

Favignana is the largest of the Egadi Islands. It has a more distinctly Arabic flavour than the others: couscous challenges spaghetti on the menu, and styles of fishing, agriculture and architecture also display their foreign roots. Favignana is famous for two things: the Florio family and the *mattanza*, the annual tunny fish slaughter. The two are inextricably linked. Not only were the Florio the first people to put tunny fish into cans (at the turn of the century), they were also responsible for radically changing and simplifying the method of catching them. But the Japanese are the canners of Sicilian tuna nowadays and the Florio factories, which once brought the family legendary wealth, are deserted and silent monuments to an effervescent *fin-de-siècle* Sicilian building boom.

The *mattanza* on the other hand is still very much alive on Favignana. Local waters are still a rich hunting ground, though the catch has been somewhat leaner in recent years. The fishermen, or *tonnaroti*, enjoy a similar status to matadors in Spain; for as long as bullfighting holds the soul of Spain, the *mattanza* will be at the heart of Favignana. (Interestingly, both areas were part of the vast melting pot of the Arab Mediterranean.)

Favignana town is the island's biggest settlement; it nestles at the junction of the western and eastern halves of the island (the one hilly, the other flat) and is dominated by leftovers from the Florio period. The Town Hall was once the family palace and there is a statue of Ignazio Florio, who bought all the Egadi Islands from the Pallavicino in 1874, standing rather bleakly in the Piazza Europa. And there is no doubt that had the island's most important bene-factor been alive today, Favignana would not look so dog-eared and down at heel as it does now: around the Punta San Nicola, even the last remaining signs of ancient habitation are threatened. People have been living on this site since the Paleolithic era but nobody has the funds to preserve properly their semi-excavated remains. Even the local Antiquarium is closed.

From Favignana, the boats continue on to **Levanzo**, once known as the 'dry' island (to the Saracens Gazirat al ya bisah) because it has no fresh water source at all. In spite of this, the little town of Levanzo has about 200 inhabitants who live mostly in the cluster of little houses around the port. They survive on imported bottled water.

Nothing stirs in Levanzo on hot summer days when the deeply penetrating heat silences even the cicadas. Nothing that is except for the odd sightseer on his way to the Grotta del Genovese – Genovese because Genoese merchant ships plied the trade routes through the Egadi islands during the Middle Ages and later; in fact Philip IV sold them to Genoa in the 17th century. Levanzo derives its name from a district of that north Italian city. The Grotta del Genovese contains Paleolithic and Neolithic drawings discovered only in 1949. Incised on its walls, the former, 6000 years old, are illustrations of animals and people – magnificent early renditions of foreshorten-ing and body movement. The Neolithic works, about 5000 years younger, are more stylized and perhaps not as skilful. This cave, like the one or two rather isolated island beaches, is most easily reached by boat from Levanzo port.

Marettimo is the smallest of the Egadi Islands with less than 100 inhabitants. Unspoilt, undeveloped and rising sheer from the sea, it has very few beaches. A boat trip around the island in a painted fishing boat reveals unreachable grottoes (unless you swim to them from the boat) and hidden coves good for nude sunbathing. There are no hotels; if you want to remain overnight, or you have missed the ferry back, you can always stay in a local homestead. Without doubt, this makes it the most attractive island in the Egadi archipelago.

Most worth having a look at (leave the port going west) is a strange little church built in the 12th century by Byzantine monks. No guide gives it a name. Its style of construction exhibits that odd mixture of Arab-Norman detail which sadly will soon be obliterated forever by quickly encroaching dereliction. Nearby are the Case Romane, the remains of a Roman settlement which, for all their great age, are better preserved than the neighbouring church. Going north from Marettimo town, a path leads to the Castello di Punta Troia, once a prison. It had a horrifying reputation for cruelty in the 17th century but was closed in 1844.

Much further away is Pantelleria (115 km from Sicily), one of those places no one seems ever to have heard of. Few visit the island and on maps it is just a speck in a large blue sea 80 km from Tunisia. Its town was flattened by the Americans in 1943, but scattered about its landscape are some intriguing survivors from the remote Arabic past.

Academics come to Pantelleria to study the ancient system of agriculture still practised here: terraced vineyards and caper plantations are enmeshed within a dense web of dry-stone walls. Scattered about are the *dammusi*, indigenous stone huts – cubes – that are most probably Arabic in origin and which the inhabitants of Pantelleria have been building here as homes for over one thousand years.

The comings and goings of the ferries from the mainland to these islands can be watched from Erice which looks down over Trapani from a height of about 750 m. The views from its ramparts (the Murray Handbook calls them 'joyous prospects') extend for miles. Some say that on a clear day you can see all the way to Cape Bon in Tunisia. In particular, you get a very good view of the peculiar land formation on which Trapani stands, and of the flat coastal plain that runs down to Marsala. To the west are the Egadi Islands. From the other side of Erice distant mountains mark the tip of Capo San Vito.

For eight and a half centuries until 1934, the citadel crammed up here was known as Monte San Giuliano. It was given its name in 1077 by Count Roger the Norman because St Julian appeared to him in a dream while he was laying siege to the Arabs holed up in it. At the time it was known as Gebel-Hamed. Before that it was known as Eryx, and Mussolini revived this name as Erice in his attempt to reanimate the imperial past.

Today the ancient hilltown on the site of the Elymian city of Eryx is a magnet for tourists. Uniquely, it has not suffered from the scourge of nearly all other Sicilian towns – the perfidious grasp of modern development that encircles their ancient centres. Nor was it a target during the Second World War; street by street it is consistently medieval with, here and there, an overlay of 16th, 17th or 18th century decoration.

In the very ancient past Erice had a famous temple dedicated to Venus, the same deity the Phoenicians called Astarte and the Greeks Aphrodite. Here she was known as Venus Erycina, and her temple was supposed to have been founded by her son Eryx. In fact the dizzy heights of Mount Eryx were the seat of her cult and her temple stood where the castle of Erice is now, (pieces of temple masonry are embedded in the castle walls), poised at the summit of a precipice on the south-eastern edge of the town. It could be seen from miles out to sea and was a noted landmark for ships. A particularly venerated enclave, the temple had female slaves called '*hierodulai*' who had their own sacred way, the Via delle Gerodule. This was Christianized as the Via San Francesco – and is still one of the main arteries through the centre of town.

The Normans were largely responsible for the disappearance of the temple; they did their best to stamp out the marks of paganism up here, building a fortress with the temple's masonry and at the same time utilizing the hotch potch of surviving Punic and Roman fortifications also on the site. You can see them all. In one part of the castle is what is called the Pozzo di Venere (Venus' Well) which must have been a grain store attached to the castle. It sits in a large, open and rather bumpy area (contained within the fortifications) thought to be the actual site of the temple.

There are no less than ten churches in Erice. The most interesting is the 14th century Duomo. Unusually this was built after the construction of its battlemented campanile which originally served the Aragonese as a watchtower. It is a strange, disjointed sort of structure, even its 15th century porch does not really seem to belong to it. Inside is a lovely *Madonna and Child* (*c*. 1469) attributed by one school of thought to Francesco Laurana and by another to Domenico Gagini. It was more probably the latter, whose siblings seem to have sprinkled their works with abandon about Erice.

In the church of San Giovanni Battista, a 13th century building altered in the 15th and the 17th centuries, there is Antonello Gagini's *St John the Evangelist* and in San Cataldo, a 14th century church with a plain, flat façade, there is a holy water stoup attributed to the workshop of Domenico Gagini (*c.* 1474). Perhaps the best amongst the Erice Gaginis is the *Annunciation* by Antonello Gagini (1525) housed in the little Biblioteca-Museo Communale along with a variety of classical remains including an early head of Venus.

7

Trapani to Agrigento and Palermo

Motya, Marsala, Mazara del Vallo, Castelvetrano, Rocche di Cusa, Selinunte, Santa Margherita di Belice, Sciacca, Calta-bellotta, Eraclea Minoa, Agrigento, Pelagic Islands, Mussomeli, Villalba, Lercara Friddi, Prizzi

The SS115 is the main south coast highway. It leads from Trapani through Marsala to Mazara del Vallo, passes Selinunte on its way to Agrigento and eventually ends up in Syracuse. After the first 20 km beyond Trapani a small, almost hidden sign between two buildings in the hamlet of Ragattisi points down an unlikely looking country lane towards the quay from which boats ply to and from the island of Motya. This is one of the most important Phoenician sites in the western Mediterranean.

Motya is littered with the ruins of a great city that once stood here, an outpost of the Phoenician Empire until it was destroyed in 397 BC by Dionysius of Syracuse and an army of 45,000 men and 200 warships. In the little Museo Whitaker are some clues to the island's Phoenician past and a way of life that, until excavations were carried out by Pip Whitaker at the turn of the century, had been buried for twenty-eight centuries.

The Phoenicians were great early traders and intrepid mariner-adventurers who first sailed out of their native land, roughly where western Syria and Lebanon are today, nearly 3000 years ago. Calling themselves Canaanites and their homelands Canaan, they eventually colonized far-flung parts of the Mediterranean like Motya.

No ancient art suffered more at the hands of later generations than that of the Phoenicians; Greeks, Romans, Byzantines and others all had a hand in the destruction of Phoenicia's heritage. What we know about Phoenicia today comes mostly from the Bible – and the island of Motya. Motya, after its destruction, was simply abandoned and forgotten and in time its ruins were to vanish beneath the sand and dust which ensured their preservation until the Englishman Pip Whitaker began to take an interest in unravelling the island's mysteries. More is known about the shadowy Phoenicians from his Motya digs than from the excavation of more prominent sites like Tyre or Sidon in the eastern Mediterranean.

Whitaker was Sicily's Croesus. Scion of the enormously rich Whitaker family whose wealth came from the Marsala wine trade, he spent his youth nipping over to Motya when his family was in residence at nearby Marsala, returning with fragments which now form the nucleus of the Phoenician collection in the Whitaker museum. He was an informed dilettante and on his earliest visits to the island in the late 1870s he had been able to make out the city's circuit wall, gates and even, he thought, temples and houses.

There was the spirit of a crusader about Pip Whitaker. Nobody – not even Professor Hermann Schliemann, the great excavator of Troy, who once called in on Motya in the hope of making a truly momentous discovery – had ever unearthed anything of any importance here. But Whitaker stoically insisted that Motya was an important site and, in an effort to prove his point, he bought the island and focussed his undivided attention on it. By all accounts Pip and his wife Tina were permanently at loggerheads over the cost of the excavations: 'The girls' future must be considered', moaned Tina (Raleigh Trevelyan, *Princes Under the Volcano*), lamenting Pip's greater love for his ruins than for his two daughters' prospects. And there was no restraining him once he had dug up the necropolis on the north side of the island. He would excitedly show his find and the trinkets from it to parties of friends who from time to time trooped around the island with him. Going to Motya was a bit like going to Ascot; it was the social event of the early summer. His daughters Delia and Norina, Tina and their friends (who on one occasion included the king of Italy) would sit about on folding seats (Delia on a Union Jack cushion) under a collection of parasols while Pip in a panama hat and a crisp linen suit directed his skivvies in sifting through the rubble brought from some nearby hole. The unearthing of the necropolis was the first indication that Motya had been a place of considerable significance and its discovery was the initial reason for founding a little museum there.

Anyone who goes to Motya today should visit this museum, but only having first walked around the island (never more than 1 km in

either direction). The frail artefacts will have more meaning if you
have seen the sites they came from. Close to the museum (to the
west – left – of the landing stage) is the 4th century BC Casa dei
Mosaici, so-called because of the black and white pebble mosaic
decoration it contains. Even further to the west (take the path from
the museum) is the cothon, an artificial dock built within the city
walls, with a paved canal which runs out to sea. The city walls themselves survive in part and can be seen just to the south of the mouth
of the canal. The north of the island has five interesting sites. The
first of these, the Cappiddazzu site, about 100 yards from the North
Gate, is thought to have been the principal building on Motya –
possibly a large temple – and is named after the ghost of an old
hermit who haunted the island wearing a hat (*cappidazzu* is the
Sicilian for hat). The North Gate, once heavily fortified, defended
the entrance to the causeway that links Motya with Birgi on the
mainland. It was built of stone in the 6th century BC and exists even
now, though submerged just below the surface of the water. North
of Cappidazzu is the old necropolis and the Tophet sacrificial
burial ground where child sacrifices took place in honour of the
Phoenician gods.

Everything in the museum is laid out in neat rows inside large
polished wood and glass cabinets and at a glance you might imagine
yourself in the small private museum of an English country house –
the kind where the ladies of the family preserved their shell collections and their butterflies. It smells of furniture polish and there is a
tangy, salty taste in the air from the sea only a couple of hundred
yards away. This atmosphere of domesticity removes the edge of
hardened scholarship that usually accompanies collections of this
kind, and it makes the visit a memorable experience. Each piece
contributes to the contemporary view of an important Phoenician
city peopled by, said Whitaker, 'the pioneers of civilisation'. From
the quantity of foreign ceramics (mainly Greek and Egyptian) dug
from the graves and the remains of the houses, it seems that the
Motyans were extremely cosmopolitan and extended their relations
with other nations by friendly trading rather than by force of arms.
This, for a civilisation in a hostile world nearly twenty-eight centuries ago, is remarkable.

The Phoenicians were excellent craftsmen skilled in ornamental
metalwork and jewellery making. Among their weaponry and their
coins are ear-rings and pendants of silver, bronze, lead and a few
objects of gold. But most fascinating of all is the glass. Fragile,

1. Fontana di Piazza Pretoria, Palermo

2. *Eleanora of Aragon* by Francesco Laurana, National Gallery of Sicily (Palazzo Abbatellis)

3. Detail of Giacomo Serpotta's stucco decoration in the Oratory of Santa Zita, Palermo

4. Ballroom of the Palazzo Gangi, Palermo, where Visconti filmed the 'ball scene' in *The Leopard*

5. San Giovanni degli Eremiti, Palermo

6. Apse of the Cathedral, Palermo – the best preserved relic of the original
Norman building

7. Present-day Palermo

8. Villa Lampedusa, San Lorenzo

9. Villa Palagonia, Bagheria

10. Alcamo

11. Detail of a *mattanza* at Solanto by Paola de Albertis (19th century)

12. The remains of the chapel at Santa Margherita di Belice

13. A telamon from the Temple of Olympian Zeus, Agrigento

14. 'The Jews' of San Fratello, Holy Week

15. The Granfonte at Leonforte

16. *The Return of Persephone*
by Lord Leighton

17. An 'apostle' at Barrafranca during the Easter Sunday parade

18. The rocks of the Cyclops, Aci Trezza

19. Detail of the façade of Gagliardi's San Giorgio, Ragusa

20. Façade of San Pietro, Modica

21. A fantasy supporting the balcony of the Palazzo Villadorata, Noto

delicate vessels were retrieved from sarcophagi and there are glass representations of the gods Astarte and Baal, the Moon Goddess and the God of the Sun.

And if it had not been for Pip Whitaker, the statue called *Man in a Tunic* would possibly not be on show in the museum now. Dug up in 1979 on the north of the island, this Greek marble is one of the greatest 'finds' ever made in Sicily. It represents a young man shifting his weight from one foot to another, clad only in a body hugging lightweight tunic. It dates from the 5th century BC and is easily on a par with southern Italy's other great classical statutes, the Riace Bronzes in the museum in Reggio Calabria. Exactly why it is on Motya, who brought it here, and whom it represents, are mysteries.

Whitaker died in 1936, by which time Motya had become a site of 'national importance'. So significant was it that the Italian government put a stop to his activities in the early 1920s. Imagine Whitaker's indignation. But it was useless for him to point out that had it not been for his considerable efforts, not to mention financial input, Motya would probably still be nothing but windswept weed-fodder for the island's goats.

It is only a short distance by road from the Motya landing stage to **Marsala** and to the adjacent ruins of the ancient city of Lilybaeum which was founded by the Carthaginians in about 396 BC. It was here that the survivors of the Motya massacre were taken by Dionysus. Lilybaeum was popular even with the Romans because it had a fine port to the north of the present city. Marsala today only partially covers the ancient city and still has a thriving port, one that Garibaldi made good use of when he first arrived in Sicily at the beginning of his campaign with his ships the *Piemonte* and the *Lombardia*.

Ancient Lilybaeum is easily dealt with in a couple of hours. There are some ruins – a bath house and some well preserved mosaics – and there are the huge warehouses of the converted Baglio Anselmi, an interesting restoration of one of the great Marsala wine *baglios* and now the Museo Marsala. This museum will take you step by step through the very confusing history of the region, which was a strategic and much coveted part of the ancient world. Not least among the artefacts on show are the remains of a Punic ship which was once manned by sixty-eight oarsmen and most probably sank during the First Punic War just off the coast between

Lilybaeum and the Egadi Islands. Preserved inside a huge 'plastic bag', it is a unique discovery. Even the iron nails holding it together seem somehow to have resisted corrosion by the sea. An intensive study of the remains found inside the ship have yielded up facts about what the sailors ate, and what they took with them into battle.

But Marsala itself is lodged in most people's consciousness because of its alcoholic connections. It is the home of the Marsala wine industry which produces a rich, warm and very strong wine easily drinkable at any time of day or night. In its early days – during the 18th and 19th centuries – the industry was nurtured by the British living in Sicily and since the days when John Woodhouse, Benjamin Ingham and the Whitaker and Florio families owned their own warehouses it has been the economic staple of the town. Down on the quay you can see the wine *baglios*. Best described as mercantile fortresses, they consist of vast warehouses surrounded by high walls centred on a small palazzo, originally the administrative and residential quarters of the owners.

All the Marsala businesses were eventually taken over by the Florios in 1929 and later by, among others, Cinzano, whose amalgamated premises are housed in the great Baglio Florio. In fact along Marsala's coast you can see the abandoned hulks of the Baglio Wood, the Baglio Woodhouse and the Baglio Ingham all of which, rather sadly, are gradually falling into disrepair. The Florio-Cinzano premises, called the Stabilimento Florio, are open to the public and contain a museum in which you will find a very good collection of drinking glasses associated with Marsala. Called the Cinzano Collection, it is easily as interesting as similar collections of glass in the Fitzwilliam in Cambridge or the Victoria and Albert in London, and remarkable for Sicily because so little glass has survived the various calamities – natural and otherwise – inflicted on the island.

Marsala wine spiralled to the dizziest pinnacles of popularity under Admiral Nelson who ordered from John Woodhouse enough barrels of it to float another fleet. The industry scarcely looked back after that and throughout the course of its history helped amass some gigantic fortunes – the one Pip Whitaker inherited from the Inghams enabled him to buy Motya. The very best Marsala not surprisingly still originates here. It is possible to buy early 19th wine bottled just a few years ago; this signifies a blend of the very earliest and best vintages. Marsala can be dry or sweet; the finer they are the dryer, generally speaking, and the paler their amber colour. The sweet, dark ones – the colour of near black resin – are the cooking ones and you might like to try dishes where veal or beef has been soaked in it (it tempers the meat's dryness). Fortified with brandy or *vino-cotto* (boiled grape juice), it is aged in casks like sherry. All the Marsalas have a distinctive, slightly sulphurous flavour and what has been called a 'mystical burnt almond aftertaste'.

Marsala the town (Mars al-Alah or Harbour of God to the Arabs), is rather less interesting. The best point of entry is from the seaward gate called the Porta Garibaldi (Garibaldi's entrance in 1860). The town was badly damaged in the last war and, although sensitively rebuilt and restored, it has lost the swarthy character that somehow attaches to seaports and which characterises for instance Trapani, or Mazara del Vallo further south.

The cathedral is only worth a quick look. It is a vast place with little appeal which, although begun in the 18th century, was only completed in 1957. A sprinkling of Gagini sculptures enliven its otherwise dull interior – there are works by Domenico, Antonino and Antonello. You might be surprised to learn that the cathedral is dedicated to San Tomaso di Canterbury (Saint Thomas à Becket) of whom there is a 17th century silver statue in the Treasury. Even stranger, the sixteen grey columns lining the nave were, according to local legend, intended for Canterbury Cathedral.

Mazara del Vallo lies at the very end of this flat coastal plain. The texture of the rough old centre is more casbah than anything else – it harks back to the days when, as the seat of the Emir Abdullah Ibn Haukal, it was the capital of the Val Di Mazara and thus one of the principal Saracen strongholds in Sicily. The narrow dilapidated streets, little hidden courtyards and alleys, and the odd hammam (Turkish bath) in the Pilazza Quarter (populated now mostly by Tunisians) are the last links with the town's Arabic past. Here and there Norman bits have survived: the Duomo for example was one of the principal buildings in Norman times. It still has its early apse although the rest of the building is mostly 17th century (see Antonello Gagini's *Transfiguration* over the altar, finished by his son Antonino in 1537). In the Piazza Mokarta are the remains of Count Roger's castle. But it is to the churches of San Nicolo Regale (11th century), in the Tunisian quarter, and the Madonna dell'Alto, once part of a Basilian convent which Count Roger's daughter Julietta founded in 1103, that you must go if you want conspicuously enduring evidence of Norman occupation.

About 21 km inland from Mazara del Vallo (take the A29) is **Castelvetrano** from which a number of different small but interesting places can easily be reached. Time and history have not endowed Castelvetrano itself with much appeal, though Antonio Ferraro's choir and chancel (1574) carried out for the Prince of Aragona and Tagliavia in the church of San Domenico is a remarkable early example of the art of the *stuccatore*. A panoply of angels, saints and putti emerge from the wall surface amongst swags, cornucopie and drapery, and are characterized by their agitated, nervous staccato gestures.

Castelvetrano was the scene of the shooting of Salvatore Giuliano by his cousin Pisciotta in 1950, and the subsequent gruesome display by his disraught mother who licked the blood off the ground where his corpse had lain. That blood later turned out to have come from a chicken; it had been put there to mislead investigation of his murder and so draw a veil over the identities of the various behind-the-scenes collaborators (one of whom was a Minister of State) for whom Giuliano had become nothing but a nuisance (see Chapter 5).

Top of the list of short excursions from Castelvetrano is the little isolated church of Santissima Trinità di Delia situated about 3 ½ km to the west of the town. This is a Norman building of the 12th century. It has that strange, hybrid mixture of Arabic, Byzantine and Norman architectural styles which is uniquely Sicilian. In its crypt are the tombs of the Saporito family who were responsible for its restoration.

But for a stronger evocation of the past in this windswept part of Sicily, follow signs to **Rocche di Cusa**, directly south of Castelvetrano. You take the road to Tre Fontane just beyond the village of Campobello di Mazara. These were the quarries from which the stone for the ancient temples and city of Selinus (Selinunte) was taken. They have not been worked since the day ancient Selinus was attacked in 409 BC; the workers simply flung down their tools, abandoned their work and fled. You can still see half completed, roughly hewn shapes that would have ended up as capitals and columns for the temples. It illustrates perfectly just how the great stones were hewn from the rock and there is a cluster of columns which were carved in their entirety but which are still attached to the ground at their base. Archaeologists believe these were intended for Temple G at Selinunte.

Selinunte itself, one of the great cities of Magna Graecia, is only about 10 km away to the east. While not much remains of the city fabric itself – apart from some incomprehensible trenches filled with rubble and some piles of old building blocks – the city's temples have 'survived' and lie toppled in heaps. It is doubtful whether the Carthaginians who destroyed Selinus (Selinunte's Greek name) in 409 BC were responsible for their destruction. It seems more likely that successive earthquakes over the centuries pushed them over.

Selinus lay on the edge of Carthaginian western Sicily, sharing a much disputed border with Segesta. In fact it precipitated a war between the two in 416 BC (see Chapter 6) which resulted in Hannibal entering Selinus in 409 BC with an army of nearly 100,000 men. The carnage that followed was not unusual: something like 16,000 people were massacred and the rest taken into slavery. A few thousand escaped and were able to return later to repopulate the city, but it never recovered its former status and in the First Punic War the remaining citizens were removed by the Carthaginians, to whom they had become subject, and that was the end of Selinus.

You have to read Diodorus to find out how such a place could possibly have succumbed to attack. A city with no less than eight temples was by no means insignificant. No doubt the element of surprise – judging from the evidence left in the Rocche di Cusa – played a large part. The inhabitants were fairly confident in the knowledge that the Athenians would not be helping the Segestans and that their conflict with their smaller neighbour would be over quickly and in their favour. On top of which, they were expecting Syracuse to come to their aid. But it was too late; the Carthaginians got there first.

How could they know that Hannibal would attack Selinus with battering rams, that he would build six towers of his own from which archers would decimate the defenders of the city? Selinus had been at peace for quite some time so possibly their defences were not as effective as they might have been. The Carthaginians soon breached the walls and the carnage began. When you walk the streets of Selinunte today in the hot sun, think of the citizens whose fingers ended up as necklaces around their attackers' necks. Men, women and children were skewered on pikes and paraded around the city, their mutilated remains later set alight and their city left to burn. The old walls and paving stones were the witnesses to these horrible events.

The old city was situated on a headland overlooking the sea. It is a strange, desolate place overgrown with acanthus and wild celery (which gave ancient Selinus its name – 'Selinus' derives from the Greek word for wild celery which was the symbol of the city). It seems hard to believe that here stood one of the greatest cities in the ancient civilised world. Judging from the remains housed in the archaeological museum in Palermo, it was a highly cultivated metropolis. That the site was never rebuilt upon in later years, that it just vanished beneath the sand dunes, is due mostly to the anopheles mosquito which bred in the marshy swamps between the present village of Marinella and the east temples, the area that was once Selinunte's port.

If you come to Selinunte in the rain, you will be overwhelmed by the melancholy of the place. It is not a proud site like the Acropolis in Athens, or even Paestum, where the magnificence of the classical past is awesome. Instead, the scene is one of total defeat; and the temples that stand only do so because they were propped up at various times during the 20th century in an attempt to recreate something of their vanished grandeur.

There are three parts to the Selinunte ruins: the main acropolis on the headland above the sea, propped up on a gigantic bastion part of which still survives – you see it on the approach road. Up here you will see the remains of Temples A, B, C, D, and O (so called because nobody is certain to whom they were dedicated). There are also some well preserved, paved streets and stumps of walls belonging to collapsed houses and other buildings. A great gate – the North Gate – leads from the Acropolis into a vast and as yet unexcavated part of the city behind which shelters the site of the necropolis. Other temples, Temples E, F and G, are to the east in a little isolated group. Between this group and the others on the Acropolis is the site of the harbour (with another on the other side of the headland), once lined with warehouses and quays. Selinunte used to be an important commercial centre but nothing at all remains to indicate that.

The massive walls that can still be seen around parts of the Acropolis date from the late 6th and early 5th centuries BC with later additions put up whenever the city's defences needed to be strengthened. The North Gate was an important part of these fortifications but it is impossible now for the casual observer to make out anything among the mounds of earth and the piles of old stones strewn about the place. Margaret Guido in *Sicily: An Archaeological Guide* says that 'as an example of military architecture it is of the first importance', so complex and so devious was its planning. See what you think.

Temple C, at the highest point of the Acropolis, is perhaps the earliest surviving temple in this part of the city (first half of the 6th century BC) with seventeen columns running down each side and a double row of six each along the front. It is thought this temple was dedicated to Herakles – and in the archaeological museum in Palermo you can see a range of fine sculpted metopes (the square space between two triglyphs in the frieze of a Doric order) that came from it – one shows Perseus killing the Medusa. Temple D, immediately to the north of Temple C, was much smaller with thirteen columns down each side and six at the front and back. It dates from around 540 BC. Immediately to the south of Temple C is Temple B, a tiny, one-roomed construction once fronted by a four-columned porch. Its neighbour immediately to the south, Temple A, was a late building – it dates from the first half of the 5th century BC. Next to it is Temple O whose superstructure no longer exists; not much is known about it except that it fronted on to a sacred area which might date from the period after the city's destruction.

The other temples, the so-called 'Eastern Temples' are more spectacular, if only because Temple E, the most southerly of the group, was partly re-erected in recent years. Massive to our eyes, in Selinunte's heyday it was not the largest. Temple G (the most northerly of the group) had that distinction and was in fact one of the greatest temples that ever existed. (See also the temples at Agrigento, Chapter 7).

Temple G, possibly dedicated to Apollo, was begun sometime in the second half of the 6th century BC. Like Temple C it had seventeen side columns, though the difference in scale is enormous. You could fit Temple C inside nearly three times. So massive was it in fact that its roof had the additional support of two rows of columns down the centre. It took so long to build – and was not complete when the Carthaginians struck their fatal blow – that even though the piles of collapsed columns and weather-worn capitals may not look much to the untrained eye, it has been possible to use this building to study the changing fashions of classical architecture: its east side is archaic in style while its west side is classical.

Plenty of architectural fragments from the temples have survived, and sculpture, ceramics and jewellery were excavated from the ruins of the city and deposited in the archaeological museum in Palermo. It is rather frustrating that you cannot see them *in situ* at Selinunte, though there is an Antiquarium in the Acropolis area and a small museum in Castelvetrano in which some of the less important fragments from the site are displayed.

East of Castelvetrano is **Santa Margherita di Belice**, a town which unfortunately found itself very near the epicentre of the Terremoto di Belice in 1968. The landscape around it has ruckled and tipped, destroying the town almost totally. This was the model for the Salina family's Donnafugata in Giuseppe Tomasi di Lampedusa's *The Leopard*. In the novel the family came here each summer to stay in their country palace. 'Beyond the short bridge leading into the town were waiting the authorities, surrounded by a few dozen peasants. As the carriages moved on to the bridge the municipal band struck up with frenzied enthusiasm *Noi siamo zingarelle* from 'Traviata' . . .; after this at a warning by some urchin on the look-out the bells of the Mother Church and the Convent of the Holy Ghost filled the air with festive sound' (*The Leopard*). In reality the palace at the heart of Santa Margherita belonged to the family of the author's maternal grandmother, the Filangeri di Cutò, and it was the favourite home of the Lampedusa family. It was built in 1680 by Girolamo, Prince of Filangeri and even though it is now a crumbling ruin it is a touchstone for lovers of *The Leopard*.

In the summer of 1860, the year of Garibaldi's assault on Sicily, the Salina family were in Donnafugata. The Prince 'loved the house, the people [and] the sense of feudal ownership still surviving there'. Tancredi showed it excitedly to Angelica, with its 'inextricable complex of guest rooms, state rooms, kitchens, chapels, theatres, picture galleries, odorous saddling rooms, stables, stuffy conservatories, passages, stairs, terraces and porticoes, and . . . a series of abandoned and uninhabited apartments which had not been used for many years . . .'. These rooms were actually inspired by those in the Lampedusa family home in Palermo (see Chapter 3).

Today only a single wall of the great palace survives, overlooking what was once the town's 'leafy square'. Even the church next door has collapsed, where they went 'according to ancient usage . . . to hear a Te Deum' immediately on arrival in the town after their long haul across the Sicilian interior; only a derelict neo-classical vault remains. You can clamber through the ruins of both buildings and the torn unkempt jungle of the magical gardens where 'the lusty ilexes which were the glory of the place' once stood. But a search for the fountains from which water was 'blown from shells of Tritons and Naiads' is fruitless: only crumbling piles of masonry remain.

You cannot help wondering what the Prince of Salina himself would have to say about the demise of family patrimony; he knew the end was in sight for Sicily's feudal aristocracy (in fact the palace and the estates were sold by Lampedusa's uncle to pay a debt long before the earthquake), but can he have imagined it would end like this? The carcass of the building lies wrecked at the centre of the old town, and on the outskirts are the concrete apartment blocks which mock and threaten to engulf it.

The road leaves Castelvetrano going east beyond Selinunte to Sciacca, a town that reassures you that not all is doom and gloom in western Sicily. Unlike most of the ports on this itinerary so far, this one does not turn its back on the ocean. The bulk of what you might want to visit is squeezed on to the side of the hill up which the town staggers in terraces, overlooking the harbour.

Beyond the main gate – the elaborate 16th century Porta San Salvatore, used by local traffic to get in and out of the place – the town is full of churches. They overpopulate the narrow alleys and winding streets of the Rabato and Cadda quarters. Their origins are Saracen. Santa Margherita in Via Federico Incisa, dating from late in the 14th century, has a side portal sculpted, it is thought, by Francesco Laurana. He is also thought to have produced the Madonna della Catena in the fourth chapel on the right inside the Duomo. This is a vast building begun by the Normans in 1108 (see the outside of the main apse) and enlarged and adapted in the 17th century. Antonino Gagini, whose *SS Pietro e Paolo e storie della Passione* (1591, with Gian Domenico Gagini) is in the right apse, was responsible for the statues of San Pietro, San Paolo, la Maddalena, San Giovanni Battista and San Calogero on the sides of the campanile.

There are more traces of the Normans here in Sciacca. In Piazza San Nicolò, in the medieval Terravecchia quarter, the little church of San Nicolò was founded between AD 1100 and AD 1136 by Julietta, Count Roger's daughter. It is an interesting place built on a Latin cross plan and once decorated with fading Byzantine-style frescos. Of the Norman castle, Castello dei Perollo in Via Castello, not much survives, but the façade of the church of Santa Maria della Giummare, reached from the Via Valverde by a flight of steps, is still dominated by its two Norman towers. Most of the rest of the church was reconstructed in the 16th century, and late in the 18th century the vaults of the nave were given an elaborate face-lift by Mariano Rossi who covered them with an Assumption of the Virgin. The building's late 18th century rococo stucco work is by Ferraiolo.

Sciacca, like any old town, especially any Sicilian one, has one or two bloody tales to tell. Any itinerary should take in the Castello dei Luna, once the headquarters of the Aragonese Luna family whose feud with the Perollo, a rival Norman clan, reduced the population by nearly half in the 15th and 16th centuries.

There are three possible small trips from Sciacca. One, to Monte San Calogero about 7 km away to the north-east, is a visit to the hot springs. Another is to the little town of Caltabellotta, while the third is to the ancient site of Eraclea Minoa about 25 km further along the coast going south-east.

On Monte San Calogero, you can see the hot vapour grotto that has been in use since the 3rd millenium BC. The site was once known as Thermae Selinuntae, Sciacca having been a spa resort attached to the baths, one much favoured by the ancients of Selinus. Nowadays Sciacca has its own thermal baths which are still in use.

About 20 km further inland, **Caltabellotta** is where the peace treaty following the War of the Vespers was signed on 31 August 1302 between Frederick II of Aragon and Charles of Valois. Unspoilt like Sciacca, the hilltown of Caltabellotta seems to have been poured down the mountain by God. In the days of the Normans it was virtually impregnable and for a while it kept secure Sybilla, the wife of Tancred (illegitimate nephew of King William the Good and the man to whom Richard Coeur De Lion, William the Good's brother-in-law, gave the sword Excalibur) who had usurped the Sicilian throne. She and her son William III hid here in 1194 shortly before they were caught by Henry VI. Tancred and Henry had been rivals for the Sicilian throne; Henry's claim was legitimate, Tancred's not. When Tancred died towards the end of the 12th century, his son, at the age of seven, became king as William III. But Henry still wanted the throne and eventually he got it, removing Queen Sybilla and her children from the castle, blinding and castrating William, and packing the whole family off to lifelong imprisonment in Germany. Henry (who was the father of Emperor Frederick II – Stupor Mundi) then dragged Tancred's corpse from its resting place in Palermo cathedral, beheaded it, and threw it on to a rubbish tip. Not much of this sad castle at Caltabellotta remains except for a gateway at the top of the town. Below is Count Roger's Chiesa Madre in whose Chapel of Santa Maria della Catena you can see an elaborate example of the stucco work of Antonio Ferraro (1598). The church also contains a statue of the Madonna by Giacomo Gagini (1536).

Eraclea Minoa, the last of the three excursions from Sciacca, was a buffer city between Selinus and Akragas (Agrigento) and as a result was always being drawn into disputes between the two. Most of what survives there – the city walls, a large theatre, and fragments of ruined houses – dates from the 4th century BC.

The only remaining major town on this route is of course **Agrigento**. Akragas to the ancient Greeks, Agrigentum to the Romans, Kerkent to the Arabs, and Girgenti to everyone else until 1927, Agrigento is one of those places where for a fleeting moment the classical world becomes tangible again. If you could wish the modern town on to another planet you would be left with the most impressive ancient Greek complex outside Greece itself.

Akragas must have been particularly coveted by the Carthaginians who attacked and destroyed it in 406 BC. At the time it had about 200,000 inhabitants, a fraction of whom were descended from colonists from Gela and Rhodes who were supposed to have come here around 581 BC. The rest were slaves who contributed hugely to the luxurious lifestyle of their masters and for which Akragas was famous. It was Plato who remarked that the people of Akragas built as if they would never die, and ate as if they had not an hour to live. Theirs was a beautiful city: according to the poet Pindar 'the most beautiful city of mortals'. Daedalus himself was claimed as founder.

It was also a great power, the only rival in Sicily to Syracuse. But the sybaritic lifestyle took its toll and when the Carthaginians arrived outside its walls, Akragas was unable to hold out for longer than eight months. Even its soldiers had been leading the life of Riley in their barracks and, according to Diodorus, they fled with the civilians leaving the city to be burnt, sacked and looted. Perhaps they had in mind the Carthaginians' horrendous deeds at Selinus earlier that century.

A string of remarkable Doric temples dating from the 5th century BC straddles a ridge south of the city, overlooking the rivers San Biagio and Sant'Anna (Akragas and Hypsas to the ancients). These temples are tributes to a range of gods venerated by the Greeks of Akragas. The Valle dei Templi, the main archaeological zone, contains five temples (in varying states of repair), tombs and the excavated site of the Hellenistic-Roman quarter of the city. Here too is one of the best museums in Sicily.

Only one temple, the Temple of Concord, remains in anything

like its original condition. This is due to the fact that in the 16th century AD it was converted into a church by the ingloriously named San Gregorio delle Rape, Saint Gregory of the Turnips. He put arches into the walls of the cella to create aisles in the building's interior and filled in the spaces between the columns. Thus it remained for 1,200 years until it was restored by the Prince of Torremuzza in the 18th century.

Its name has no historical validity. It simply derives from a Latin inscription found on the site. Doric (thought to have been built about 430 BC), with fluted columns standing directly on a stylobate, it is thought to have been one of the first temples in Sicily to be built with subtly different spaces between its columns. They narrow as they march towards the corners. Another interesting refinement is the slight inward slant of the columns. In comparison to the temples at Selinunte (Temple C for example), the metopes on the Temple of Concord may have been decorated with painted rather than carved mythological scenes (likewise the pediment), and covered with white stucco below the level of the capitals.

Following the line of the old city wall going east, you will find the Temple of Juno (or Hera). It is not unlike the Temple of Concord, except that only bits of it, including twenty-five columns out of the original thirty-four, have survived. The rest of the building fell over the edge of the hill in a landslide. Although nature did her bit, the building also suffered at the hands of the Carthaginians when they sacked Akragas. In fact you can still see traces of fire damage on some of the stones where the heat of the flames turned them red.

West, past the Temple of Concord, is the Temple of Hercules (or Herakles) of which a handful of columns re-erected in the 1920s now stand. Dating from late in the 6th century BC, this is the earliest of the temples. South, beyond what was thought to have been the tomb of Theron the benevolent tyrant of Akragas, is the Temple of Aesculapius, a somewhat mysterious figure who was the divinity of healing. It once contained a statue of the god by Myron, stolen by the Carthaginians, rescued by Scipio Africanus, then stolen again by the hated Gaius Verres, Governor (or Praetor) of the Roman Province of Sicily between 73 and 71 BC. He was tried in 70 BC for gross misconduct. At this event Cicero declared that 'the island was the first to teach our ancestors what a fine thing it is to rule over foreign nations'.

To the west of the Temple of Hercules is one of the biggest (if not *the* biggest) Doric temples ever built: the Temple of Zeus. This was a massive undertaking which continued for years until either the manpower dwindled in exhaustion, or funds were diverted elsewhere. Anyway, in 406 BC it was still unfinished. It was so enormous that in addition to the gigantic columns required to keep it standing, its architects incorporated giant stuccoed and painted telamones (over 6 m high) which supported the architrave of the building with the help of invisible iron beams running from column to column. The earthquakes – or perhaps the Carthaginians – tipped these creatures to the ground, where one of them remains to this day, its arm locked forever in a position of support for the entablature it once held up.

In its time the construction of this temple was revolutionary. Not only was its scale quite without equal, but the method of its wall construction was new. First the inclusion of the telamones made for an elevation which was rather different; second the building was constructed using smaller individual elements instead of the usual huge, unwieldy blocks. Where the various sections met, stucco sealed the joints so the observer would never have known the difference. The only problem with this, from a 20th century point of view in particular, is that the building automatically became more vulnerable not only to earth tremors but to local builders, who over the centuries have been able to carry away its stone.

A kind of Via Sacra connects this huge white elephant with the so-called Temple of Castor and Pollux. This in fact is an incorrect reconstruction of modern times using a variety of bits and pieces rescued from different buildings. Nearby are various other shrines including the Sanctuary of the Chthonic Divinities. Here the forces of nature were worshipped in a rite that was intended to ensure that the crops did not fail. Archaeologists have unearthed other altars on this site, some of which predate even the ancient Greek ones; they are probably older even than Akragas.

There are a great many things to be seen in Agrigento itself: the Giacomo Serpotta stuccos in the church of Santo Spirito are worth a long look. In the nave are large perspective reliefs (c. 1693–5) of which *The Presentation in the Temple* is thought to be the finest as well as one of only two – the other is *The Flight into Egypt* – entirely by the master. In the nave of the church of the Purgatorio (otherwise known as San Lorenzo) are some Serpotta attributions (1704–7), allegorical works surrounded by a delightful ornamental array of stucco busts, masks and undergrowth.

Santa Maria dei Greci, south of the Via Duomo and hidden

amongst a succession of alleyways, is one of Agrigento's most interesting churches. It was built on the remains of a temple possibly
dedicated to Athena – you can examine the ruins underneath the
north aisle and in the apse are some fragments of its early pavement.
Agrigento's Duomo most probably occupies the site of an early
temple as well. The earliest religious sites were often assimilated by
later Christian ones, just as the functions of some Christian saints are
often interchangeable with those of the deities of pagan antiquity.
This building shows an eclectic combination of styles: founded in
the 14th century, it features a crazy mixture of Arab, Norman and
Catalan detailing, and there are alterations dating from the 16th
and the 17th centuries as well.

Agrigento is the point of embarkation from Sicily to the **Pelagic
Islands** (Linosa and Lampedusa). Most people leave the area without
ever visiting them or, if they absolutely have to go there, they take a
plane from Palermo to Lampedusa. Porto Empedocle on the coast
south east of Arigento is the maritime gateway to these islands. It is a
brute of a place, famous only as the birthplace of the writer Luigi
Pirandello, whose home at the nearby village of Caos is now a
museum.

Linosa erupting from the Mediterranean about 42 km north of
the better known island of Lampedusa, gives new meaning to the
word remote. It was here that the Italian government once banished
some of the more illustrious Mafia chieftains to kick their heels and
contemplate their futures in complete isolation. There is no escape
from Linosa, its total area is only about 10 square km and there is
nothing whatever to do apart from swim and struggle along the
dusty paths and tracks which criss-cross the island and the flanks of
its three extinct volcanoes. Volcanic activity in the past accounts for
the black sand and dust which settles on the skin, turning it a pale
grey. Enforced seclusion apart, and even though it is breathtakingly
hot in summer, it provides welcome respite from the turmoil of the
20th century; it has only a handful of shops and less than 10 km of
roadway.

Lampedusa is a scraggy deforested limestone lump that pokes
out of the sea just 110 km from the coast of Tunisia. In fact, this
island has more in common with Arab north Africa than with
southern Italy and not for nothing is it known as 'Africa's gift to
Europe'.

The island gave a title to the Tomasi family, of which Giuseppe,

Prince of Lampedusa and author of *The Leopard*, was the most illustrious member. The family received the island in 1630 from Charles II of Spain; one of their descendants, Princess Carolina, tried to sell it to Queen Victoria. An appalled Ferdinand II, realizing its strategic worth, quickly offered the family a higher price so that today it is still a part of Italy.

People often say that the coastal waters of Italy and its islands are filthy, that there is not a single stretch that remains unpolluted. If this is true, Lampedusa's coastline is the exception, perhaps because until now the island has been relatively free from tourism. In 1985 an organization called Mare Nostrum came into being with the aim of protecting the ecology, the landscape and the artistic patrimony of places like Lampedusa, in the knowledge that they would inevitably become more popular as the years went by. Its coastline is rugged and dry, and translucent sea and sandy beaches alternate with windswept stretches of rugged cliff lurching dramatically into the water.

Lampedusa was at different times inhabited by the Greeks, the Romans and the Saracens. Not much survives from these periods though past excavations have revealed a variety of tombs, long defunct water tanks and coins. The town of Lampedusa itself is interesting if only because there is nothing really Sicilian about it at all. Its labyrinthine alleys reek of the casbah (as well as the sardines and the anchovies which have made it famous) and its inhabitants are ruddy-faced Tunisian fishermen; whatever happened to the descendants of the ninety men and thirty women imported from Sicily in the middle of the 19th century as part of Ferdinand II's colonization programme?

In the middle of the island is the sanctuary of the Madonna di Porto Salvo in which is kept a statue of the Virgin which, according to a legend which sounds all too familiar, arrived on Lampedusa during a storm. The Pisan ship bringing it from its sculptor's studio on Cyprus in the 8th century AD put in at Lampedusa for safety, and the statue remained. She is brought out for an airing on 22 September on which day there is a procession followed by two weeks of festivities in her honour.

Agrigento lies at the southern end of the old SS189 which weaves its way from Palermo through the interior of the island. For the most part this is a desolate and remote landscape but, if you have time, there are a handful of small towns and villages to be reached from it which are worth more than just a passing glance: Mussomeli, Villalba, Lercara Friddi, Prizzi.

Mussomeli, crammed on to an impregnable crag, is dominated by the huge Castello Manfredonico built by the powerful Chiaramonte family in the 14th century. To its east lies **Villalba**, a small, ancient town that existed in the days of the Normans, possibly founded by the Arabs. During the second half of the 18th century it grew rapidly as the labour base of the vast feudal estate of Micciche on which it was centred; it is a true product of rural feudalism. Like so many other rural towns in Sicily it has two churches vastly out of proportion to the rest of the place which is poor, mean and rather bedraggled. But Villalba played a crucial role in the renaissance of the Mussolini-gagged Mafia at the end of the Second World War. And it is worth paying a visit just to see the memorial tablet on the grave of Don Calogero Vizzini, a genius who masterminded one of the most unfortunate and far-reaching episodes of modern Sicilian history.

The Duce, through the services of his Prefect, Cesare Mori, had managed to throw most of the Mafia rank and file, as well as some of their leaders, into jail, effectively reducing Mafia power for the first time in its history. (All, that is, except for Don Calogero who had outsmarted even Mussolini, and other Mafia brains who conveniently turned Fascist.) Mussolini's success was partly due to his willingness to string people up from lampposts without any tedious trials. Some were torn apart (say the rumours) in Mori's enthusiastic revival of excrutiating tortures favoured by the Spanish Inquisitors, (in *Le Parocchie di Regalpetra* Leonardo Sciascia writes that his methods would have shocked even the Inquisition), and others were dumped into penal servitude on the remote Mediterranean island of Linosa. In 1927 Mussolini was able to announce to the Fascist parliament that the war against the Mafia was over.

It was not. There were still *mafiosi* submerged in the community and the Americans undid all Mussolini's work, inviting them to collaborate in the 1943 invasion of Sicily. Recognizing that the cunning *capo-mafia*, Don Calogero, was still a man of enormous influence, the Americans – using Lucky Luciano, the infamous head of the American Mafia whose connections and contacts naturally extended to Sicily – came directly to him as soon as the invasion had begun, and used him and his subordinates to pave the way to a bloodless capture of western Sicily. It was relatively simple for Don Calogero and his band to pressurize what was left of the Italian army to abandon their strongholds; General Patton subsequently announced the 'fastest blitzkrieg in history' (Norman Lewis, *The Honoured Society*). Moral considerations aside, it was an effective strategy: the British Army, tramping through the east where the Mafia was less influential, took more than two months to achieve the same objective. For the Mafia, it meant liberation from Mussolini: for Luciano it meant the commuting of a long prison sentence and deportation to Italy.

From then on, perhaps unwittingly, perhaps not, America played into the Mafia's hands. In 1943 it allowed Vizzini to become Mayor of Villalba and, having done so, were then handed a list of Vizzini's recommendations for mayoral posts in other parts of the island. 'He compiled a list of suitable candidates for the office . . . many [of whom] . . . as Don Calò pointed out, had spent long years in confinement. No one seems to have had time to investigate his claim that his nominees had suffered for their political ideals, rather than for crimes ranging from armed robbery to multiple homicide' (Norman Lewis). As a result, all over Sicily, country towns woke up to find themselves ruled by a bunch of hoods. Thus began the history of post-war Sicily.

Don Calò was a wily old hoodlum whose funeral notice proclaimed him 'great in the face of persecution, greater still in adversity', and his memorial tablets laud his tirelessness in the defence of the weak and his 'status' as a gentleman.

All the gloom of Corleone and Partinico can be found in Villalba. It penetrates this mountainous enclave, long the haunt of brigands, all the way to **Lercara Friddi**, birthplace of 'Lucky' Luciano. Friddi (from *freddo*) means cold. The town is over 660 m above sea level and certainly feels the occasional icy blast.

To the west of the SS189 is **Prizzi**, reached from Lercara Friddi by penetrating a desolate rocky mass known as the Monte Carcaci. It crowns the summit of a low hill not far from the Lago di Prizzi. This dark little town broods all year round until Easter, when it erupts in an annual manifestation of that melding of pagan and Christian ritual so characteristic of Sicily.

On Easter Sunday a strange and ancient dance performed by Death (dressed in a yellow outfit with a leather skull-like mask) and the Devils (in red with brown tin masks) symbolizes the attempt of the forces of Evil to vanquish the forces of Good, represented by statues of the Virgin Mary and of Christ. The dance of Death and the Devils takes them all over the town and at specific points they come face to face with the Divinities borne on the shoulders of the citizens. At one point, Christ is supposed just to have risen and the forces of Evil dance about in front of Him in an attempt to prevent His meeting His mother. When the Virgin's cloak falls from her shoulders, it means she has recognized her son and Evil retreats. In days gone by this ritual, a seasonal drama, was reassurance to the people living in the harsh, mountainous interior of the island that the forthcoming agricultural cycle would bear fruit. It helped them spiritually to rise above the harsh life that has always been their lot.

The festival has an atmosphere of restrained violence and even desperation. In these communities there was a very fine line between economic survival and destitution. The more precarious the situation the more violent the dances would probably have been. Nowadays it has all been ritualized: man's techniques for dominating nature (read struggle between light and darkness, life and death, Good and Evil) are no longer primitive and backward. What is interesting however is that the all too real 'struggle' that plays out before you in the streets of Prizzi today, to a background of piped pop music, is the very latest in a long line of rituals that have probably been taking place on this spot since the ancient communities of the Greek civilization peopled the island.

PART THREE

CENTRAL SICILY

8

The Tyrrhenian Coast:
Palermo to Mistretta

Bagheria, Solunto, Capo Zafferano, Caccamo, Termini Imerese, Cerda, Cefalù, Castelbuono, Santo Stefano di Camastra, Mistretta

It is fairly difficult to tell where the sprawl of suburban Palermo ends and where the old satellite towns and villages, once set amongst olive groves and vineyards, begin. The coastal road – the SS113 running east from Palermo – starts amongst the palms on the Foro Italico, beneath the imperious gaze of the Palazzo Butera. It stumbles and bounces over pot-holes as it struggles out of town past the former villages of Romagnolo, Bandita, Acqua dei Corsari and Ficarazzi all the way to Bagheria about 14 km to the east. Of the old villages, Romagnolo is perhaps the most interesting. Once a small fishing village, its strange neo-Arabic pavilion designed in 1906 by Ernesto Basile for the Florio family (this languishes between the shore and the main road, recently rescued from near extinction by Salvare Palermo) and the 19th century Gothic seaside villas teetering at the roadside a hair's breadth from collapse, are the only indications that this was once a fashionable district.

Nowadays the SS113 is the less daunting of the two main eastern exits from Palermo; the motorway (the A19), just a few blocks to the south, is a half-built race track dotted with bloated dead dogs and burnt-out Fiats. Take your pick of the two roads: the former is more scenic, the latter quicker.

Bagheria is the first place of interest east of Palermo. It emerges gradually from the bedraggled tangle of orchards and olive groves of what must once have been an exotic landscape. You see outlying villas first, some turned into cow sheds, then maybe a large set of ancestral gates emblazoned with the arms of some long extinct family, and perhaps a park wall signifying a nearby estate. Some of Bagheria's villas are still private and frequently in use, often by the descendants of those who built them. Not too far from the sea, the town provides relief in summer from the stench and the overbearing heat of the capital. In the 18th century the Palermitan aristocracy moved here *en masse* for the summer months, and their wealth is everywhere displayed in the remnants of Bagheria's magnificent architecture. Of course much has changed today: Bagheria is a notorious Mafia stronghold, and large areas of its peripheral parklands, vineyards and orchards have been built over. But the centre, if your mind's eye can prise off the 20th century overlay, is still a fairly homogenous 18th century country town.

The first villa was built here in the 17th century by Giuseppe Branciforte, Prince of Butera. Parts of it still survive at the very top of the Via Butera, along with what was known as the Certosa, a late 18th century neo-classical pavilion in its gardens, which once contained a series of wax portraits of famous people including Louis XVI, Nelson and King Roger II.

The rest of Palermitan aristocracy followed the Prince of Butera's example in the next century and in 1769 another of the Branciforte family put forward a plan to formalize Bagheria. The Via Butera became the main street – its ascent to the top of the low hill given a certain dignity by the florid façade of the Butera villa at its summit – and another street, now the Corso Umberto, was created at right angles to it. In this street are Bagheria's chief surviving glories: the Villas Valguarnera, Palagonia and Trabia, all privately owned.

The Villa Valguarnera, uniquely, is still set within its own parkland. Owned by the Alliata family, it is still very much in use today, though sadly you cannot see around it and nor can you see it from the street. Both this and the Trabia villa are a source of frustration to the Mafia anxious to get their hands on the land.

The Villa Trabia is divided into flats, each one occupied by a different member of the Trabia family (a branch of which still owns the Palazzo Butera in Palermo (see Chapter 2). The Villa Palagonia on the other hand is no longer lived in (other than by a caretaker whose flat is in the basement) and is owned not by the Palagonia family (profligate spending mostly on the villa used up their huge fortune) but by a Palermitan professor. This one is open to the public. Its gates, flanked by grotesque stone monsters, stare across

the piazza beyond a petrol station at the entrances to the Valguarnera
and the Trabia villas, the former hidden from view beyond the
undergrowth of its gardens, the latter screened by a large ornate
wrought-iron gate. The Villa Trabia is the one that looks like a very
old wedding cake. In its forecourt behind the pampas grass is Ignazio
Marabitti's crumbling statue of Abundance.

Both the Valguarnera and the Palagonia villas are the work of
Tommaso Maria Napoli, a genius with a flair for architectural invention, and the Palagonia (begun in 1705 for the formidably rich
Prince Ferdinando Francesco Gravina, Prince of Palagonia) in particular is a masterpiece of ingenious planning. The principal rooms
are arranged around a curved axis, their shapes unusual and varied,
and their distribution asymetrical about an oval entrance hall. The
piano nobile is approached by a complex open-air staircase which
changes direction subtly and in unexpected ways as you ascend it.
But the brilliance of this plan can be overlooked because nowadays
you enter the property from the back. Originally, visitors would
have approached by way of a long thin avenue, flanked by high walls
laden with statuary, to the other side of the house. The 'out-
stretched arms' of the curved wings would have welcomed them.
Beneath the stair, a vaulted open passageway led the entrance axis
under the house and through to the back of the property, to the gate
by which visitors now enter.

This building's remarkable architectural qualities are also over-
shadowed by its slightly later, and much discussed, adornments –
most notably the grotesque monsters on the walls enclosing the
building. Everybody seems to have heard of these. What is known
about the Villa Palagonia's 18th century appearance derives from
traveller's journals. It amused Brydone and horrified Goethe; by
the time of their visits the owner, Ferdinando Gravina, the grandson of its builder, had already created what Goethe called the
'Palagonian madhouse'. The bizarre stone monsters, dwarfs and
strange beasts – like the horse with human hands – were already in
place. Many are still there, sitting on the curving garden walls,
overlooking the cacti and the flowerbeds. It is not known what
caused Gravina's mania but, according to Swinburne whose account
of the place was published in 1790, the monsters were based on
Diodorus's descriptions of the strange beings which emerged from
the slime of the Nile when the heat of the sun was particularly
intense.

Within, the look was just as strange. All that survives now of the decoration in the main rooms on the *piano nobile* is the facetted mirrored ceiling in the ballroom and a fantastic series of oval, bust-length portrait medallions, (said to represent family members), but reports by Brydone, Goethe and the French artist and traveller Jean Houell tell of strange furnishings made of fragments of broken porcelain. They describe columns and pyramids made from Chinese teapots and bowls. In dismissing them as the product of an inspired lunatic perhaps they were right: the prince's guests certainly felt his eccentricity when unwittingly they sat on seats with concealed spikes beneath their cushions.

There are other villas scattered around the town, all in advanced states of dilapidation, but none in the crazed vein of the Palagonia. At the end of the Via degli Oleandri, for example, is the Villa Villarosa, a vast neo-classical edifice attributed to Marvuglia and dated vaguely to the 1770s by Anthony Blunt. Built for the Notar-bartolo Dukes of Villarosa, it seems deserted (though you can never tell in Sicily where pseudo-dereliction is reckoned to deter intruders). At the bottom of the Via Butera (turn right near the railway station) is the gigantic 18th century Villa Cutò, while further on (going left at the bottom of the Via Butera) is the Villa Cattolica, an early 18th century villa which is now an art gallery.

Shielding Bagheria from the sea is Monte Catalfano on the eastern seaward slope of which are the remains of **Solunto**, a town built by Timoleon in about 350 BC to replace Solus, which was destroyed by Dionysius of Syracuse in 397 BC. Solus lay a few kilometres to the south-west of the Solunto site and, along with Palermo and Motya, was an important Phoenician commercial centre. Finds from it can be seen in the archaeological museum in Palermo, but virtually nothing remains to be seen at Solus itself, so concentrate on Solunto where there is a small museum. Among the surviving ruins there, which include some from the Roman period, are traces of the agora (the open space in a Greek or Roman town used as a market place), a theatre, a small odeon, as well as a district of excavated shops and houses. In the Via Bagnera are the remains of a fairly sumptuous Roman house which still contains mosaics and wall paintings.

The views from the side of Monte Catalfano are spectacular. Beyond the old olive trees and the broken boulders the coast runs north to the old lighthouse on **Capo Zafferano**. This is one of the few untouched, unspoilt stretches of coastline near Palermo, and a good place to swim.

East from Solunto, the coastal road joins up with the A19 which hugs the shore all the way to Cefalù. On the way it passes Monte San Calogero on whose eastern flank lies an interesting and remote hilltown called **Caccamo,** dominated by a magnificent and many-towered 12th century castle. Once the property of the Dukes of Caccamo, this state-owned fortress has been partially restored – frustratingly, bits of it are still obscured by scaffolding. The local Chiesa Madre should be visited as well if only to admire the sculpted relief panels around the sacristy door which are thought to be by Francesco Laurana.

North of Caccamo on the coast is the spa town of **Termini Imerese,** where the hot thermal waters from the mountains flow into the sea. Termini's baths have always been important; the Romans called the place Therma Himera. And as usual there is a mythological explana-tion for their existence: the Cyclops lies crushed beneath the weight of Sicily. His mouth is under Etna, his shoulders are at Syracuse and the Straits of Messina, his feet are beneath Monte san Giuliano at Erice, and his loins lie under Monte San Calogero 'distilling for-ever', says Carlo Levi in his *Words are Stones*, 'these beneficial waters'.

Ancient Himera survives in fragments about 9 km from Termini. Among its ruins is an important Doric temple which, dedicated to Zeus, is supposed to have been built on the site which witnessed the great battle in 480 BC between the Carthaginians and the Greeks. The Greek victory was an important milestone in the rise of their power in Sicily. Hamilcar, the Carthaginian leader, died during what was by all accounts a terrifying slaughter: of a Carthaginian force composed of, so they say, 300,000 men, Diodorus claims that only enough to a fill a single small boat survived to return home and tell the tale.

Hamilcar's nephew Hannibal took his revenge on the Athenians in 409 BC, by razing Syracuse to the ground and murdering thou-sands of its inhabitants. The survivors fled, settling where Termini Imerese is nowadays while Himera, broken and ravaged, sank into oblivion. The finds from the site, which include the temple's lion-head water spouts, can be seen in the archaeological museum in Palermo.

The A19 forks about 15 km beyond Termini Imerese: one branch continues on to Cefalù, the other snakes inland to Enna bypassing

Cerda, famous only as meeting place of the Seventh Army advance columns during the Second World War. This was Cerda's one moment of fame. It is a town 'grey amid a naked expanse of fields and surrounded by that same colour of earth and stubble, that same air of silence and of long-established malaria' writes Carlo Levi. Sicily is full of places like this.

Cefalù on the other hand is quite different. It is one of the most interesting towns anywhere in Sicily, a small fishing port dwarfed by a great Norman cathedral and with a labyrinthine old quarter out of which noisy alleyways clamber up towards the great Rocca di Cefalù. Way above the town, on the Rocca, are the ruins of the so-called Temple of Diana (actually a megalithic structure adapted by the Greeks in the 5th century BC), and the town's tumbledown medieval fortifications. The awesome splendour of this great rock meets its match in Cefalù's magnificent cathedral, just beneath it at the summit of the town. This is decorated by possibly the best medieval mosaics in Sicily. Nothing, not even the Antonello da Messina portrait in Cefalù's Museo Mandralisca, can eclipse their otherworldly magnificence. On any shortlist of ten essential expeditions anywhere in Sicily, they ought to rate near the top. Frustratingly the cathedral has incomprehensible opening hours: be warned.

The cathedral springs into view immediately if you approach Cefalù from the west. It stands out way above the medieval town, its twin-towered façade facing the sea, its backdrop the craggy face of the Rocca. It has a dignified monumentality about it and a strangely defensive character. Its builder was Roger II who, according to a local tradition, was shipwrecked somewhere off Sicily's north coast in 1129. To avert a possible watery grave, he is supposed to have vowed to build a church dedicated to SS Peter and Paul should they intervene to save him and his crew; it would be built at whichever spot they guided him to. Thus at Cefalù in 1131 work began on what is without doubt one of the most awesome Norman structures in Sicily.

Legends like this one are part of local folklore all over Italy. This one is just a red herring; the cathedral is too grand a building for such a small and insignificant town. The real motive for its construction was political, and the so-called vow was a smokescreen for the adroit scheming of its royal builder.

The building is thought to rest on the foundations, or perhaps the stump, of a Roman basilica. When it was first built, the Normans placed in its east end two porphyry sarcophagi which were to have been the tombs of the king and his wife. Their presence instantly raised the status of the building to royal pantheon, underlining the *opus principale* of the entire project. A charter of 1145 officially bestowed the tombs, as well as the town of Cefalù, on the church, aggrandising the Bishopric of Cefalù. During much of King Roger's reign, Cefalù and not Palermo was the citadel of the state church.

The King's motive was to create a bulwark against the power of the Church in Rome. Roger regarded the regulation of church affairs in his own kingdom as a royal prerogative – an idea which infuriated the Pope. He regarded himself as a 'priest-king', and a mosaic in the Cappella Reale in the Palazzo Reale in Palermo shows him receiving his crown from Christ himself and not the Pope. Even the positioning of the two thrones in the cathedral at Cefalù underlines this thinking: in the choir the mosaic-adorned episcopal (on the left) and royal (on the right) thrones are given equal status. This expresses Roger's belief that the Norman kings, like the local bishops, held power by divine right.

In a country of three distinct cultural groups, Roger made an effort to please all of them in order to maintain a peaceful equilibrium. Because of the Byzantine Greeks living in his midst, he humoured the schismatic creeds of Constantinople when he needed to, and yet still paid lip service to Rome when it suited him. When, early in his reign, the Papacy was divided by the Anacletan schism, a rather deceitful Roger got the anti-pope to approve his kingship of Sicily and to reinforce the bishopric of Cefalù. The cathedral with its royal tombs was an effective symbol of the King's defiance of the Pope. Rome in a rage excommunicated Roger who responded by capturing the legitimate Pope, Innocent II. After an inelegant period of bartering, Innocent agreed to withdraw his terrible indictment in return for the power to invest Sicily's bishops.

In practice Roger went on electing his own bishops whether the Pope confirmed them or not. By 1150, however, Roger seems to have come to a compromise with the next Pope, Eugenius II, and by the time the King died in 1154 the reasons for which Cefalù had originally been established had lost all force. This put an end to any further privileges for Cefalù. But because there was in fact no legislation nullifying the charter of 1145, Cefalù pestered King Roger's heirs to honour its terms, and to bring his body, which had

been buried in Palermo Cathedral, to its rightful resting place here
by the sea. Cefalù was not going to give up its coveted position
without a fight.

Roger's son William I, a master at the art of procrastination,
always said that consecration of the cathedral would have to take
place first, and that this was impossible until building work was
finished (the mosaics were in place by 1149 but the west façade
wasn't completed until 1240). After William's death Frederick II,
equally reluctant to confirm the 1145 charter, took the empty tombs
from Cefalù to Palermo where you can see them to this day. He
simply seized them, having made sure the coast was clear by first
sending the Bishop on some spurious long-distant errand.

Though the cathedral's intended function was never realized, its
magnificence has never been eclipsed. Even now the mosaics are
practically as they were when they were first installed on the walls of
the apse and the choir. Of all the mosaics of the period, these lead
the way in artistic quality. Their influence is recognizable in other
Sicilian works, in particular those of the Cappella Reale and the
Martorana in Palermo, and of course in the cathedral at Monreale.
Incidentally, these too are all redolent of the politics of the day.
Roger II saw himself in the same mould as the Emperor Justinian,
and not for nothing are the mosaics often celebrated as purely Greek
works on Sicilian soil.

The principal figure at Cefalù is a huge, staring Christ
Pantocrator, frozen in an act of benediction in the conch of the
central apse. He holds an open Bible on whose pages is written 'I am
the Light of the World' in Latin and Greek. Beneath him is the
Virgin flanked by Archangels, and below her are the Apostles, six
on either side of the window. On the side walls flanking the apse are
rows of patriarchs, prophets and saints. What potent images these
must have been at the time of Roger's dispute with the Pope. Rome
must have seemed light years away.

Scattered about the cathedral's conspicuously Norman interior
are one or two other interesting things, including sixteen antique
Roman columns which divide the nave from the side aisles. Pointed
arches spring upwards from Roman and Byzantine capitals and up
above is an open timber roof whose beams still bear the traces of
13th century paintings. Until the late 1970s, the interior of the
building was festooned with a baroque overlay which was wildly out
of place in the context of the majestic Norman structure. All of this
is being removed. Outside are two towers with pointed pyramidal

roofs dating from the earliest building period. They flank the west front and are joined by the 13th century arcaded porch. Blind arcading runs around the building at window level, and there is a cloister which seems to anticipate a very much more beautiful one at Monreale.

Across the road from the Piazza Duomo, in the Via Mandralisca, is the Museo Mandralisca which houses Antonello da Messina's *Portrait of an Unknown Man*. Once the property of Baron Enrico Piaino di Mandralisca, the portrait is a three-quarter length work of the Flemish type (see Antonello's other works at Messina (see Chapter 11), Palermo (see Chapters 2–4) and Syracuse (see Chapter 14)). Typically of his portraits, the sitter has a very lively, almost mischievous expression and, like his altarpieces, the painting shows a wonderful combination of attention to detail (evidence of contemporary Flemish influence) and an Italian clarity and solidity. Alongside it in the little museum are the Baron's collections of coins, shells, and Greek and Arab pottery. In particular see the 3rd century BC Sicilian Greek vase on which a fish merchant slices up an enormous tuna fish. Go to the fishmonger anywhere in Sicily and the scene will hardly have changed.

In the 1920s Cefalù was well known all over Sicily for the curious antics of a certain Edward Alexander Crowley who chose the town as the setting for his 'Abbey' of Thelema, the headquarters of a magical 'religion' that he had founded. Crowley was the man who inspired Somerset Maugham's *The Magician*. Known as The Beast, he was in the mould of Sir Francis Dashwood (who anticipated Crowley and his Abbey by two hundred years with his Hell-Fire Club). But while Sir Francis would never have pretended that his Abbey was for anything other than frolic and debauchery (the entrance to the Hell-Fire Club's temple was shaped like a vagina while beyond were statues with pornographic inscriptions), Crowley intended his cult as the eventual 'successor' to Christianity. His demonic vision was anything but terrifying: 'my house is going to be a Whore's Hell, a secret place of the quenchless fire of Lust and the eternal torment of Love', he announced on arrival in Cefaù. In reality the Abbey was a not very distinguished place – a sort of semi-surburban cottage with no sanitary arrangements. Now dilapidated, it survives in the Portera district of Cefalù in a large overgrown garden not far from the Rocca. You can look at it from the outside, but it is not open to the public.

The cult's history is bizarre. Crowley had a coterie of disciples upon whom he bestowed a variety of favours. One of his favourites, was Raoul Loveday, another was Leah Faesi, otherwise known as the Scarlet Woman. Along with the other Thelemites, she spent her days experimenting with drugs, mixing potions, breeding, and doing unspeakable things to herself and others using various 'magic' icons and a goat. The walls of the villa were covered with pornographic murals; some of these survive and you can see them today if you are lucky enough somehow to get into the building, which is mysteriously owned by a 'widow from Palermo'.

The trappings of ritual magic – like the circle painted on the floor – still existed in the 1960s, although their exact purpose is not known. The brethren probably never indulged in human sacrifice though they did once ritually kill a cat (having anaesthetised it first), and five sparrows were sacrificed to invoke Mercury. The Beast himself crucified a toad and ate it; afterwards, not surprisingly, he suffered from boils. Most days (and nights) were spent in maniacal worship of 'jolly Priapus', wrote Crowley's biographer Julian Symonds in his book *Great Beast*. Priapus' 'cudgel . . . beat him [Crowley] around the head and drove him mad, so did the opium, cocaine, ether, morphine, heroin and hashish . . . '.

His friend Raoul Loveday, an earnest disciple who dedicated himself 'body and soul' to Crowley's new religon, died in 1923 after sipping the blood of a dead cat – according to local newspaper reports. This rumour was propagated by his wife Betty May, chief cook and baby watcher at the Abbey, who loathed Crowley. The reality was quite different: having drunk some dirty water he expired after a bad attack of gastroenteritis. Loveday's funeral was a popular occasion. The Beast arranged to have him buried outside the local Catholic cemetery and the news of the event spread quickly around Sicily. The Abbey was so well known that hundreds of peasants flocked in from the countryside to witness Crowley the High Priest bury his magical 'son'. 'All around perched on the rocks, they watched and waited', wrote Symonds. 'Perhaps the worship of Priapus, which had continued in southern Italy into the 19th century, was still being performed . . . '.

Crowley was finally frogmarched from Cefalù on Mussolini's orders and deported from Italy with his children Hermes and Dionysus. The people, by all accounts, were sad to see him go. They had grown used to seeing him loitering with his offspring in the streets of the town and up on the Rocca near the ruins of the ancient Temple of Diana (with which he had a spiritual fixation), his head shaven, his earrings glistening in the sun. And they loved to listen to the reports of the mysterious acts of 'sex-magic' that he performed with one or other of his concubines.

Edging inland from the Rocca, just south of Cefalù on the fringe of the Monti Madonie, is an attractive little town called **Castelbuono** whose chief attraction is a chapel dedicated to Sant' Anna within the local 13th century castle. In it an ebullient array of stuccos thought to have been the work of Giacomo Serpotta is well worth a detour.

Adjacent to the Monti Madonie, further east, is another range of mountains called the Nebrodi which constitute the highest part of north-eastern Sicily. The gateway to this area is the coastal town of **Santo Stefano di Camastra**, famous for its ceramics. From here one of the most preposterous mountain passes imaginable leads on up into the mountains and the town of **Mistretta**. Not much traffic goes this way, just a clutch of Fiats each day and some old Piaggio three-wheelers carting vegetables to and fro. The modernity and scale of the road leads one to imagine a great 20th century city as its destination. But Mistretta is not very big and the towns futher inland on the same road are tiny places which no one ever thinks of visiting. Mistretta has the feel of any rural town in southern Europe – deserted on weekdays but crammed on Sundays and feastdays when the population of the outlying farms and villages crowd into town in search of entertainment. It does not have that black, oppressive broodiness which hangs like a cloud over so many Sicilian towns.

Mistretta grew up in the Middle Ages around a castle strategically placed on a route between the Tyrrhenian Sea and the interior of the island. The very last fragmented remains of this building wobble on the edge of the rocky hill above the town. From here there are wonderful views north out to the Aeolian Islands. Not much has happened at Mistretta through the course of its history and even though it is thought to be in the Mafia camp, there have been no dramas to upset the quiet pace of its country life. Its palaces and churches have survived relatively unscathed.

The most prominent of these are in the Via Libertà and the Piazza Vittorio Veneto in the town centre which is dominated by the Chiesa Madre. Lodged into the main façade of this lumpen edifice is a statue of the *Madonna and Two Saints*, dated 1494, said to be by Giovanni da Milano. The foundations of the building are far more ancient than this, though in its present form the church is only about 360 years old, having been rebuilt in the 17th century when Mistretta became a fairly wealthy town.

The patrician glamour of that period survives in a number of small but magnificently adorned palaces, each one a monument to the notion that overblown external decoration is a sure sign of affluence within. This is nothing exceptional: you see it all over Sicily, most memorably in Noto, Nicosia and Erice. The inhabitants of the Palazzo Russo, opposite the church of San Sebastiano (recognizable by the stucco figure languishing in an upper niche stuck full of arrows), were perhaps only fairly wealthy, while the occupants of the Palazzo Scaduto further along in the Via Libertà were probably extremely rich. The Palazzo Scaduto's current use as the Gran Bar belies its original magnificence although nothing the bar might put into its windows could ever eclipse the great pot-bellied herms holding up its entrance portal. Within, the original double stair survives, now ignominiously propping up cupboards and pots of bedraggled palms.

Many other old residences are scattered about the town, richer or poorer, some with surprisingly ebullient carvings around a door or a window, each one worked enthusiastically by provincial carvers only vaguely aware of current artistic trends in the capital. They concentrated on making bunches of fruit seem more fecund, grimaces uglier and pot-bellies more bloated. It is sensuality at the expense of sophistication out here in the provinces.

9

Mistretta to Enna

Nicosia, Troina, Agira, Sperlinga, Gangi, Petralia Soprana,
Petralia Sottana, Polizzi Generosa, Collesano, Leonforte, Enna

---

Beyond Mistretta, still in the Monti Nebrodi, are clusters of antique
hilltowns of which Nicosia and Enna are the most important. Going
west from Nicosia, the SS120 creeps back into the Monti Madonie,
leading to Sperlinga, Gangi, the two Petralie – Sottana and
Soprana – and Polizzi Generosa, all scraggy little towns with interesting and colourful celebrations during Easter Week. Go east from
Nicosia and you find Troina and Agira, hilltowns once coveted by
the Normans and hardly changed since. All of these towns survive in
varying degrees of decrepitude, their castles and churches mouldering quietly, their inhabitants watchful and superstitious. All are
formidably high, and all have enviably wide-ranging views of the
surrounding countryside.

Nicosia is a dusty, sun-parched place which was shaken vigorously
in an earthquake in 1967. Not much has been done to repair the
damage and a great many of its buildings, like the Cathedral of San
Nicola, are held together by scaffolding. San Nicola is a wonderful
old wreck. Successive conquerors of Sicily adorned it in their own
particular fashion: the building is largely 14th century, but there is a
discreet overlay, particularly on the entrance portal, of the baroque.
Facing the piazza, San Nicola's lateral flank has a 15th century
portico. Inside, a few treasures resisted destruction, best of which
are a wooden crucifix by Fra Umile da Petralia and a Gaginiesque
marble pulpit in the nave.

At the highest point of the town is the church of Santa Maria
Maggiore, wedged between enormous boulders tossed up in some
primeval eruption. Built in the 13th century, reconstructed in the
18th after a landslide had demolished most of the town, it was
nearly destroyed again in 1967. The earthquake left the church bells
lying in a heap by the door, where they remain to this day; if you

hear bells ringing there now, they are only electronic recordings. A lovely carved entrance portal opens to a dank interior whose principal treasures are an elaborate marble triptych by Antonello Gagini (1499–1512) and a throne on which Charles V sat when he passed this way in 1535 on his way home from Tunis.

The way up to Santa Maria Maggiore goes along the Via Francesco Salmone, a silent old street lined with honey-coloured palaces heavy with carving. One in particular, No 37–9, sports vivacious, squirming herms, Titans and gargoyles gouged from its stone façade. The artists and craftsmen working on buildings such as this will probably never be identified, but the eclecticism and passion of their carvings is typically Sicilian. It seems that the artists were simply having a good time, enjoying their materials.

In various quarters Nicosia, like a great many other Sicilian earthquake-stricken towns of great age, has suffered from unattractive and bland modern infill. Ancient streets have been jerked from their fusty daydreams into the 20th century and suddenly confronted by stark new apartment blocks, or even abandoned building sites. And nobody seems to care, least of all the lazy old men sitting about in the afternoon shadows picking their teeth and swatting the flies off their brows. Sadly Nicosia is another Mafia town and the preservation of old towns is not one of their concerns.

Earthquakes have hardly affected **Troina**, a little town east of Nicosia. The development of its core stopped sometime in the 17th century and most of what you see high on its solitary peak is, if not medieval, certainly no newer than 400 years old. Here and in Agira, just to the south, it is the 17th century buildings that 'violate' the early townscape.

The core of Troina dates from Count Roger's time. In fact it was in Troina in 1062 that Roger, his first wife Judith and about 300 of their knights nearly met their ends. It was summer and they had just arrived from Calabria. Leaving Judith in charge of the small garrison, Roger laid siege to Nicosia. In his absence the Greeks and Saracens living in Troina overpowered the Norman force and took Judith hostage. Horrified, Roger returned to rescue his wife but was himself beseiged. For four bitterly cold months the Normans were holed up on this impregnable mountain top 1200 m above sea level. John Julius Norwich reports in *Normans in the South* that Judith had to share a woollen cloak with her husband. Once they had burned all the wood they could find, eaten all the horseflesh they could stomach, and found themselves with nothing left to drink, desperation stirred their courage. One snowy night in early 1063 they stole silently through the Saracen barricades to a victory only made possible because their beseigers, also frozen, were intoxicated on the local brew. Norwich relates that – with a quick act of contrition to Mohammed – they had consumed it 'for its calorific properties'.

If you are here on a wintry day, when the wind fills Troina with icy blasts from the snow-capped peak of Monte Etna, spare a thought for Roger, Judith and their knights, languishing in the freezing, spectral gloom of the vaulted passageways around the cathedral.

Count Roger built the cathedral (1078–80) and Troina became an important strategic point for the Norman campaign in Sicily. Heavily fortified, it became their treasury. A single poignant relic survives to this day in the cathedral treasury: a square ruby ring that Roger presented to the cathedral at the end of the 11th century. This was no incidental act of generosity. Troina was the seat of the very first Norman bishopric in Sicily, and was much favoured.

The cathedral was rebuilt in part in the 15th and the 18th centuries – some not very exceptional baroque work obscures heftier Norman handiwork beneath – but there are still parts of the building which are distinctly Norman. The crypt, the elongated proportions of the interior of the building and the external blockwork of its lower walls are the most impressive. The blockwork is best viewed from the dark, vaulted passage to the right of the building – it burrows its way under the church tower and runs down to where the castle once was and where you can still see traces of the old city walls, dating from before even the Normans. They are thought to be Greek, built when Troina was known as Polis Tyrakinai, and was possibly the place Pliny knew as Tyracinensis.

The houses around this upper piazza, and those lining the Via Conte Ruggero as it rambles down through the town, are tall and clifflike with ancient, silent doorways. Steps straggle off on either side between them to hidden streets on lower levels in which are dim, closed churches and rustic undercrofts filled with chickens and great empty ceramic jars once filled with olives or oil. The church of San Silvestro contains Domenico Gagini's statue of San Silvestro (whose tomb is also here) and near the Portella Sant'Ippolito, in the Contrada Amoruso, are the ruins of the Saracen mill that Count Roger, after his victory over the Saracens of Troina, presented to the cathedral.

South of Troina is **Agira**, one of those many places whose lofty position earned it the title *Belvedere di Sicilia*. Agyrion to the Greeks, it is said to have been the birthplace in the 1st century BC of the historian Diodorus. In his time Agyrion's chief deity was Herakles who, in the early Christian years, is thought conveniently to have been transformed into San Filippo d' Argiro, a local 'saint' credited with some fairly impressive miracles. The John Murray Handbook has him driving out the devils which haunted the pagan sites in and around the town and converting many of its inhabitants to Christianity. The church of San Filippo in the lower town is filled with dedications to his saintly person and there is even a wooden choir by Nicola Bagnasco inlaid with scenes from his life as well as a statue of him by Giambattista Amendola in the crypt.

There are one or two other interesting works of art in the town: San Silvestro has a painting on marble thought to be by Willem Borremans; here there is also a statue of the *Madonna dei Poveri* by Amendola (1593). The churches of San Salvatore and Santa Maria Maggiore sport their Norman origins to differing degrees: while the former has had added a 16th century façade overlain with the usual baroque tat, Santa Maria Maggiore has an impressive array of unspoilt Norman features including some lovely decorated capitals. And if you cannot see it on display, ask to be shown the elaborate 13th century mitre kept in the Treasury of San Salvatore. Its surface has been worked with gold thread and pearls which hold in place small painted enamel panels of the saints.

On the other side of Nicosia, the SS120 leads to **Sperlinga**, just a few terraces of old cottages lining a great calcareous rock sticking out of the fields in the middle of an arena of mountains. On top is a castle whose deepest recesses – dungeons and bolthole chambers – have been gouged from the innards of the rock itself. It has a near-360° view of the countryside around it and there are bastions – half solid rock, half stone-built – that reach from the bottom of the mound to the top. The fortifications seen there today date from about 1283 and were built mostly by the Chiaramonte family who owned the castle at the time. The fortress remained in private ownership until 1970 when it was sold to the state for much needed restoration.

The history of the place revolves around the hated Angevin rulers of Sicily. When the rest of the country rose against them during the bloody excesses of the War of the Vespers in 1282, the Angevin garrison of Sperlinga, alone with Calatafimi, remained untouched, a fact recorded with some pride on a stone above the lower entrance to the castle. While their compatriots were having their throats slit, the Sperlinga garrison was also allowed a safe passage out of the district to Messina from which a boat took them back to Anjou. And if anyone had dared to attack them in the castle, they would have found the entrance booby-trapped. One spectacular trap survives: at the very highest point of the castle, on a rampart bounded by recently restored crenellations, are a series of gaping holes in the pavement. These were once obscured by trap doors which fell open under pressure, precipitating whoever was unfortunate enough to step on them down into Stygian rock chambers below. There they were left to rot.

The innards of the rock are riddled with a labyrinth of inner passages and tomb-like chambers. Some were living quarters, others were defensive positions, prisons, weapon foundries or granaries, and some were almost certainly home to the ancient Sicani, Sperlinga's earliest inhabitants. Some of the rooms were occupied until about ten years ago by local residents too poor to afford anything better. These troglodytic dwellings often opened from the backs of cottages at the base of the rock and were shared with the livestock. Freezing and smoke-filled in the winter, damp in the summer, each was a testimonial to the domestic horrors of Sperlinga in the Middle Ages. One section has been preserved and is rather grandly called an Ethnographic Museum; it contains pretty local ceramics, a quaint old bed and rough-shod wooden tables and chests made of a few bare planks knocked together.

Sperlinga grew in the 17th century when it became the feudal property of the Natoli, Princes of Sperlinga. At that time the single spired Chiesa Madre was built. There is only one piazza – the Piazzale del Castello – which faces the church of Santa Maria della Mercede at the top of the town. This is lined with buildings whose back walls were linked to form a continuous defensive barrier. It had, and has, only one entrance – you reach it via a steep flight of steps.

The road from Nicosia to Sperlinga continues to **Gangi**, birthplace of the painter Giuseppe Salerno (1570–1632) whose works can be seen all over Sicily. Beyond, it leads to Petralia Soprana and Petralia Sottana, the one high, the other lower in the valley, and on to Polizzi Generosa, Caltavuturo and Sclafani Bagni. These small hilltowns strung along the sides of the Monti Madonie are easily covered in a

day, unless you spend time here during Easter Week when there is
a lot to see.

In the Madonie Easter is a serious event. If you were to spend
Easter Week at Gangi, or at one of the Petralias, Polizzi Generosa
or even further afield at, say, Collesano (between Caltavuturo
and Cefalù), you would notice at once the interchangeability of
sacred and profane. It is this, spiced with a healthy dose of fantasy
and legend, which, says Herbert Kubly in *Easter in Sicily*, is the
Sicilian peasant's way of escaping the brutish reality of his material
life.

To the outsider it can sometimes seem that Christ is only incidental, that the Easter story is just a convenient way of explaining the
magic of the death and subsequent regeneration of vegetable life.
You feel in these mountains that any sort of god will do just as long
as he, she or it ensures the successful passage of seedlings to bounti-
ful harvest. Instances where the Church has had to intervene to
forbid certain practices are not unknown. It comes as no surprise to
find that the reigning deities in these parts in the past were
Demeter, the fertility goddess, and her daughter Persephone. The
countryside between the Madonie, Troina and Enna is immensely
fertile. The hills are blanketed with wheat fields – 'the navel' of
Sicily and the breadbasket of the classical world. Over this paradise
ruled Demeter from her temple on Enna's Rocca di Cerere.

Demeter was known to the Romans as Ceres (whom modern
cynics know as the Virgin Mary). The cathedral in Enna has a side
chapel dedicated to the Virgin, and its decoration in stucco is of
voluptuous cascades of fruit and flowers tumbling off the vaults
of the roof; this was not simply some virtuoso excercise by the
stuccatore but homage to the earth's fecundity and the Virgin's role
as the Great Mother. Legend has it that Demeter's daughter
Persephone departed into the underworld in the autumn and
reappeared in the spring, bringing with her fresh buds and a new
lease of life for nature. The celebration of Persephone's emergence
from the underworld was at one time just as important as Easter –
the most important date on the island's ecclesiastical calendar – is
now.

All over Sicily you will find symbols intended to ensure the
regeneration of the plant cycle. One is the *lavureddi* in which plates
of lentils, chickpeas or barley are left to sprout in complete darkness,
the seeds interwoven with ribbons. (Recently in Agrigento province
the bishop forbad this, though staunch practitioners ignored him.)

The palm is central to Holy Week festivities at Gangi, as it is in many small towns all over Italy. It symbolizes the victory of the Redeemer over death. Leaves of the tree are carried in bunches which have been blessed in a church on Palm Sunday. In antiquity the palm was thought to possess powers which could deflect evil and misfortune; all over Sicily you still see little palm crosses in bedrooms over the matrimonial bed, in shops, on the dashboards of cars, even in buses. It is still said to have power over the evil eye.

Of all Sicily's Palm Sunday events Gangi's are the most colourful. Members of the local confraternities – lay religious brotherhoods – dress in their individual 'uniforms'; if you happen to belong to the Compagnia del Carmelo, for example, you wear a white robe with a brown hood, while the members of the Compagnia delle Anime Santa del Purgatorio wear black. Others wear light blue or red while some wear confraternal finery embroidered with gold and silver thread. The ritual uniforms are mostly ancient, handed down from father to son within each confraternity.

A large cross is carried through the town at the head of the procession, followed by the confraternities in order of their foundation, each one clustered behind a leader who holds aloft its emblem. From the Piedigrotta church the procession wends its way through the town, through the narrow crowded streets, up to the Chiesa Madre and on to the church of SS Salvatore (home to a magnificent *Crucifixion* by Fra Umile da Petralia – see the high altar). Lining the route are drummers, each one dressed in his confraternal kit, announcing the impending arrival of the procession.

Even though the distances between the various towns shut away in the Madonie are so very small, the variations in the Easter rituals between neighbouring towns are surprising. On Palm Sunday, for example, in contrast to Gangi's processions, both **Petralia Sottana** and **Petralia Soprana** stage an enactment of the 'meeting' between Christ and the Madonna. And while in Gangi on Easter Thursday, homage is paid to the *fasciddati* (loaves of semolina flour in the shape of lambs, laid out on a table in the respective chapels of the individual confraternities), the faithful of Petralia Soprana proceed around the town's churches visiting the *saburca* (offerings of fruit, nuts, money etc.) in order to re-establish the contract with God violated by the sins of mankind throughout the year. This act is of exceptional value in Sicily: it is supposed to open the way for men to make peace with their enemies.

Further afield, the people of Scillato (a village between Caltavuturo and Collesano) celebrate Palm Sunday with a wake, while at **Polizzi Generosa**, about 15 km away, there is a huge feast called the 'unleavened supper' at which everyone eats lettuce, oranges and *u picuruni*, the Easter lamb made from marzipan. You see these and other ritual confectionery – birds (doves, or chickens each with an egg under its wing) and flowers – all over Sicily. Size, shape and colour varies from town to town though the lamb is generally accompanied by a little red banner signifying the Redeemer, and each one is gaudily 'made up' – red lips, jewellery – with candied fruit in order to look its best for the sacrifice.

Good Friday celebrations also differ from town to town. While at Gangi a procession weaves through the town supporting either single statues or tableaux of the sacred events of Christ's life leading up to the crucifixion, at **Collesano** they hold a penitential procession called the *cerca* (search). This really begins the night before, when the locals go around the town 'looking' for Christ. Wielding torches, their role is gradually subverted and ironically they end up as Christ's executioners. At their core are the members of a confraternity called the Santissimo Crocifisso who carry in their hands the symbols of Christ's sacrifice – the cock, the hammer, the pliers, nails, the crown of thorns, a sponge, dice, and a lance. There is also a sun and a moon, even a ritual loaf carried on the end of a spear, and before the *cerca* takes place a roasted lamb is eaten at a banquet. On Good Friday a woebegone figure playing Christ, a chain on his foot, drags a cross through the streets of the town followed by Roman soldiers and the brethren of the Santissimo Crocifisso dressed in smocks, hoods and crowns; and in the evening there is another procession, of Christ, his grieving Mother, St John and Mary Magdalen.

Some of the peripheral events are more mystifying than others: at Petralia Sottana for example, on the Wednesday before Easter, there is a peculiar event called the *trimuliu du li cannili* (the trembling of the candles). The local priest gives a sermon timed to coincide with the gradual sputtering out of the candles on a fifteen arm chandelier placed on the high altar. Everyone is plunged into total darkness. Even more incomprehensibly, the priest then bangs the pews, first on his own for a minute or two, then joined with gusto by the congregation.

Even without the help of Easter Week, most of these little towns are attractive and interesting in their own right. Paintings by the workaholic painter Lo Zoppo are generously scattered about. San Nicola at Gangi has a *Last Judgement* (1629) which is considered his best work, and there are others in San Francesco at Petralia Sottana, in the Chiesa Madre in Polizzi Generosa (which once had seventy-six churches), and Petralia Soprana. While in Gangi, visit the church attached to the Castello di Gangi; it has a barrel-vaulted ceiling which could be, according to Anthony Blunt, the work of the Gagini, and a rare instance of the early 16th century Florentine style of architecture in Sicily, and circular reliefs of putti from the della Robbia workshop. Domenico Gagini sculpted a bass relief of the Last Supper for the Chiesa Madre in Polizzi Generosa, and in Petralia Soprana's Convento dei Minori Riformati is a *Crucifixion* by Fra Umile da Petralia who was a native of the town – see his monument at its centre.

South again from Nicosia the road wends its way down to **Leonforte**, a remarkable little town hemmed in on its knoll by cornfields. At its base, facing the mountain eyrie of Enna, is a strange fountain called the Granfonte. It was built in 1651 by one of the Branciforte princes, Nicolo Placido, whose feudal seat was here, and it makes a grand architectural statement – while simultaneously dispensing water into troughs for washing; its construction (in golden stone to match the surrounding cornfields) was an isolated act of benevolence at a time when feudal dependants were more likely to be given a kick in the teeth than fresh running water. The water troughs are backed by a scenographic wall topped by a strange sculpture showing what looks very like an oriental carpet partly unravelled. The water jets out from little pipes into the troughs which are just the right height for a donkey. Even now the odd labourer drops by to fill water jars.

Up on the hill, the rear of the Branciforte palace looks over this quaint rural cameo. The palace, surrounding a vast courtyard, is nearly derelict, the Branciforte having long departed. But San Giovanni Battista across the road contains some of the tombs of the family, which was once the richest in the country. The church was built by Ercole Branciforte slightly earlier than the Granfonte.

Like a great many country towns once at the centre of vast feudal estates, Leonforte expanded in the 17th century. However it was unusual for a landowning family to show anything more than a passing interest in their property. Unlike their peers, the Branciforte actually visited Leonforte and this must be the reason why it is more elegant and ordered than most of the ragged little country towns in

Sicily. Piazza Regina Margherita for example is circular, bisected by
the Corso Umberto. And from it there are vistas, at right angles to
the Corso, which terminate in a flight of steps. Only beyond those
can you see the normal spaghetti-like passages and alleys.

Enna is visible from Leonforte, its bulk partially eclipsed by
Calascibetta. Both lie about 19 km further south, Enna, a much
coveted fortress town with a long and eventful history, rising to a
dramatic 933 m.

Enna was among the last towns to be taken by Count Roger from
the Saracens. Their name for it was Kasr Janni. Corrupted, this
became Castrogiovanni, a name it retained until Mussolini changed
it back to Enna, the modern version of its classical name Henna
which the Romans had altered to Castrum Ennae.

The Normans found the Saracens enormously difficult to dis-
lodge. The Saracens themselves had only conquered it from the
Byzantines, in 859, by climbing one by one through a city sewer.
By 1086 Count Roger had taken Agrigento, but even with much of
Sicily under Norman control – Palermo itself had been theirs
since 1072 – Enna remained inviolable. However, on the fall of
Agrigento, Count Roger found that among his prisoners were the
wife and children of the Emir of Enna, Ibn Hamud. Reluctantly, or
so it seemed, he agreed to meet Count Roger to discuss a safe
passage for his family. In fact knowing that his position was
untenable, he had to give up. But he couldn't be seen simply to
hand Enna to the Normans.

Hence, it is thought, when Roger and Ibn Hamud met they
formulated a plan whereby the Emir and his party, having left the
fortress one day, would be captured by a force of Norman knights
who just happened to be lying in wait for them behind a rock. Subsequently Roger took Enna, and Ibn Hamud's wife and children
were returned to him; but not before he agreed to adopt Christianity
as his faith. He was given an estate in Calabria by Roger and there he
retired with his new name – Baron Ruggero di Camuto, Ruggero
after his godfather and Camuto, well, who knows? It isn't a far cry
from Hamud.

There are two good places from which to view the countryside
surrounding Enna. One is the Piazza Francesco Crispi and the other
is the Rocca di Cerere. From the former you can see all the way to
Leonforte, Nicosia, Cerami and Troina – all of which are better seen
at night when, lights ablaze, they resemble a diamond necklace

garlanding the Nebrodi Mountains. From the Rocca di Cerere the views stretch away past Frederick II's Castello di Lombardia to Etna.

It was at Enna that in 480 BC Gelon erected a temple to Demeter; it was the sacred seat of the cult of Demeter and Persephone her daughter who, according to legend, was abducted by Hades in the meadows to the south-east, on the shores of Lake Pergusa through which he then took her to live with him in the underworld. This event is commemorated by a copy of Bernini's famous statue *The Rape of Persephone* (the original is in the Villa Borghese in Rome) in the Piazza Francesco Crispi.

It seems Persephone loved to play in the fields and meadows around Enna. It was a place, says Ovid, 'where Nature decks herself in all her varied hues, where the ground is beauteous, carpeted with flowers of many tints'. (While this may once have been the case the vicinity of Pergusa itself has since been raped by developers and today the hunt for an unspoilt meadow would be long and fruitless. Spring in the rest of Enna's province is, however, very beautiful.) After Persephone's abduction, a bereaved Demeter left Olympus and wandered the earth vainly searching for her. On her travels, she found out what had happened and that Zeus (who some say was her husband, others her brother) had given his consent for the abduction. In a fury, Demeter refused to return to Olympus and brought a blight on Sicily: the island would remain barren until Persephone was returned to her. Zeus conceded, as did Hades though he allowed her to return to earth only for a few months each year. She would spend eight months in the underworld – from October to June – re-emerging in the spring when the seeds are sown and the natural cycle begins afresh. Satisfied, Demeter then made Sicily the most fertile place on earth.

Even though time has obscured the exact rites of this cult, there are one or two events in the local church calendar which seem to hark back to the legend of Demeter and Persephone. In Enna, for example, on her feast day, the faithful place bundles of hay and flowers before the statue of the Madonna delle Grazie (the Madonna of all the Graces). Is this a continuation of the custom of making offerings to Demeter and her daughter in the temple on the Rocca? The Demeter-Madonna relationship is a very satisfying one simply because the connections seem so obvious. Its manifestations are legion: on Easter morning at nearby Caltagirone, a cloaked statue of the Madonna is trundled out into the nearby countryside to 'search' for her son. The similarity with the pre-Christian legend is striking.

These rituals are not confined to Easter. Jean Houell in his *Voyage Pittoresque* of 1785 noticed something strange when he witnessed a harvest festival near Catania: 'The peasants celebrate the wheat harvest with a sort of orgy, a popular festival of thanksgiving for the good harvest they have gathered. Young people dancing in a circle; they are followed by a man riding on an ass and beating a drum; five or six men similarly mounted parade after him carrying long poles decorated from top to bottom with sheaves of wheat; in their midst another man, also mounted, carries a large banner which floats majestically in the breeze. A young woman, dressed in white and seated on an ass, comes next; she is surrounded by men on foot who carry bunches of wheat on their heads and in their arms, and who seem to be paying her homage. An entire crowd of country people follow this procession, playing on different musical instruments.

The most educated people in Catania have assured me that this is a very old custom, of which the origins are unknown; but they do not doubt that it is a remnant of the ancient festivals dedicated to Ceres [Demeter], and that the young woman represents this goddess, to whom the harvests thought to have been obtained through her good will are offered.'

If you had come to Enna nearly twenty-five centuries ago, you would have seen Demeter's temple newly built on a wide ledge above a tremendous drop. Her statue was, according to Cicero, extremely large and accompanied on its rock by one of Triptolemus the hero of agriculture. It was he who witnessed the rape of Persephone. This venerated spot, once a wonder of the classical world, is now a flat, empty space with only a few mounds and a couple of stony foundations.

There is a lot to see in the town of Enna. The principal attraction is, as usual, the Duomo, an early 14th century building with the march of the centuries written across every surface. Even the holy water stoup sits on a base thought to have come from the Temple of Demeter. Its most treasured external adornment is a side entrance in the Chiaramontese style and, inside, some lovely, rather battered choir stalls thought to have been carved by Filippo Paladino. This was once one of thirty-five churches in Enna. One of these, called Santa Spirito according to a great many early 20th century guides, contained an old cooking stove, the very one, the credulous were told, at which the Virgin was preparing her dinner when the angel of the Annunciation appeared to her.

Enna to the Piana di Catania

Caltanissetta, Pietraperzia, Mazzarino, Butera, Gela, Piazza Armerina, Aidone, Caltagirone, Piana di Catania

South west of Enna is **Caltanissetta**, a town noted chiefly for the sagging ruins of a castle built by Frederick III of Aragon on a fantastic rock nearby. Caltanissetta is not an important place – not even a very beautiful place. It was bombed in the last war and the only things of any interest there nowadays are the contents of the Museo Civico, specifically those that came from Sabucina, a Hellenized Sikel settlement to the north-east, fortified by the Greeks and destroyed by Agathocles around 311 BC. In particular see the 6th century BC terracotta model of a temple from Sabucina and an early Bronze Age sculpture thought to be the earliest protrayal of a human figure yet found in Sicily.

Caltanissetta is the starting point for what Italians call a *giro*, an easy roundabout tour, to a handful of minor but interesting places deep within central Sicily. The shortest *giro* – a walk from the town – is to the Badia Santo Spirito, a triple-apsed basilica founded in the 11th century by Count Roger and his third wife Adelaide, whom he married when he was approaching sixty.

While a small country road (SS122) goes north-east towards Enna and the *autostrada*, an even smaller one (SS191) leads out of Caltanissetta going south, cutting round Monte Gibil Gabel, then going east to **Pietraperzia** where there is an interesting if battered Norman castle (1088) enlarged over the years by the local landowners. Beyond, after about 9 km, the road forks: one branch runs south past Barrafranca, while the other continues east to Piazza Armerina, a haphazardly baroque town famous above all for the Roman mosaics unearthed at Casale on its eastern outskirts.

The Barrafranca branch of the SS191 struggles through some of the harshest landscape in Sicily, bounces over pot-holes and gaping fissures in the tarmac, and continues down to **Mazzarino** and Butera. Mazzarino, another *ex-feudo* of the Branciforte family (see Leonforte, Chapter 9), was the home town of a band of notorious *mafiosi* Franciscans who in 1962 were brought to trial charged with crimes ranging from extortion to murder. These startling accusations gripped the country at the time and most fascinating were the revelations that the monks were deeply interested in pornography, and not just as voyeurs. Their involvement from the conceptual phase right down to distribution of the finished product engendered some hilarious headlines in the local dailies.

But the realities of their lifestyle were more sinister: the Abbot was the *capo-mafia* of the whole valley, and some of the good fathers in his monastery carried guns. Hardly what St Francis would have envisaged. The fathers also bought and sold property and loaned money at high interest. It was also revealed at the trial, according to Norman Lewis (*The Honoured Society*), that the monks had used the confessional to transmit their threats. Needless to say the accused were acquitted of all charges, though three laymen accused at the same time got thirty years each. Norman Lewis wrote in *The Honoured Society* that their invulnerability lay partly in their appeal to the Sicilian subconscious: 'To this, the fact that the monks were immoral would be unimportant. What was important was that they were the human vehicles of magic power. The supernatural offices they performed were in no way lessened in their efficacy by the monks' own extreme human fallibility. The Medicine Man or the African Head of Bush Society is not expected to be virtuous, but to be a successful practitioner in the art of compelling rainfall or driving away devils ... It was, and still is, the power of exorcism that counts. The monks were not good men, but they were powerful men, and it was their power to which the Sicilian subconscious automatically responded.'

About 16km further south, **Butera** is another picturesque town also at one time a part of the domains of the Branciforte Princes of Butera. Beyond it, with its wonderful views, is **Gela** and Virgil's Campi Geloi, the wide fertile plains in which, says the Murray Handbook, the poet Aeschylus met his end. An eagle flying overhead carrying a tortoise mistook his head for a stone and dropped the unfortunate creature on to it.

Gela was briefly one of the most important cities in Sicily. It was founded in 688 BC but its power only lasted until Gelon, its ruler, transferred his seat to Syracuse in the 480s. After a brief renaissance, it finally succumbed to the Carthaginians and the Mamertines and was razed to the ground in 282 BC.

'Anyone who is interested in Greek antiquities should not fail to visit Gela,' says Margaret Guido in *Sicily: An Archaeological Guide*. Much of what remained after the devastation of the ancient city was subsequently covered–and hence protected–by shifting sands, so that the archaeologists working on the site have made some very startling discoveries. Not only are there extensive Greek fortifications from the 4th century BC, but the remains of Gela's public baths of the same date have survived in part, making them the only example from Greek times to have survived in Sicily – even the seats still exist. Vases, coins, sarcophagi and assorted architectural fragments from the site are housed in Gela's Museo Archeologico which can only be seen if you brave the horrible town that Gela now is.

Of all the routes from Caltanisetta, the one to **Piazza Armerina**, with the Casale mosaics, is the most interesting. Here, excavated from beneath a landslide, are some of the finest mosaics to have survived from Roman antiquity. It is not known who commissioned them, or who lived in the villa now known as the Villa Imperiale. It was obviously somebody's summer home, a very grand hunting lodge.

It was partially uncovered in 1761, but systematic excavations only really began after 1950. Not much survives of the original fabric apart from floor mosaics. The wall and vault paintings have been destroyed and the mosaics today are protected by a superstructure that aims to provide some kind of comprehensible setting for the ruins. There are about thirty major points of interest about the place; while on-site plans give some idea of the gigantic scale of the building, a route around it ensures that everything worth seeing is covered on a single tour. The circuit around the villa takes in public rooms, private apartments, hot and cold baths and a large colonnaded portico.

Since the 1950s all sorts of guesses have been hazarded as to who lived here; it is rather a learned dispute, and one that has filled pages in history books. Briefly however, there is strong evidence that Maximianus Heraclius, Diocletian's co-Emperor between AD 286 and 305, may have built it, that it was further decorated by his son

Maxentius who became Emperor in AD 306, and that it was taken over by Constantine after Maxentius's death in 312.

The strongest evidence to support Maximianus's claim relates to a beautiful mosaic called *The Labours of Hercules*, which is located in a room of its own – a dining room possibly – surrounded by three apses. Such is the importance of this mosaic that, for a while during the early excavations, the villa was called the Villa of Hercules. At the time the villa was built, says Volkried Schuster, the Roman world was divided into an eastern and a western half. Diocletian realised that the gigantic scale of the Empire was impractical, that it could no longer be governed from a single centre. There should be one ruler for the west and another for the east. To allow the tetrarchy to become reality, he abdicated and called on his co-Emperor Maximianus to do the same. Diocletian withdrew to his well recorded palace at Split, and perhaps Maximianus's equivalent of this was the villa at Piazza Armerina.

It is known fact that Maximianus identified himself with Hercules. Hercules is supposed to have been a mortal with special powers of triumph over chaos – certainly here he is seen coming to the aid of the gods threatened by giants on Olympus – see the second apse. The gods cannot defend themselves, so Hercules shoots his arrows at the five giants who fall to their deaths. In the neighbouring apse is the apotheosis of Hercules, and in the third apse you see Ambrosiana and Lycurgus, the former liberated from the power of the latter – youthful forces triumphing over chaos and decay. These portrayals of Hercules have an almost Michelangeloesque power.

Could these scenes be mirroring contemporary political events? The idea has been put forward that the Hercules mosaic was completed after Constantine, Maximianus's great general, had resubjugated Britain for him. It might be that the mosaic is expressing his jubilation at this successful campaign.

The owner of the villa can, it is thought, be seen in the hunting scene in the nearby ambulacrum, a 60m long corridor closed at either end by an apse. He stands, bearded, leaning on a stick, a pillbox hat on his head, his cloak more decorated than those of his companions.

Look out for what is thought to be a portrait of the Imperial family in the vestibule (called the Vestibule of the Imperial family) and, more memorably, the bikini girls in what is known, unsurprisingly, as the Room of the Bikini Girls. Here, ten females prance about in what look very like – yes – antique bikinis.

Most intriguing about the mosaics is the attention to detail in every one of them: notice the dress of household attendants, soldiers and hunters and the range of different hairstyles, landscapes filled with wild animals, household gods, mythological scenes, and scenes from marine life. Everyday activities are enchantingly portrayed, in particular the *Sacrifice to Artemis* in the Room of the Small Hunt and the love-making scene in the Dormitory. In the former a miniature statue of Artemis stands on a plinth set up between two trees. At its base a fire has been lit – the coals are red hot – and a servant tries to control a yapping dog while two important person-ages stop and, holding on to their horses, pray. In the love-making scene, a nearly naked female kisses a naked youth; her cloak is slipping off, revealing her bottom. Rather more exotic is the scene in the ambulacrum of the wild animals and birds being loaded on to a galley presumably for transportation from Africa to Italy. Attendants stagger up the gangplank clutching what may be ostriches.

All the mosaics belong stylistically to what is known as the Roman-African School (early 4th century AD), recognizable by its exotic elements and its rather free, almost impressionistic style. These mosaics were known to the Normans; in fact King William the Bad had Piazza Armerina destroyed in about 1160 for the part it took in a rebellion. He may also have helped at the same time to destroy the villa. Prior to that, the villa was open for all to see; in fact it was occupied until the Arab period, and maybe the Norman kings used it from time to time. Certainly, the similarities between these mosaics and those of the Sala Re in the Royal Palace in Palermo are often remarked upon.

Beyond Piazza Armerina is **Aidone** (see the lovely wooden crucifix by Fra Umile da Petralia in the church of Sant' Anna) outside of which are the remains of the now ruined city of Morgantina, an important site about which not very much is known. Not much has been excavated, but it is known that a city was founded here in the late 7th century BC on the site of an even older one founded four centuries earlier. In the 6th century BC it was destroyed, and in the late 4th century BC once more rebuilt, continuing to develop under the strong Syracusan influence of Hieron II. What survives on the site belongs mostly to this last period – there are remains of a theatre and an agora, the latter unusually constructed on two levels, and there are a great many Hellenistic houses of which one, the House of

Ganymede, contains 3rd century BC mosaics. One shows Ganymede being carried away by Zeus's eagle.

The portable remains of Morgantina's past are kept in the antiquarium in Aidone – those, that is, that have not been plundered from the site. Morgantina only ever gets a mention in relation to tomb robbers. The Getty Museum in Malibu, California, contains a statue of Aphrodite which is thought to have come from Morgantina and while many see the Getty and the Aphrodite, hardly anyone goes to this solitary site in the hills east of Piazza Armerina.

South of Piazza Armerina is **Caltagirone**, a town famous for its ceramics. It is impossible to miss them: they crowd two museums – a collection of modern ceramics in the Museo Civico – a barbaric, unpleasant looking place, a former Bourbon prison – and a more general but comprehensive collection in the Museo della Ceramica. Ceramics decorate the façades of many of the buildings; they adorn the Ponte San Francesco and they even line the risers of the 142 steps of La Scala, a staircase which clambers up to Santa Maria del Monte on the top of one of Caltagirone's hills at the very centre of the town. They gleam in the sunlight, each one decorated with a scene or figure from Sicilian mythology.

Caltagirone makes some of the grandest baroque statements yet encountered on this tour of Sicily. Wandering through the spaces around the junction of the Municipio, the Chiesa del Gesù and the Duomo, you would be forgiven for imagining you were on stage. The dramatic effect of these vast façades is enhanced by the scarcity of traffic in this part of town; only pedestrians are allowed into it. Opposite the Duomo is the Corte Capitaniale, the façade of which is punctuated with carvings by the ever-prolific Antonello Gagini, helped by a relation, Gian Domenico.

From Caltagirone, the SS417 leads through the fertile **Piana di Catania**, the Plain of Catania (once the haunt of the mythological cannibal Laestrygones), all the way to Catania itself. It is a fertile place nowadays, filled with fruit trees and pasture for grazing. But in the 19th century, the novelist Giovanni Verga, who came from Catania, recorded, in *Malaria* (one of his *Short Sicilian Novels* set in this region), that 'in vain the villages of Lentini, Francofonte and Paternò [towns on the edge of the plain] try to clamber up like strayed sheep on to the first hills that rise from the plain, and surround themselves with orange groves, and vineyards, and ever-green gardens and orchards; the malaria seizes the inhabitants in the depopulated streets, and nails them in front of the doors of their houses whose plaster is all falling with the sun, and there they trem-ble with fever'. The Lake of Lentini, he continued in *The Properties*, was 'like a piece of the Dead Sea'. There was nothing in it, nothing moved there, and nothing grew there either. It was just an unpro-ductive swamp.

It is still deserted today, though cultivated now for the first time in its history since the Cassa del Mezzogiorno took it in hand to drain it. As the road continues north-east from Caltagirone, between Ramacca and Palagonia, it enters the plain – 'an immense campagna' – and there are no other towns really until Catania itself. The legacy of the malarial past is such that even now there are practically no farmhouses or outbuildings here. Just a 'great silence'. The plain is shut in by mountains – Etna in the north, the Monti Iblei in the south and south-east, and in the west the foothills that lead away to Enna, Nicosia and the Nebrodi Mountains.

The Short Sicilian Novels were first published in 1883 as *Novelle Rusticane*, when Sicily was one of the poorest of the Italian states. The advances of the Industrial Revolution had had little effect on it and feudal agrarian life continued much as it had for centuries. In Verga's stories the Piana di Catania becomes a microcosm of the ills of the rest of the island. In his peasants dwells the same rustic stoicism found in Hardy's characters, and there is an epic grandeur as of Greek tragedy in their struggles. Says Eric Lane, who introduces the Dedalus edition (1984) of this work, 'Verga ennobles them by turning the misery and squalor of their life into art'.

It is very easy, driving through a great many smaller Sicilian towns and villages, particularly those stuck out in the middle of nowhere, to make scathing comments about the poor condition of the ancient, crumbling houses, the lack of amenities, the stares of the inhabitants. Maybe the church is locked and nobody can find the person who knows the man who keeps the key. If there is no specific monument, no great painting, and the people in the bar fall silent when you enter, it is very easy to drive on cursing. Sicily is an exclusive place; it can alienate you and shut you out. But Verga's stories illuminate those dark little homes in the Sicilian hilltowns. They familiarize you with the inhabitants, their gestures and banter as they hang out of windows screeching at each other in a dialect that few Italians even will understand. Verga gives a glimpse into the minds of the old men sitting about in the piazza, or the labourer dragging behind him a donkey laden with brushwood. He demystifies the life of rural Sicily that has barely changed in over a century.

PART FOUR

EASTERN SICILY

11

The Tyrrhenian Coast: Messina to Santo Stefano di Camastra

Messina, Milazzo, the Aeolian Islands, Tyndaris, Patti, Frazzano, San Marco d'Alunzio, Sant'Agata di Militello, San Fratello, Santa Stefano di Camastra

'The approach to **Messina** is the finest that can be imagined,' wrote Patrick Brydone in a letter to William Beckford on 15 May 1770, as the ship bringing him from Naples skirted the straits between Calabria and Sicily and sailed into the port of Messina. It still is one of Europe's most magnificent waterways, even from the decks of the shuddering Tirrenia car ferries that plough their way back and forth from Villa San Giovanni in Calabria to Sicily's 'Gateway'. The landscape surrounding Messina has not changed very much since the 18th century though the city itself, ravaged by a series of calamities, Brydone would find quite unrecognizable.

Behind Messina are the Monti Peloritani and to the left, beyond Capo Taormina, is Monte Etna capped with snow even in the summer and languidly billowing smoke all year round. To the north of the city straggle the little fishing villages of Pace, Paradiso and Contemplazione (Peace, Paradise and Contemplation) until the island falls away into the sea at the Punta del Faro, a finger of land poking into the straits at a point where the Tyrrhenian and Ionian Seas meet. Somewhere out here is the legendary whirlpool of Charybdis, that constant threat to safe entry into the harbour at Messina which so taxed Odysseus. In reality it was the violent meeting of different currents passing through the straits. Scylla was the six-headed sea monster facing Charybdis, in reality a rock on the mainland side of the straits which emitted strange sounds when the wind howled around it; together they created what Edward Hutton calls 'the tremendous double adventure' (*Cities of Sicily*).

Just over two miles wide at their narrowest, these straits separate two of the most beautiful stretches of coastline in Italy. The view of it from the top of the hill above Messina is, said Brydone, 'beauty beyond description'. From up there, he saw the straits as an 'immense majestic river'. Taking the Circonvallazione a Monte, the road which runs up the side of the mountains behind the city, look back out to sea and beyond to the Calabrian headlands; it is particularly glorious during very hot weather when the landscape on the other side succumbs to the effects of the Fata Morgana, a mirage which distorts and exaggerates its profile.

'And the key [sic] exceeds anything I have ever yet seen,' Brydone continues, noting the magnificent buildings 'four storeys high and exactly uniform' lining the landward quay of Messina's harbour. These were the palaces built by Simone Gulli in the 17th century and joined together as a monumental terrace known as the Palazzata. Brydone saw them thirteen years before the great earthquake of 1783 shook them to bits. And Goethe saw them five years later: they were still in ruins. In his diary he said they looked 'revoltingly gap-toothed and pierced with holes'. He also noted that while their interiors were in ruins their façades were still intact – due to shoddy construction behind more solid frontages.

They were rebuilt with the rest of the city and Bernard Berenson saw them in 1888 on his first visit to Messina. But by 1908 they were gone again, obliterated along with the rest of the city by an earthquake that lasted about thirty seconds but killed over 84,000 people. Berenson, retracing his steps, wrote sadly in his diary on 20 May 1953: 'I recall rather nostalgically the Messina that I first visited . . . with its noble architectural front, called the 'Palazzata' and parallel with it streets lined with big and small palaces, each of their windows with a balcony caged in with gilded wrought iron'. By then, whatever had survived the tremors had been destroyed by Second World War bombing. Messina saw the Germans' last stand in Sicily and they hung on with a tenacity that almost matched the determination of the Allies to oust them.

The Palazzata stood facing the crooked arm of the city's harbour (shaped like a sickle, the *Zankle*, which gave the town its name in the 8th century BC). Nowadays they have been replaced by modern blocks which, while lacking the elegance and the grandeur of their antecedents, at least preserve the general effect of a long terrace facing the sea. And it does not really seem to matter that they are built of concrete; the fact that they exist at all has helped to preserve

Brydone's 'key' so that a stroll along it at the water's edge and under the gaze of a vast statue of the Madonna called the *Madonnino del Porto*, on the other side of the port, is almost as lovely as ever. Unlike Palermo, Messina never turned its back on the sea.

Having heard that Messina has been sacked over the years, toppled by earthquakes and flattened by bombs, strangers to the city drive on quickly, either south to Taormina or west to Cefalù and Palermo. Messina and the dog-eared remains of its illustrious past are left behind. However, quite a few old monuments have survived despite the *terribilità* of fate. There are perhaps five really important things to be seen in the city today: the Museo Regionale, the scarred little church of SS Annunziata dei Catalani, the Duomo founded by Roger II in the 12th century, Montosorli's polygonal Fontana d'Orione (1547) in front of it, and his Fontana di Nettuno (1557 – and later rebuilt).

The Museo Regionale has become the 'safe house' for Messina's art treasures; most of the city's churches have vanished, but quantities of their contents are now kept here in a rambling building on the edge of the city, once a monastery. There are classical remains, mosaics, Norman sarcophagi, architectural fragments, and frescos, and there are bits of old Messina lying in heaps in the garden. But the real treasures here are the paintings of Antonello da Messina and Caravaggio.

Antonello da Messina was the only great Renaissance painter to have emerged from Sicily. Much of the Renaissance simply passed Sicily by, but Antonello contributed to Italy's artistic mainstream both stylistically and technically. According to Vasari he went to Flanders and subsequently introduced the art of painting in oils to Giovanni Bellini; the effect of this timely event was to spread the technique throughout Italy. While art historians no longer believe this story to be true, they have never actually disproved it.

Not much is known about Antonello, a mysterious figure who seems to have been working in and around Messina from 1457 to 1465. In 1465 he painted the *Salvator Mundi*, now in London's National Gallery, and after that his name disappears from the records. But it emerges in 1473 in Messina with the San Gregorio Polyptych, an altarpiece in a central or north Italian form, which is in the Museo Regionale today. Where he went during the missing years is a question which intrigues art historians – hence the theories about a stay in Flanders.

The San Gregorio Polyptych shows an attention to detail more common in contemporary Flemish paintings than in Italian ones. In particular, the properties of reflected light (notice the transparent jewellery in the Virgin's crown) suggest he may even have had some knowledge of Jan Van Eyck's work. Vasari, the great and often inaccurate recorder of the lives of the painters, says that Antonello studied with Van Eyck before going on to Venice. And yet at the same time his figures begin to show an awareness of volume, his backgrounds an awareness of architectural form, as though the painter had recently seen the work of for instance Piero della Francesca in central Italy. The experts think it unlikely that he ever went to northern Europe and it is now accepted that his initiation into Flemish style and technique took place in Naples where he will have known the work of Colantonio, an eclectic painter with a pseudo-Flemish style.

Antonello's later pictures show the much clearer assimilation of both Italian and Flemish influences which can be seen in the *The Annunciation*, held in the Museo Regionale in Syracuse. He is believed to have been in Venice after 1473, and his stay there was a major catalyst in his development from provincial artist to master working in the Italian style (see his later works in the Palermo museum). He died in Messina in 1479, painting there, possibly in 1477, a Crucifixion (now in the National Gallery, London) which not only has a Belliniesque landscape but a new Venetian light and colour as well.

There are also two huge Caravaggios in this gallery, both commissioned by the city in 1604 – *The Adoration of the Shepherds* from the church of the Cappuccini and *The Resurrection of Lazurus* from the church of SS Pietro e Paolo dei Crociferi. Perhaps the lasting legacy of Caravaggio's Sicilian works is the influence he had on local painters like Filippo Paladino and Pietro Novelli whose works are here in Messina and scattered all over the island.

While the churches of the Cappuccini and SS Pietro e Paolo have both vanished, the little church of SS Annunziata dei Catalani still exists to exhibit the typical eclecticism of 12th century Norman architecture. The exterior is richly decorated with blind arcading and bands of chequered patterns in polychrome marble, and there is a dome. It is a strange survival, half buried below road level and hemmed in between much later buildings. Further on, in the Via Garibaldi, is another church, a ruin too fine to demolish. This is the 13th century church of Santa Maria degli Alemanni, which, even in its present state, is an unusual example of the Sicilian Gothic style.

Not far from SS Annunziata dei Catalani is the Duomo. It is possible that not even its founder would recognize it today, so severe are the changes that have taken place to its ancient fabric. Although its exterior has a 'period' look about it, it was in fact totally rebuilt after the devastation of the last war. Guidebooks call it a 'restored' Norman building, one of the most splendid on the island. Well, it may have been Norman, and certainly its reconstruction was a noble effort, but the accumulated gloom of the centuries has evaporated and it no longer reeks of the past. The ghosts of Joan of England, Richard Coeur de Lion's sister, and her husband King William the Good, who were married here in 1177, no longer languish in the shadows. Even the twenty-six gigantic granite columns taken from a nearby classical temple to line the nave no longer exist.

Sadly there is little to see here now apart from a restored sculpture of the *Baptist* by Antonello Gagini and the tomb of Archbishop Palmer of Messina, who was responsible for having arranged the marriage between Joan and King William. And above the altar is the portrait of the Virgin, painted, we are told, by Saint Luke. This is Messina's *Madonna della Lettera*, the Madonna of the Letter, so called because of the letter (Il Graffeo) that she wrote to the Messinese on the occasion of their conversion to Christianity by St Paul. It is supposed to have been given to an embassy from Messina in AD 42. The original vanished in the 13th century, though the Duomo still has a copy of it.

In front of the Duomo is a large fountain designed in about 1547 by Fra Giovanni Angelo Montorsoli, a native of Florence who collaborated with Michelangelo in Rome and Florence, then later worked in Perugia, France, Naples and Bologna. His Fontana d'Orione, in a version of the High Renaissance style, is one of the finest works of its kind from 16th century Sicily. Although reconstructed, it is important chiefly because its magnificence as a civic project is evidence of Messina's standing as a commercial city – the commercial counterpart in Sicily of Genoa or Venice on the mainland. It is in keeping with the desire of the Messinese to be regarded as the first city of Sicily. Dedicated to Orione, the legendary founder of Messina, it is thought to have been built to commemorate Charles V's triumphal entry into Messina a decade earlier. The fountain's sculptural decoration which includes the four reclining figures representing the rivers Nile, Ebro, Camero and Tiber, is suggestive of those erected temporarily for festivals and triumphal entries.

The decoration of the Fontana di Nettuno in the Piazza Unità d'Italia (it has been moved – it used to stand in the harbour) relates to an earlier fountain. 'Taken together' says Sheila ffoliott in *Civic Sculpture in the Renaissance: Montorsoli's Fountains at Messina*, 'the fountains create a Messinese epic celebrating Messina's foundation, position in the world, and destiny to be an ideal modern city and home for the arts and letters.'

The figure of Neptune, in its original position, follows in a long tradition of statues of gods placed in harbours, of which the ancient colossus of Rhodes is the most famous example. Ffoliott also gives an interesting insight into a less obvious significance of figure and fountain: around the late 15th and early 16th centuries, there was a great deal of interest in the appearance of the ancient port of Ostia, which at one time was dominated by a statue of the Emperor Trajan who had rebuilt it. Taking this as a prototype, not only did the Messinese locate their statue by the waterside, but invoked imperial associations with a Latin inscription on it setting forth Charles V's descent from the ancient Roman Emperors. All this was rather appropriate because, in the manner of his 'ancestors', Charles had his imperial treasury contribute to the rebuilding of Messina and its port as well.

The Messina-Palermo *autostrada* (the A20) cuts through the Monti Peloritani and heads for the north coast. This inaccessible mountain range is full of ravines that the sun never reaches and skeletal peaks bleached of all colour. In the distance is the sea. Here and there are old olive groves and clumps of oleanders inexplicably in flower though the terrain around them is scorched brown and wrung dry of moisture.

The A20 leads to **Milazzo** and the Capo di Milazzo, a promontory that leans out towards the Aeolian Islands. Milazzo, according to Idrisi, Count Roger's Arabic geographer, was 'a marvellous citadel with elegant lines, solidly built ... an impregnable fortress.' Greatly enlarged by Charles V, it survives in part, dominating the town. From Milazzo ferries leave for the **Aeolian Islands** of Vulcano, Lipari, Salina, Stromboli, Panarea, Filicudi and Alicudi.

These islands are a mass of extinct, and nearly extinct, volcanoes which jut up from the sea about 45km from Milazzo. Some offer little more than solitude – **Alicudi** and **Filicudi** for example, the most westerly islands – while others like **Panarea** (the Capri of the archipelago) are fashionable holiday destinations for wealthy

Milanese with second homes. **Stromboli** is the most dramatic: its volcano erupts drowsily almost every day. A rather melancholy place, it only has about 500 inhabitants. **Salina**, the second biggest island, has the most inhospitable landscape from which the vines have been coaxed into producing an extremely good sweet malvasia wine. **Lipari** is the most popular with a pretty port and plenty of cafés, bars, shops and hotels with their own swimming pools. Lipari has the added attraction of being keeper of most of the remains of the Aeolian past; it has an excellent collection of Neolithic artefacts housed in the local museum. There is also what is known as an Archaeological Park in which an uninterrupted sequence of life from the Neolithic period to the present day has been reconstructed from local evidence. In addition to this, its Hellenistic Acropolis encloses the oldest thermal bath equipment in the world.

On **Vulcano**, if you can bear to venture there and imbibe the evil sulphur smells emanating from fissures in the ground, the great attraction is to wallow like a hippo in a mire of hot stinking mud. Apparently its restorative powers are second to none.

Back on Sicily itself, the A20 runs along the edge of the Golfi di Patti before diving into a mountain on whose summit are the remains of **Tyndaris**, very nearly the last Greek city to have been founded in Sicily. It was built by Dionysius the Elder in 395 BC and initially settled by a few hundred exiles from the Peloponnese War, driven from their homelands by the Spartans. The name Tyndaris is theirs – given in honour of the Peloponnesians' native divinities, the Tyndarae brothers of Helen of Troy, Castor and Pollux. Evidence of their cult survives in the finds of coins and mosaics.

Cows and goats now graze amongst the ruins of this illustrious city which once guarded the Tyrrhenian coastline and was as strategically important here as Taormina was to the Ionian seaboard. The site, having been built over by the Romans, retains very little that is Greek except for the old city walls which face the approach to the citadel site from the valley – beautifully cut stones in layers which, after nearly twenty-three centuries, are as stout and as crisp as if they had been completed fifty years ago. Under the Romans Tyndaris flourished until according to Pliny great parts of it vanished over the cliff during an earthquake. The surviving theatre is Roman; so is the monumental partially restored (1956) basilica which opened on to the agora. This is now partly covered by the large modern

Sanctuary of the Madonna di Tindari. Sculpture which once stood in the niches of the basilica found its way into the Archaeological Museum in Palermo but there are other pieces from the site, including a large head of Augustus, housed in the small antiquarium just by the gate to the excavations. There are partially excavated grids of streets and along one of them is a fully uncovered Roman house with a mosaic floor.

Tyndaris is extremely popular nowadays for its black-faced Byzantine icon – the Madonna Negra or Black Madonna – housed in a grotesque extravaganza of kitsch stained glass and gaudy mosaic. It arrived by sea rather mysteriously in a barrel, runs the legend, and since then has been responsible for a number of startling miracles, not least of which is saving a child from certain death after it fell over the cliff. Through the intervention of the Black Madonna – she sent a mattress to soften the child's landing – the victim was saved, and today pilgrims come in their droves to pray to the venerated image for happy solutions to less obvious private agonies.

Not far from Tyndaris is **Patti**. Here, in the right transept of the cathedral, is the tomb of Adelaide, the third wife of Count Roger. She died and was buried in Patti six years after she had gone as a widow to marry King Baldwin of Jerusalem. He was attracted by her great wealth, a large portion of which – gold, silver, purple (precious cloth), gemstones, beautifully worked vestments, weapons and shields of gold – was transported eastwards in seven ships as her dowry. Albert of Aix, (one of the most informative of the historians of the First Crusade), who chronicled her departure, marvelled at all this wealth, describing the glittering ships (with gilded masts) that carried the wedding party to the Middle East. Although Adelaide was magnificently received, she was badly treated by her new husband who suddenly revealed an existing wife. After five years Adelaide was unceremoniously repatriated minus her wealth and she died a year later in 1118.

Although the present tomb dates from the Renaissance, the effigy on it is from the 12th century original. Adelaide lies on her side facing the altar, her head leaning on her hand. The inscription on the tomb not surprisingly makes no reference whatever to her ordeal in Jerusalem. Although Patti Cathedral had originally been built by Adelaide's son Roger II to house her remains, it was rebuilt in the 18th century; not much survives from the Norman period except for some recently discovered stonework on its entrance façade.

There is one other thing to see in this small, ancient hilltown cruelly dragged into the 20th century by an explosion of concrete housing around its edges. This is what remains of a 4th century Roman country villa discovered when the A20 was built – in fact the A20 had to be raised on stilts to avoid it. In the spring wild poppies growing from the rubble and along the edge of the road give some idea of the Arcadia this rural retreat once was. Only partially excavated, it offers remains of polychromatic floor mosaics with designs of animals, birds, flowers and vines.

The main road continues along the coast past Capo d'Orlando and then suddenly terminates in a ditch; from here – Rocca Caprileone to Cefalù – it still awaits construction. Take the small tortuous country road that climbs up the mountainside to the little hilltowns of Capri Leone, Mirto and **Frazzano**. A few kilometres outside the last, on the right of the road, is the convent of San Filippo di Fragalà, a lonely, forgotten relic built nearly 1000 years ago, by Count Roger.

Every day an old rustic unlocks a side gate in the hope that someone may drop in for a look. Few outsiders know it exists, and wandering through the empty cells and down the rickety corridors of its upper floors, you will almost certainly be alone. The abbey buildings with their stone-carved window surrounds are mostly 17th century, but Count Roger will have known the little church with its characteristic decorative brickwork, its three apses, and the squinches constructed like stalactites which hold up the dome. Its cavernous interior still has traces of the Byzantine frescos which once illuminated the interior as if by supernatural means.

Continuing up the track beyond the convent, the road soon peters out on a ridge overlooking a valley which stretches way into the distance. At the far end is the hilltown of **San Marco d'Alunzio** where Queen Adelaide and her son Roger often whiled away the summer months. Not much is left of their castle – the first the Normans ever built in Sicily (1061). Beyond is **Sant'Agata di Militello** and, just further inland, **San Fratello** where Adelaide founded a Lombard colony. In fact a direct link with Count Roger's widow still survives here in the local dialect in which experts have been able to discern traces of ancient Gallic-Italian. Just 21km further on is **Santo Stefano di Camastra**, famous for its ceramic workshops. Beyond, the road leads on to Cefalù and Palermo.

12

The Ionian Coast: Messina to Taormina

Mili San Pietro, Itala, Savoca, Taormina, Giardini Naxos

From the southern limits of Messina, the motorway dashes down to Taormina along a shelf, just before the Peloritani mountains drop into the sea. Between Messina and Taormina are some strange little towns as well as solitary Norman churches and monasteries straddling the sides of crumbling ravines. Mili San Pietro and Badia are two hamlets each with a peculiar ancient church and there is another remote one between Savoca and Forza d'Agro hidden away on a ledge in the arid cactus-filled Val d'Agro. Each is a beautiful architectural oddity that exhibits a blend of the Islamic, Byzantine and Norman.

The village of **Mili San Pietro** is only about 7 km from Messina. Spiritually, it is aeons away, a wreck of a place that still warrants the most disparaging criticisms ever uttered by fastidious travellers to Italy in the past. One assumes that true squalor and wretchedness have practically vanished in the last half of the 20th century, but Mili San Pietro easily fits the following description by a 19th century visitor to a place in northern Italy. He describes the town as seen 'to greater advantage in distant view than in close approach to it. A poetical contemplation, that might otherwise have been lulled with romantic wanderings . . . must wake up in fright on finding itself . . . confined to the minutae of one of these filthy places'.

Quite so, but Santa Maria di Mili, another of Count Roger's foundations for the Basilian fathers (1082), lies a few hundred yards beyond the village. Derelict, a tenacious survivor nonetheless, it has been abandoned to romantic decay beside a lean-to containing a large pig. You can ask for the key at the nearby farm. From the road it appears more Byzantine than anything else: there is a series of blind arches above which windows and niches alternate with each other all the way around the building. These details and the tiny orange bricks with which it was built indicate its origins – nearly obscured by a face-lift in the 17th century, added to a variety of other 15th and 16th century adornments: see the 16th century marble entrance portal with a tondo of the Madonna and Child on its architrave. Inside you can still see a stone that records the death and burial here of Count Roger's illegitimate son Jordan, who died of natural causes – narrowly avoiding having his eyes gouged out by his father as reward for leading a rebellion against him in 1083.

The little church of San Pietro at Badia, a hamlet folded away into crevices of Monti Scuderi (about 12 km from Mili San Pietro), a tortuous 1½ km drive into the mountains above Itala, is in better condition. Its hybrid design and basilical shape can be examined with greater ease than Santa Maria di Mili's because it is open for Sunday mass. But perhaps the church of SS Pietro e Paolo in the Val d'Agro is the most extraordinary church of the three. Another Basilian foundation and once part of a convent, it defies generic identification: is it Norman, Arab or Byzantine? Is this Sicily, you might wonder, noticing the cacti in the untidy fields nearby and on the gravelly slopes that tower above it? The little flat domes are strikingly reminiscent of Greece or Turkey.

This building, currently undergoing restoration (but still open), is oriented in a typically Byzantine manner with an east-west axis and a triapsidal transept. But it has a Latin basilical plan and perversely its domes are mosquish. The multi-coloured exterior of alternating black lava and white limestone blocks, and the decorative blend of red brick and the light blue mortar, would look very much at home in the Middle East where the decorative trend was, and is, more prominent. The blind arcading of pointed arches marching around its exterior, on the other hand, its assertive verticality and its powerful solidity could only be Norman. Not surprisingly, the *capo-maestro* of the building works was a Norman called Gerard the Frank though the plaque above the main door addresses him in Greek hieroglyphics. There is also a date: 1172 (the date of the restoration of the building, 57 years after King Roger II endowed it in 1115).

Gerard the Frank is the only builder from the Norman period whose name is known to us. He was either an imported artisan who had the ability to blend the characteristic features of the Byzantine and the Arabic or, more probably, was the master in charge of a number of artisans all working under their own steam on the site. They created not merely a mixture of styles but a new style with its own unmistakable Sicilian character.

To the east of the Val d'Agro is the little town of **Savoca** draped across the ridge of a low mountain and surrounded by some demonic boulders. It overlooks Santa Teresa di Riva on the Ionian coast, and on the landward side the views stretch away to the Val d'Agro. On a clear day you can see all the way to Monte Etna about 40 km away.

Nobody ever comes to Savoca; nobody, that is, except the people who live in Santa Teresa and Casalvecchio Siculo, hamlets further up the valley. The truth is that Savoca's buildings have for years been slipping down the hill among the wild flowers. Nobody seems to notice or care. They make the journey up here on hot summer evenings to taste the *granita di limone* which is a speciality of the Bar Vitelli in Piazza Fossia on the edge of the town. In fact there is nothing to beat it on a summer evening when the breeze from the Monti Perloritani is cool and r freshing and the Ionian Sea takes on a glassy shimmer as the sun sets on another stifling day.

The *granita* machine which takes up two thirds of the bar is a much coveted piece of equipment dating approximately from the 1930s; it is fridge, sink and *granita* machine all rolled into one. When he was in Savoca to make *The Godfather* Francis Ford Coppola tried to buy it and ship it back to America, but the stalwart Savocesa behind the bar would not let it go. It is as essential a part of the Bar Vitelli as is the 1950s wireless, the old cane sofa with a rug flung over it and the groceries that have been lining the shelves since they were put there very nearly twenty years ago.

Coppola immortalized the Bar Vitelli when he turned it into the country house for the scene of Michael Corleone's wedding feast. The building, the dusty piazza in front of it, and the village behind, were found to be more appropriate to the director's requirements than anywhere else in Sicily, Corleone itself included. On a wall in the building, a comely, squat 19th century house, is a photo of Marlon Brando.

Savoca became the district's principal town when Count Roger took it from the Saracens in the 10th century. Then, it was known as Kalat Zabut (which roughly translated means 'fortress of *sambuco*' – a name which derives from the many elder – *sambuco* – trees in the district around Savoca; its name became Sabuca, then Savoca). Before the Saracen occupation, when Savoca consisted of a huddle of huts clustered along the side of the hill, it was known as Pentifur (probably a corruption of *penteforio*, five hamlets), an impossibly antique name which lingers on today in the name of the castle – Castello di Pentifur – whose remains crown the great rock above the town. The remains of the castle are thought to date principally from the Norman period, though there were additions over subsequent centuries, most notably those at the beginning of the 15th by the Aragonese rulers of Sicily. If you take the Via Pentifurri round to the back of the hill you will see a series of windows whose character is more Spanish than Norman.

Savoca must have been a fairly prosperous place judging from the handful of buildings surviving there. It was a feudal town which, along with about twelve other villages in the immediate vicinity, belonged to the Barony of Savoca until the beginning of the 17th century. With the abolition of the feudal system in the early years of the 19th century, Savoca went into a decline as the inhabitants gradually moved away to the bigger coastal towns in search of work; inevitably it also suffered along with Messina when earthquakes struck the area. Large parts of the town survive as nothing more than heaps of stone. History does not relate what the now vanished churches were like, but some of their treasures still exist in the surviving churches of San Michele Arcangelo, San Nicolò di Bari and the magnificent Chiesa Madre. We can be sure they were far from insignificant.

You enter the town via the 12th century city gate, the Porta della Città, at the bottom of the Via San Michele which leads up to San Michele and San Nicolò di Bari. It lies just beyond the Bar Vitelli clustered around which are the remaining medieval homes of today's Savocese.

San Michele's principal treasures are its external adornments: two Gothic portals, one framing the main entrance to the church (beneath a small round window), the other a side door. The first, dating from the early 15th century, has stone oak and holly leaf decorated capitals on the top of striated columns. There is a theory that this doorway was taken from the Chiesa Madre further on up the hill – a credible theory because its scale is far greater than little San Michele Arcangelo can comfortably accommodate. The church was re-oriented in the 17th century, gaining a longer nave running south-north and a new tower. It had to have a new door and since the Chiesa Madre was being renovated (and given a new entrance portal) at the time, it is conceivable that this 'old fashioned' doorway was moved down here. Originally you entered San Michele from the east (by the other door) so that the rising sun entered the church with you and fell on the altar at the end of the nave. San Michele still has an altar in this position though nowadays it is only secondary to the main one in the north.

If you get inside the church, there is a gilded and painted wooden pulpit to be seen – the building's loveliest piece – dating from the 18th century. It has scenes of Savoca's other churches painted on its sides. There are also some lavish but crumbling 17th century putti and cornucopie around the interior walls, plenty of faded paintwork and gilding, and some flaking, half ruined frescos. Enough survives amongst the dust and the decay for you to imagine a sumptuous interior. Why does somebody not restore it?

San Nicolò – built facing the sea – is dedicated to San Nicolò di Bari, the protector of fishermen, and is much better preserved than San Michele. The landslides earlier this century hastened restoration when they dramatically bit off its seaward end, dragging the choir and the altar over a precipice and leaving a very much truncated nave. It was partly rebuilt from local cimina stone after the 1908 earthquake, and that dark other-worldly mustiness that ought to fill an interior of the late 15th century has vanished under pots of apricot paint and brash new gilding. However the church is still full of treasures: see the solid silver statue of Santa Lucia (often kept in the local bank) and the two 17th century painted wooden statues of the same saint (the church was once dedicated to her – see the ancient stone head on its external entrance façade). But most important is the painted and gilded 14th century panel of San Michele, once the glory of the interior of San Michele Arcangelo.

Continuing up the hill along the Via San Rocco, past the priest's house, the Casa del Parocco, (where you obtain the keys to the churches) the ruins of some old mansions poking out from under the weeds, the remains of a religious foundation called the Frati Conventuali and the mid-15th century church of San Francesco dell' Immacolata, eventually you arrive at the Chiesa Madre, overlooking a vast panorama of foothills and sea, and clinging to a narrow ridge linking two hills.

Dating from the 14th century, it has a richly decorated and rather eclectic exterior adorned with a variety of details: a Norman-Arabic doorway on the extreme left, a 16th century rose window and central door, and an Aragonese door on the right. Inside, the decoration is equally heterogeneous: a fine interior, laden with the relics from vanished churches. There is a 16th century choir, an early 19th century altar and a series of carved stone capitals dating probably from the early Aragonese years. Underneath the left hand side of the church is a mysterious covered passage that leads down to a now vanished quarter of Savoca. Adjacent to the Chiesa Madre are the remains of a monastery whose principal treasure after the bulk of the building collapsed in 1908 is a single biforate window dating from the 15th century.

The road leads past the Chiesa Madre and a handful of cottages to Monte Calvario with its own Via Crucis along which, on Good Friday, a devotional procession wends its way. At the summit of the hill, still in the devotional mode, are the remains of a very antique hermitage.

The bigger houses in the lower town, behind the bar, are still occupied by the local gentry, the kind of people who in Sicily are referred to as Don – (a title of Spanish origin) and who you see in the piazza in the early evening all over the island wearing the ubiquitous felt hat. They occupy posts in the local *comune* such as that of Podestà (mayor). One family in particular, of whom this kind of description fits are the Trimarchi, small time landowners and traditionally *gabelotti* for a large local estate. *Gabelotti* would lease an estate from a landowner for a number of years and, instead of working it themselves, would parcel it out between share-cropping peasant farmers on the most extortionate terms. Not unlike Don Calogero Sedara in *The Leopard*, they were upwardly mobile peasants. Nowadays the Trimarchi have the distinction of being able to prove their worthiness within the local community because the corpse of one of their ancestors, dressed in exquisite 17th century finery, languishes in the catacomb beneath the local Convent of the Frati Minori Cappuccini on the road to Casalvecchio Siculo, about ten minutes walk from the centre of the town.

Not more than a short line mentioning this burial chamber appears in guidebooks to the island, if any appears at all. Strangely, this perfectly preserved small catacomb (or grisly sepulchre depending on how enchanted you may be by decaying corpses, some of them over two hundred years old), contains the unbeautiful and usually unvisited remains of roughly thirty-five of Savoca's inhabitants from the 17th and 18th centuries – lawyers, abbots and other local worthies. Most of the corpses are dressed in their own clothing, and they parade the full range of dress from the formal (silken breeches and embroidered waistcoats) to the humdrum. Some are propped up in a niches around the wall and are held in place by a strap, mouths agape, limbs grotesquely twisted. Others lie naked in glass-topped coffins stacked on the floor or slotted on to ledges like books on a shelf.

The catacombs fill up during the Festival of the Dead, or I Morti, when families commune with their dead ancestors. At the beginning of November each year the dead are supposed to leave their burial place to walk in procession through the town distributing presents to children who have remembered them in their prayers. On 2 November, the culmination of the festival, the descendants of the deceased assemble to pay their respects in the catacombs, which have been swept out and laden with flowers for the occasion. This rather macabre experience is extremely popular, all the more so because the presence of a 300 year old ancestor 'in the flesh' is a source of great pride.

There are plenty of little villages not unlike Savoca in this region. But while Savoca is undoubtedly the most interesting, Casalvecchio Siculo and Forza d'Agro are also worth a visit, the former for its Chiesa Madre, the latter for the remains of the Norman castle and for the ancient streets of stone cottages. Forza d'Agro gives some idea of what Savoca must once have looked like.

By contrast, **Taormina**, just 15 km away, is a worldly metropolis where the locals, urbane and sophisticated, are used to dealing with the foreign public. Everyone seems to have been to Taormina. In 1770 Brydone led the way, finding the Teatro Greco particularly inspiring. He trotted around 'the once famous city . . . reduced to an insignificant burgh' under an umbrella to protect him from the sun. Later, Goethe noted that art as well as nature had been responsible for the incredible beauty of the theatre. He hardly mentions the surrounding town that he could see through an inpenetrable barrier of cacti whose prickly spikes were a 'painful obstacle' to his progress. In the 19th century, Cardinal Newman breakfasted at Taormina and remarked after seeing the view from its ramparts that it was the 'nearest thing approaching Eden'. He felt sure that he would have been a better and more religious man if he had lived in the town.

D.H. Lawrence chose to make it his home for a while, preferring it to Palermo, and a certain Baron von Gloeden drew Taormina to the attention of frustrated northerners in the 19th century – particularly the English – with his photographs of its young men posing in a variety of local beauty spots clad in nothing but garlands of ivy. As a result the town's popularity soared and lonely singles flocked here in search of what life in the frozen north had for years been denying them. (The town's *tabacchi* are still filled with reproductions of these notorious photographs.) Since then Taormina has never really looked back. The Christmas to Easter period is the best time to visit. That is when the Sicilians fill the town, well before the influx of hearty Germans and coachloads of elderly females from the English south coast.

Taormina's popularity is more than justified. The theatre – the largest in Sicily – and the stupendous views from it to Etna, are perhaps its greatest attractions. The theatre dates from about the 3rd century BC and was rebuilt by the Romans a century later. Ninety-nine per cent of the visible remains are thought to be Roman; the scena is in unusually good repair, and there is a deep trench – the orchestra – built to accommodate the animals, fighters and the foundations of the stage – the proscenium. The wings – the parascenia – have also survived, so have the porticoes at the back and some seats in the cavea.

The Roman brick construction obscured everything Greek. The scena with its niches, arched gateways and its monumental construction even obscured the view of Monte Etna. Impressive though their bulk may have been, one suspects that the Greeks may have better exploited the stunning natural backdrop. Their idea of a theatre was of course more erudite than their successors'. The Romans used it for gladiatorial dramas: the equivalent of ice skating in the National Theatre. The full glory of its natural surroundings has only been revealed since the scena began to disintegrate. The Arabs kept it blocked up – in fact they converted the building into a palace which a noble family, the Zumbo, were given permission to use in 1465 on condition they did not damage the old fabric. Later it sank into obscurity until a Dutchman Jacques D'Horville brought home a description of it in 1764.

Brydone's descriptions and Houell's and Saint-Non's views of it (1782–7 and 1781–6 respectively) reawakened curiosity about the theatre's origins. In the 19th century it was incorrectly restored – for example the granite columns on the scena (still there now) are wrongly positioned. They were simply fished out of the ruins and erected in the first place that suggested itself. Houell and Saint-Non only drew their stumps and their bases. Perhaps somebody will be bold enough to remove them.

Various other bits of ancient Tauromenium are scattered about all over the town. From the theatre, the Via Teatro Greco leads to the Piazza Vittorio Emanuele and comes to a halt in front of the late 14th century Palazzo Corvaia. This piazza was the site of Tauromenium's Greek agora and subsequently the Roman forum. Here, in the Roman days, stood a statue of a Roman Prefect, Gaius Verres, which, says Cicero, the angry citizens overturned after an infringement of their agreement of alliance with Rome. This area was dominated by a temple, possibly dedicated to Apollo, and it was also the site of the Odeon whose broken remains, behind the church of Santa Caterina, are known as the Teatro Romano. Both Santa Caterina and the Palazzo Corvaia next to it were constructed using cut stone from earlier buildings.

Parallel to the Corso Umberto, just beyond Santa Caterina and on the seaward side of the road, is the so-called Naumachia, thought by some to have been a huge cistern probably once connected to the city baths. Jean Houell drew it as a massive wall with a series of niches cut into it. It has not changed much since his day and forms a terrace-buttress for the Corso and the buildings on it. Some describe it as a nymphaeum (literally a 'temple of the nymphs', a sort of pleasure establishment with fountains and statues) of the Hellenic type, others say it is all that remains of the Gymnasium, once famous for its unbeatable athletic records. It was most probably a mixture of all three. Its structure spread out southwards, possibly in terraces down the hill and after the Teatro Greco it is the most important ancient construction in the town.

There are some other antique bits and pieces traceable among later constructions: if you look along the roadside flank of the church of San Pancrazio just outside the Porta Messina, you will see some very hefty building blocks just above the road line. These are the remains of the cella of a once famous Temple of Isis.

After the classical remains, Taormina's palaces are the next most worthwhile places to visit: Santa Stefano (14th century), Corvaia (late 14th and 15th centuries, built around an earlier Arabic tower), and Ciampoli (1412). These are the town's principal secular monuments; each one is rather singularly adorned with a variety of very Spanish looking biforate and triforate windows.

The Palazzo Santo Stefano is undoubtedly the most beautiful of the three. It was owned by the Dukes of Santo Stefano who, having bought it from its original builders in the 15th century, sold it to the state in the middle of the 20th. The biforate windows on the first and second floors are distinctly Gothic while the polychromatic bands around the façade are a manifestation of a Sicilian-Arabic inheritance.

Palazzo Corvaia (which was the scene of the Sicilian Parliament in 1411 – it met in the large hall overlooking the piazza), was badly knocked about over the years and eventually left for derelict. It is the result of two phases of construction in the 14th and 15th centuries. Four pretty biforate windows face the piazza and its exterior is enriched not by polychromatic stonework but by fantastic Gothic forms whose origins are Catalan. Spanish influences were slow to penetrate Sicily but by the end of the 15th century were well established. The ogee arch capping the door at the top of the inner court-yard stair dates from this period, as does the portal – with its 'basket-handle' arch and moulding, here supported by two short half columns – which opens from the street into the internal court-yard. This is a much more exaggerated Catalan-Gothic and at one time was not an uncommon sight in both Taormina and Messina. There are others like it in Taormina, particularly in the Corso Vittorio Emanuele – see the Casa Paternò (No 190) and the Casa Gullotta (No 170).

Taormina's other great survival is the early 15th century Palazzo Ciampoli – also showing a distinct Spanish influence. It sits at the top of a long flight of steps just off the Corso. There was at one time a large courtyard in front of it – a gateway to which, built partly of Taormina marble, survives to the left of the building. Of the five biforate windows on the main façade only the pair on the extreme right are original. The building is thought to have belonged to Damiano Rosso, standard bearer to Frederick of Aragon; Rosso's coat of arms is over the door.

Taormina's churches are unexceptional, small and provincial. The Duomo, dedicated to San Nicolò di Bari, is more fortress-like than ecclesiastical. It has medieval crenellations around the top which are somewhat at odds with its 17th century façade. Inside, a large single chamber is pierced at the rear by a series of chapels: the Cappella delle Grazie (on the right of the main altar) has a lovely 15th century alabaster statue of the Madonna in front of which the figure of Christ seems inexplicably to be floating in mid-air; Cappella Sacramento, to the left, is built partly from marbles plundered from the theatre. Other artistic fixtures are paraded around the walls. Of these, in the south aisle just inside the main entrance, an early 16th century polyptych in an intricate and delicate Gothic frame is the most beautiful. This is the work of Giovanni de Saliba, a well known 15th century wood sculptor and great uncle of the painter of the polyptych, Antonello de Saliba, whose work was heavily influenced by no less than Antonello da Messina, Giovanni Bellini and Cima da Conegliano. A work by another of Sicily's chief exponents of the Antonello da Messina school, the tryptych *The Visitation* by Antonio Giuffrè, is also in the south aisle. Quiet contemplation of these is effortless in a building entered by none but those in need of solitary prayer.

Taormina is well placed for exploration of the east coast and its hinterland. In January 1921, at five in the morning, D.H. Lawrence left Taormina by train for Palermo: 'It is full dawn – dawn – not morning, the sun will not have risen. The village [Taormina] is nearly all dark in the red light, and asleep still . . . One man leading a horse round the corner of the Palazzo Corvaia . . . And so over the brow, down the steep cobble-stone street between the houses, and out to the naked hill front. This is the dawn-coast of Sicily. Nay, the dawn-coast of Europe. Steep like a vast cliff, dawn-forward. A red dawn, with mingled curdling dark clouds, and some gold. It must be seven o'clock. The station down below, by the sea. And noise of a train.' (*Sea and Sardinia*). At **Giardini-Naxos**, on the sea front below Taormina, is an extravagantly decorated railway station designed by Ernesto Basile. 'I hate the station, pigmy, drawn out there beside the sea' – Lawrence had eyes only for the landscape and for Etna, 'indescribably cloaked and secretive in her dense black clouds'.

Beyond Giardini-Naxos is Schisò, a little fishing port that replaced ancient Naxos, a Greek colony of about 750 BC, the very first to have been established. Occupied and destroyed by the Syracusans three centuries later, its inhabitants moved to Tauromenion (Taormina). Only parts of it have been excavated, any finds deposited in the little museum on the quay. Its most magnificent remains are those of the ancient city walls made of enormous polygonal basalt blocks locally quarried.

13

Taormina (via Castello di Maniace) to Catania

Randazzo, Castello di Maniace, Adrano, Catania, Acireale, Aci Castello, Aci Trezza

---

From Schisò the SS185 runs inland to Francavilla di Sicilia, and a subsidiary branch then leads south via Castiglione di Sicilia to the SS120 and the road to **Randazzo**. From Randazzo, an interesting town built of purplish-brown lava, the SS120 continues on to the Castello di Maniace, while the SS284 skirts the lower slopes of Monte Etna (and is the route to take for the best view of the mountain). It runs on to Bronte – a run-down, shabby place – and Adrano.

The **Castello di Maniace**, now a museum, was originally part of an ancient Benedictine convent endowed in 1173 by Margaret of Navarre, mother of William II, Count Roger's great-grandson. In fact Margaret's chapel survives inside the castle compound and is currently being restored. On this spot the great Byzantine general George Maniakes defeated the Saracens in 1040, and here Count Roger and Adelaide built a commemorative chapel – the one that Margaret of Navarre enlarged. However Castello di Maniace is more famous for its links with Admiral Nelson.

Castello di Maniace was the centre of the 30,000 acre Bronte estate which Ferdinand III gave to Admiral Nelson, along with the Dukedom of Bronte, in return for having whisked the king and his family to safety during the revolution at Naples in 1798, and for helping him to regain his throne. Nobody thought to tell the new duke that although he was now owner of some of the most fertile land on the island, it was also generously strewn with volcanic rock and the castle manor house was a picturesque ruin. Apparently for some days Nelson declined this honorium, from 'a fear that his acceptance of so great a gift would expose him to a suspicion that he served the king from an ignoble motif' (*Horatio Nelson*, T. Pocock). He yielded after a timely interval, fully intending to live there one day in quiet retirement with Emma Hamilton (who called him 'My Lord Thunder', Bronte being the mythical giant who forged the thunderbolts for Jupiter). In the meantime Nelson practised writing his name: should he call himself 'Bronte Nelson of the Nile', or would it be 'Nelson and Bronte'? Unfortunately he died before ever seeing the place.

This gift, however, brought Nelson an annual of £3000, (half of it given to his father for his lifetime), which did not endear him to the workers on the estate or the inhabitants of the wretched town of Bronte. Benedetto Radice in his *Memorie* says that the two greatest evils afflicting Bronte were Etna and the Duchy. The constant threat of death under a flood of lava was hard enough to bear but to have to live as a serf subject to the feudal jurisdiction of the landlord – who was not only absent but a foreigner as well – was almost more than they could stand. Nelson was never a hero in the eyes of the people of Bronte; he was the one who in effect had saved Sicily for the old regime. They regarded him as part of the process that helped the country escape the social upheaval of the French Revolution.

Bronte survived as the property of Nelson's descendants, the Earls of Bridport, well into the 20th century, though they sold it to the *comune* in the 1970s. Nelson's great-great-nephew, who became Duke of Bronte in 1904, laid out the gardens and altered the house so that it became more like an English country home. It is not large – a handful of reception rooms and a long barrel-vaulted corridor off which open a series of bedchambers large and small. Outside are a smattering of outbuildings, and Margaret of Navarre's chapel. In the middle of the courtyard is a large Iona cross beneath which is buried Fiona MacLeod, the pseudonym used by the writer William Sharp who died in 1905.

The Castello is a little piece of Sicily that will always be distincly English. When the Bridports departed they were forbidden to take with them the heirlooms that had descended to them via Nelson's niece Charlotte. They even had to leave behind Nelson's grant of titles by George III as well as the last glass from which he drank on board HMS *Victory* at the Battle of Trafalgar. Rooted to a pedestal beneath a glass-topped case inscribed Nelson-Bronte, a stopperless decanter sitting beside it, it is one of Bronte's last physical links with the Admiral himself.

You might enter the house expecting an interior of faded damasks, polished wood and the musty atmosphere redolent of old port. Not a bit of it. Most of the furniture has vanished and the one or two old Sicilian pieces that remain are piled high with ancient copies of *Country Life* and *Burke's Peerage*. On the walls vast canvasses of Nelson's sea battles compete for prominence with rows of terrible cartoons from *Punch*. Chintz curtains and battered lampshades are incongruous in the rough little town of Maniace and the sun-parched feudal landscape of Sicily stretching away for miles into the distance.

From Bronte, the road continues south through the petrified lava flows to **Adrano**, the modern version of the Adranum founded, says Diodorus, by Dionysius the Elder in 400 BC. From Hadranum to Adranion to Adarnu' and Aderno, the most interesting thing about Adrano today is the 11th century castle in its midst, a gigantic blockhouse founded by Count Roger on top of a pre-existing, possibly Saracen, building subsequently converted by the Bourbons into a jail. In it is a small but rather eccentric museum explaining Adrano's past. It includes a collection of pre-historic ceramics and identifies the range of nearby sites from which they came.

On the second floor is the old chapel of Adelaide, Count Roger's third wife. It is decorated with a series of purplish-red lava columns and capitals running around the walls. It presides over a small collection of artefacts, the most interesting of which are some stone Roman heads; the Countess would no doubt be scandalised to see them deposited on her altar.

The building is surrounded by a 'terrace' which is the best place from which to survey what is left of the town centre. On one side is the Giardino della Vittoria – inhabited by an array of exotic palms and clutches of old men in felt hats – and facing it is the vast 16th century monastery of Santa Lucia now long since turned into a school. On the other side of the castle is the pathetically ruined Chiesa Madre, an enormous church built using sixteen basalt columns that are thought to have come from a nearby temple, perhaps the very sanctuary whose doors, says Plutarch, mysteriously flew open during a local battle around 344 BC. If they are one and the same, then this is the temple in which, during the same event, the metal statue of the god Adranus, to whom the building was dedicated, was seen to perspire and his javelin to quiver.

From Adrano, the road continues via Paternò and Misterbianco,

skirting the northern reaches of the Piano di Catania to **Catania**. The
quality of life in Catania cannot have changed much since the writer
Verga's time (see also Chapter 10). It is one of the most colourful
places in Sicily – noisy, fast, crime-ridden and characterized by an
awe-inspiring blend of Italian, east Mediterranean and north African vivacity. Here too is some of the most magnificent trail-blazing
baroque architecture in Sicily. Few modern buildings have been
allowed to encroach on the old core of Catania which was completely
rebuilt after a vigorous earthquake in 1693. At that time nothing of
importance survived except for one or two of the more solid portions
of Count Roger's cathedral (1094), still visible today, and Frederick
II's Castello Ursino.

As a result Catania has a remarkably homogeneous city centre
and its successful rebuilding led Brydone to remark that it was 'so
noble and beautiful'. The most important architect to be called in
at the initial stages of the rebuilding programme was Alonzo di
Benedetto (the only architect to have survived the earthquake), and
operations were directed by the quick witted Bishop of Catania, who
was also governor of the city. The first major constructions were in
the Piazza Duomo – the Archbishop's Palace next to the Duomo,
the Seminario dei Chierici opposite and connected to it by the Porta
Uzeda (1696), and the Palazzo dei Principi del Pardo in the south-
west corner. Easy to notice, all are very similar stylistically: each
has a flat façade on which decoration has been restricted to the
window surrounds and the massive pilasters. These are delicately
ornate buildings which look as fragile and impermanent as if they
had been cut out of cardboard. Decoration is restrained in comparison with what was to come just a few years later under Giovanni
Battista Vaccarini and Stefano Ittar: the calm before the storm as it
were.

It was Vaccarini who unleashed the full vigour of the Roman
baroque on Catania. He was appointed architect to the city in 1730
and he brought with him knowledge and ideas gleaned from the
Rome of Borromini and Bernini. Each of his buildings is full of
novelty and invention.

Vaccarini's first Catania project was the Municipio on the north
side of the Piazza Duomo. The ground floor had already been
started (1695) by the time he took over (1732), and the differences
between Catania's first baroque phase and the second are easily dis-
cernible by comparing the ground and the floors above. Vaccarini's
contribution has an almost sculptural quality which, as the century

proceeded, became more monumental. Here his entrance portal and the windows above it seem almost to lean out and away from the façade.

The façade of the Duomo is also Vaccarini's; he took over reconstruction in 1736, adorning what remained of the original Norman building. Notice how the movement of its external parts is beginning to quicken – there are canted columns and curved pediments – so that by the time he designs Sant'Agata (opposite the lateral flank of the Duomo in Via Vittorio Emanuele, and built 1748–67) he treats the façade as a squirming S-curve. This building is probably his best work. Inside, rarely for Catania, its decoration is rococo; it was done after Vaccarini's death.

There are two other Vaccarini buildings in this street. Where it cuts the Piazza Cutelli is a late work – the Collegio Cutelli – with its lovely round courtyard. The other is the Palazzo Valle on the corner of the Via Landolina. This is easily recognizable by its billowing entrance portal topped by a wrought-iron balcony and a window whose pediment thrusts its way out of the wall. There is no known date for this building though its wrought-iron balcony was mirrored all over Sicily, particularly in the east and south-east. The shape in this case was dictated by the fall of the women's dresses.

In the same quarter of the town, and not far from the Palazzo Valle, is the Palazzo Biscari. To get there, take the Via Museo Biscari which goes off at a tangent from the little piazza in front of San Placido (behind the Duomo). San Placido, by the way, is an important work (c. 1768) by Stefano Ittar (d. 1790, see Appendix 2). It carries on the tradition set by Vaccarini, but in Ittar's own personal style. The monastery attached to it lies opposite the Palazzo Biscari. This vast rambling building was built originally for Vincenzo Paternò-Castello, Prince of Biscari and father of Ignazio, who showed a grateful Goethe around his important archaeological collection in 1787. Parts of it are now in the Civic Museum housed in the Castello Ursino and it would be possible to see it if the museum were not perpetually closed for restoration. In the collection Goethe inspected a collection of 'marble and bronze figures, vases and all sorts of such-like antiquities'. In particular a torso of Jupiter held his attention; it had 'greater merits than one would guess' (he had seen a cast of it elsewhere). Goethe does not mention the astonishing decoration both inside and outside the building, he calls it simply 'a one-storey building on a high foundation.'

Well, it does have a high foundation – at the back – facing what

was once the harbour. On top of a high bastion, either a part of the
city wall or of the city's sea defences, is a one storey wing which is
the building's oldest portion. What is so remarkable about it is the
richly exuberant decoration surrounding the windows. Putti and
cornucopie burst out of the stone and squirm around the windows
to the cornice above. These details are typical of a local provincial
style of architectural ornament before the advent of Vaccarini, and
probably date from the early 18th century. They are thought to be
the work of Francesco Battaglia (1710–88, see Appendix II) who
built the little chinoiserie pavilions at either end of the same terrace.

Battaglia was certainly responsible for the principal courtyard
of the palace which opens out of the Via Museo Biscari, though the
low stair and the portico are unfinished. This was once the main
entrance, leading to a series of rooms which nowadays are used for
concerts (although the palace is still private). The end room contains
one of the freest pieces of rococo decoration in Sicily. It dates from
the middle of the 18th century. It has a stretched oblong shape and
above it is a coved ceiling pierced in the middle by an oval beyond
which is an outer dome. Between the two ceilings is a row of windows giving light to what was the minstrel's gallery. While the lower
ceiling is alive with rococo stucco, the upper one is decorated with an
allegorical fresco. The gallery is reached from a side room by an
extraordinary stair of rough rococo work and an ornate handrail
spiralling up to a little door at the top. At one end of the *salone* a
niche once contained a ceremonial bed in which princesses of the
house received ceremonial visits a few days after the births of new
children.

The Palazzo Biscari is preparation for a visit to Catania's monastery of the Benedettini, a building so vast that the monks who commissioned it ran out of money during its construction. It was never
completed. It was begun in 1704 by Antonino Amato, and Brydone
was filled with admiration and wonder on seeing it: 'I spied a
magnificent building at some distance,' he says, 'which seemed to
stand on the highest part . . . My curiosity led me on, as I had heard
no mention of any palace on this side of the city. On entering the
great gate [designed by Carmelo Battaglia in the first half of the
18th century], my surprise was a good deal increased on observing a
façade almost equal to that of Versailles; a noble staircase of white
marble, and every thing that announced royal magnificence. I had
not heard that the kings of Sicily had a palace at Catania . . .'. Indeed
they did not, and Brydone was even more amazed when he went

around the building and saw another front of 'equal greatness'. On going home to his lodgings he was told 'that it was no other than a convent of fat Benedictine monks; who were determined to make sure of a paradise at least in this world, if not in the other'. A great many of the Benedictines' treasures – perhaps Brydone saw those too – have ended up in the Civic Museum collection in the Castello Ursino.

Clamped to the side of it, facing the baroque Piazza Dante, is the equally enormous church of San Nicolò, designed by Antonino Amato in 1730 though the works were carried out largely by Battaglia. The Sicilians call it the 'mastadon' – whether in honour of its gigantic scale or the extinction of its original purpose as the conventual church, history does not relate. It is however the largest church in Sicily, even though, like the monastery, it never reached completion. It still has gigantic half-made stumps of columns framing its main door. Inside there is nothing of interest, though the sheer scale of nave, transept and vaulting is awesome.

The principal façade of the monastery, the east façade, has similar richly decorated window surrounds to the Biscari palace. Inside is the very first neo-classical staircase in Sicily, begun in 1794 by Antonio Battaglia, and obviously replacing the one Brydone saw. There is also a central courtyard full of palms and a highly decorated summer house now, sadly, falling to bits. The whole white elephant of monastery and church is in rather poor condition, but if you creep in past the man at the gate and clamber through the archaeological dig taking place in the courtyard, an illicit potter will be well rewarded.

There is one other important street in Catania that remains to be visited. This is the Via Crociferi, lined with baroque palaces, churches and convents. It was built on top of a lava flow in the 17th century, and is currently being excavated in part in an attempt to reveal the ancient city below. The Via Crociferi opens off the Via Teatro Greco that runs from the southern end of the Benedettini monastery going east past the ruins of a theatre built by the Romans – enter from Via Vittorio Emanuele (there are also ruins of an amphitheatre thought to date from AD 2. These lie in Piazza Stesicoro). In it are four churches – San Francesco, San Benedetto (first quarter of the 18th century), the Gesuiti (1754) and San Giuliano (begun 1739). Of these, perhaps the last is the most inventive. Its façade, designed by Vaccarini, is based on a single convex curve and, says Anthony Blunt, both San Placido and the Collegiata

in the Via Etnea (by Ittar *c.* 1768) evolved from it. San Benedetto is
the odd one out: its façade is riddled with ornament and statues and
it is closer to what you would expect to find in Syracuse, where the
architecture is more ebullient.

Catania falls prey to rampant piety annually on 5 February. The
citizens don their finery and set off to worship Sant'Agata, the
virgin matyr who lived in Catania in the 3rd century AD. Legends of
her life are many and varied. Briefly, when she spurned a suitor, a
consul called Quintain, he turned on her, punishing her for her
Christian beliefs. She suffered the gamut of horrific tortures and
finally, after being rolled over hot coals, she was visited by St Peter
in her small stone cell – the one which you can see in the church of
Sant'Agata al Carcere – and her wounds were miraculously healed.
To increase further her suffering her persecutors cut off her breasts,
and to this day paintings of St Agata depict her carrying them on a
plate like two jellies straight from the mould. On her feast day you
can buy little breast-shaped loaves and cakes in honour of her
memory.

The Duomo in Catania is dedicated to Sant'Agata; it contains her
shrine in a small chapel to the right of the main altar. Festooned
with multicoloured marble interspersed with gilded stone, her
effigy (covered in precious jewels donated in honour of her intercession by grateful citizens over the centuries) reposes behind a large
grille on one side of the chapel. Her mortal remains are kept here
and once a year are brought out and whisked around Catania for an
airing. Such was the power her remains were thought to possess that
she would be taken to zones of the city imperilled by the threat of a
new flow of lava from Etna. Brydone was present at one of these
events and witnessed the impassioned pleas to the saint from the
owner of a threatened property. The owner rushed to the limits of
his land and fixed an image of the saint to a fence facing the mountain. Verga's Don Marco (in *The Gentry* from *Short Sicilian Novels*)
was eating macaroni when a flow of lava started moving towards his
vineyards: 'The man who looked after the vineyard was carrying
away the implements of the wine-press, the staves of casks, everything that could be saved, and the wife had gone to fix canes bearing
images of the saints who should protect the place, at the boundaries
of the vineyard, mumbling Ave Marias'.

When the image of Sant'Agata was not enough, out came the
veil which she is thought to have inherited from Isis. This had
special properties but because there was only one of its kind, little

pieces of cotton and linen were fixed to it which, after being blessed by the bishop, were supposed to have absorbed enough of the veil's power to save at the very least a person's house and garden. Inevitably, however, the sacred relic fluctuated in local esteem as from time to time the lava flow ignored saintly intervention and swept into town obliterating everything in its path.

The remains of old, even ancient lava flows are inescapable in the vicinity of Catania, especially around the towns of **Aci Castello, Aci Trezza** and **Acireale**. Etna has heaped its burning innards on to the coastline with frightening regularity, and the last serious eruption was as recent as 1979. On this occasion the flow of hot lava stopped just a short of the village of Fornazzo on Etna's eastern flank, narrowly missing Giarre, a town of about 27,000 inhabitants, about 4 km away.

Terribilità has always pervaded this stretch of Sicily where rumblings of the earth's insides are often a sinister forewarning of eruptions and earthquakes, of rivers that vanish and reappear as the earth gyrates, and of a coastline that recedes and advances as the lava extends or buries it. These natural calamities intrigued the ancients and the mythology of this landscape is full of violence. The various towns whose names begin with Aci remind one of the story of Acis who was in love with the nymph Galatea. Jealous of him, the Cyclops Polyphemus, the one-eyed giant, squashed him with a huge rock hurled out of his volcanic crater. Seeing his blood flowing out from beneath the rock, Galatea turned it into a stream of water, and today the river Aci flows out to sea near Acireale, its mouth somewhere near the little port of Santa Maria alla Scala. The Cyclops' violence was also thought to account for the Isole Ciclopi, a series of inhospitable rocky lumps poking out of the sea just off the coast of Aci Trezza. According to Homer, a furious, blinded Cyclops flung these rocks at Odysseus when he made his escape from the giant's cave.

Acireale is the biggest of these coastal towns. Its centre is dominated by a vast 17th century cathedral dedicated to SS Annunziata and Santa Venere (the latter the patroness of the city). Its façade was redesigned in the 19th century by Giovanni Battista Basile in a vaguely Gothic style, though the interior is original – here there appears to be not a single surface undecorated. Where the stucco runs out, painted decoration takes over.

Next to this church is SS Apostoli, another 17th century building, and further on, in the Piazza Vigo, is San Sebastiano, wobbling with over-ebullient decoration; it gives some idea of the style of architecture that must have been common along this coastline prior to the 1693 earthquake. San Sebastiano is the focus of a festival in honour of its dedicatee on 20 January when a wooden statue of the martyr, bound to a pillar and stuck with arrows (he died, shot full of arrows), is taken out of the church and dragged around the town on a huge silver litter by members of the various local confraternities. At the saint's side are two silver arms: reliquaries containing, so it is said, bits of his body.

Acireale's two main streets are the Via Vittorio Emanuele and the Corso Umberto. On either side, dark brooding alleys slope off downhill towards the sea, each one paved with lava and, where the adjacent buildings are not blackened with the stuff, they are sooty from the all-pervasive diesel fumes of passing traffic. Great banks of wrought-iron balconies, heavy ornate portals and window surrounds edge outwards over the street, and here and there a dusty geranium squeezes out a bloom. One of these streets, the Via Romeo, leads east from the Piazza Duomo, past SS Apostoli and the ornate Palazzo Comunale, to a dramatic stone walkway called the Strada delle Chiazzette that connects Acireale with the sea and with the little seaside village of Santa Maria alla Scala.

Aci Trezza and Aci Castello can be seen from Santa Maria a la Scala. The former, dominated by the Cyclops' rocks, is the less interesting of the two, while Aci Castello is only worth a visit if the geological museum in its castle is open. This building, constructed in the 13th century for Roger of Lauria, one of Frederick II's rebel admirals, was gouged out of a wedge of dark purple-black lava and is a perfectly preserved example of the architecture of its period. Frederick II ignored its apparent impregnability, taking it by building a wooden tower of equal height alongside it.

14

South-east Sicily and Syracuse

Augusta, Megara Hyblaea, Syracuse, Pantalica, Palazzolo Acreide, Akrai, Ragusa, Comiso, Vittoria, Modica, Scicli, Noto

The south-east of Sicily is a strange and fascinating area, a large part of it taken up by the hills and the mountains of the Val di Noto. There you will find remote necropoli of the Stone Ages, magnificent ruins and archaeological sites from the days of Magna Graecia; those at Syracuse are the biggest and most extensive, and there are others at Megara Hyblaea and Palazzolo Acreide, to mention only the most important. There are towns – Noto, Ragusa, Modica – whose baroque architecture, certainly unmatchable in mainland Italy, is more vivacious even than famously extravagant Palermo's. It is the hottest, most Greek part of Sicily. It has abundant summer sunshine and a mild winter climate, and there are lots of unpolluted beaches. This corner of Sicily has everything, and what could be more satisfying than to know that even the reptilian gaze of the Mafia is somehow deflected away from this charmed enclave?

South-east Sicily is a reminder of the days when the island was regarded as Europe's breadbasket. The myth of Demeter and Persephone is never far away, even now. While deforestation and bad management of the land have badly affected other areas of Sicily, in the south-east, still an especially fertile and highly cultivated area, the myth persists. Early in the summer the roadsides, fields and fruit orchards, divided into a patchwork by dry-stone walls, are awash with wild calendula, camomile, wood sorrel and poppies, and the cornfields are rudely healthy in spite of the fact that the south-east has Sicily's lowest rainfall.

The south-east, in particular the Val di Noto, is famous for its olive oil, the soul of Sicilian cooking (olives were first introduced by the Greek colonists), and for its almonds, carobs and citrus groves. The farms around Ragusa and Modica produce giant tomatoes (the kind you eat like apples) while the market stalls of nearby Comisa and Vittoria groan under the weight of locally grown peppers, aubergines and peaches. Here you can also buy fragrant honey from the purple June flowers of the wild thyme growing in the Iblaean Mountains. The Greeks loved it too, it was their primary sweetener.

It is the Greek heritage of the south-east that distinguishes it from the rest of the island; the north-west in particular, with its Phoenician and Carthaginian antecedents, was never really Hellenized. Even after the Romans, the Byzantine Greeks reaffirmed the Greek tradition and stuck to the ancient Greek cities while the Arabs who succeeded them concentrated their power in the west and north-west. In fact the heritages of the two cultures, Greek and Arabic, are deeply engrained in local custom even now in spite of liberal doses of the subsequent 'civilizing' influence of Normans, Angevins, Aragonese and Spanish.

If you went from Palermo to Syracuse on the *autostrada*, a three hour journey, you would notice differences between the two cities which epitomize the dissimilarity of these two parts of Sicily. The two cities seem as distant now as they did when separated by the winding pot-holed tracks that meandered across the centre of the island a hundred years ago. Palermo is closed and secretive and languishes, decrepit and crime-ridden in the shadow of the Mafia. It does not invite you to walk through it. By contrast Syracuse is well kept, bustling with activity and, Mafia-free, far less troublesome. A weeping plastic Madonna makes the headlines here, not murders.

Even industry thrives in the south-east, miraculously expanding and developing alongside the notorious apathy that prevents it flourishing elsewhere in Sicily. Not surprisingly the easterners are quick to point out the reasons why: they are commercially enterprising as opposed to parasitic, honest as opposed to *mafioso*.

A clue to the strength of Mafia influence outside the south-east and its weakness within is the oriental character of the inhabitants of the former and the Greekness of those in the latter. Or so they say. Tricky and secretive, the former are at odds with the open, forward-looking south-easterners whose refined and gentle character is unique in Sicily.

The first stop on a tour of the south-east is coastal **Augusta** (south of Catania) whose outskirts are festooned with one of the heaviest concentrations of industry found in Sicily. If you can be bothered to wade through it, you will find that Augusta is rather a fine old port sitting in the shadows of one of Frederick II's castles. The town's charm undoubtedly lies in its oldest quarter squeezed on to an island (Augusta's equivalent of Syracuse's Ortygia) which is connected to the mainland by a bridge.

Not far from the town, and shrouded by the smoking chimneys of the petrochemical plants, are the ruins of **Megara Hyblaea**, one of the very first Greek settlements of ancient Sicily (*c.* 750 BC). Destroyed in 482 by Gelon, it was resettled in the 4th century BC only to be ruined again in 214 BC by Marcellus on behalf of the Romans. But it is the 4th century remains that are most in evidence nowadays and they constitute a rare example of a near-complete Archaic city. The site museum with its diagrams and maps gives an excellent overview of Megara Hyblaea although the principal artefacts found here are now in the archaeological museum at Syracuse.

Marooned along with Megara Hyblaea amongst the industrial trappings of the 20th century is another much more ancient site – Thapsos. It lies not far away at the bottom of the Golfo di Augusta on the tiny sandy Peninsula Magnisi. Here, almost at the water's edge, can be seen a fascinating collection of Bronze Age, domed tombs cut into the rock – about 400 of them – and the remains of the round and rectangular huts of the peninsula's earliest settlers who established trading links with the people of Malta and Mycenae. The tombs are the highlight of the site: each was once filled with skeletons buried alongside pottery vases, beads and weapons. Of these, the most interesting so far to have come to light are those imported from Mycenae. But none has been dated post-1270 BC; in other words trading with Mycenae stopped abruptly at this time. According to Margaret Guido, this implies that Thapsos was abandoned around this date as it and other villages in the vicinity were threatened by invasions from the Italian mainland, probably by the Sikels. The people of Thapsos took to the mountains for safety and Pantalica to the west, high in the Monti Iblei, was most probably one of their refuges. Excavations there have shown that its first inhabitants arrived around 1270 BC.

About 16 km south of Thapsos is **Syracuse**, one of the most important cities in the ancient classical world, considered by Cicero to have been the Greeks' most beautiful. The city today is in two distinct parts, one of which, Ortygia, occupies a small 'island' cut off from the mainland by a narrow stretch of water and reached by the Ponte Nuovo. Ancient Syracuse also occupied both zones, though Ortygia was more attractive, having certain natural advantages: being an island it was more easily defensible; it had its own freshwater springs; and it had (and has) two natural ports, one on either side.

Syracuse was settled in 733 BC, a year after the founding of Naxos, near Taormina. According to Thucydides its first inhabitants were colonists from Corinth and they were no doubt attracted by the natural advantages Ortygia had to offer. Thus began the history of a city that has enjoyed more periods of prosperity than any other in Sicily, which in its heyday eclipsed the power and prosperity even of Athens, and which nowadays is relatively free from the ills suffered by the other major cities such as Catania and Palermo.

For most of its early history Syracuse was subject to the rule of the tyrants, some of whom were enlightened and who engendered periods of peace and cultural and economic prosperity. On the whole, however, they were warlike, savage and cruel in the extreme.

From 480 BC when, in alliance with Akragas (Agrigento) and Gela, the Syracusans crushed the Carthaginians at Himera, Syracuse began what was to be a long process of expansion. These were the years of the tyrant Gelon, and it was a period in which the city was enriched with new temples (for example the Temple of Athena which was to become the present-day Cathedral), theatres, and dockyards. Under Gelon's successor, his brother Hieron I, the intellectual ambience of the court was greatly improved; it was graced by the presence of well-known poets and philosophers among whom were Pindar and Aeschylus, who may have seen the production of (or indeed produced himself) his last plays *Prometheus Bound* and *Prometheus Released* in the theatre here. The presence of this pair is not an indication of the intellectual leanings of Hieron himself; to the contrary, historians tell that tyrants such as he had inflated ideas of their intellectual capacity and that this was normally in direct and inverse proportion to their awfulness as human beings. In this connection, Diodorus said that Hieron I was 'an utter stranger to sincerity and nobility of character'.

Nobody could have been a more terrible ruler than Dionysius the Elder who came to power after a longish period during which Syracuse was ruled, unusually, on democratic principles. In Denis Mack Smith's opinion, he was not a man to baulk at human suffering. He was the most powerful figure of his day in the Greek world, personal power at home and abroad being his overriding aim. He was responsible for the first of the great fortifications along the Epipolae ridge to the west of Syracuse, building there the first of the

Euryalus forts. But Dionysius was in some ways the saviour of the Sicilian Greeks. When he came to power, Syracuse was at a low ebb, despite having a few years previously (413 BC) defeated a vast Athenian army and navy that had been sent from Athens in 415 BC to put a stop to their ever-increasing power and influence.

This episode in the history of the Sicilian colonies of Magna Graecia involved both Segesta, Selinus and the latter's ally Syracuse (see also Chapter 6). The subsequent battle was described by Thucydides as 'the greatest action we know in Hellenic history – to the victors the most brilliant of successes, to the vanquished the most calamitous of defeats'. In a great show of bravado the Athenians under Nicias had sailed a huge fleet of ships into the Great Harbour (the western of Ortygia's two harbours) in an effort to intimidate the Syracusans. They hung about too long trying to avoid engaging in battle; the relief force sent from Athens to help them was routed by the Syracusans by which time Nicias had decided to withdraw. Unfortunately the Syracusans blocked the harbour mouth ('with a line of triremes broadside on, and merchant ships and craft at anchor' – Thucydides). The ensuing sea battle was one of the saddest in ancient history: the Athenian force was decimated and 7000 of the original 25,000 men were taken captive and incarcerated in the large quarries ('*latomie*') just outside Syracuse where they languished until they either died or were sent into slavery, branded on the forehead with the mark of a horse.

In spite of the Syracusans' victory, the fortunes of the city were severely depleted, a situation which did not go unnoticed by the Carthaginians who were anxious to grab any opportunity they could to increase their own Sicilian holdings. Aware of this, Dionysius concluded a treaty with them which saved Syracuse and, during the subsequent hiatus, built up his state into a formidable economic and naval power.

Like Hieron he managed to attract a bevy of distinguished figures to his court, and of these the most illustrious was Plato, who tutored his son Dionysius II. According to Plutarch, even so eloquent a teacher had very little effect on this useless creature who, after a period of spectacular non-contribution to the affairs of Syracuse, was dispatched to Corinth where he ended his days 'loitering about in the fish-market, or sitting in a perfumer's shop drinking the diluted wine of the taverns, or squabbling in the streets with common women'.

This inglorious episode in the city's history was not to last however and Dionysius II's successor Timoleon revised the old democratic codes, introducing reforms, injecting life into the local economy and inaugurating an era of urban growth and prosperity. Yet like his predecessors he could be ruthless, autocratic and brutal in exercising power.

The rule of Agathocles, Syracuse's next tyrant, was memorable for the bloodthirsty coup that brought him to power: there was a savage uprising during which, according to Diodorus, more than 4000 people were murdered, people 'whose sole offence was that they were of better birth than the others'. Not much is known about his domestic rule although he is thought to have redistributed the land, making him everlastingly popular with the masses. He strengthened the external defences of Syracuse and, by the time he died in 289 BC, most of Sicily was under his control.

Under Hieron II, the last tyrant before the advent of Roman power in Syracuse, the city flourished as never before. His was a very long reign during which monuments like the Ara di Ierone II (a huge sacrificial altar) were built, and the Teatro Greco was enlarged. The district of Neapolis was laid out anew, and policies introduced for improving the amenities of the city as well as the cultural life of its people. Archimedes was living in Syracuse at this time, and his talents were directed towards designing ingenious machines for defensive and offensive action – put to good use during the Second Punic War in the defence of Syracuse against the Romans. However in 211 BC Syracuse fell to Marcellus's army; the city was ransacked, much of its sculpture and paintings shipped to Rome – and Archimedes accidently hacked to bits. From this point onwards, Sicily was nothing more than an appendage of Rome.

Syracuse became just another city in the province of Sicily – an administrative headquarters – though it did flourish as a trading post. It became important for the early Christians and the Byzantines; it was the latter's main Sicilian base (as Palermo was to be the Arabs) though it fell to Arabs in AD 878. There followed a miserable period in which the city was sacked, burned and its citizens massacred, and never again was Syracuse to enjoy the power and influence it had held for virtually the whole of the preceding 1500 years.

The Normans embellished it, as did the Hohenstaufens, (Frederick II built the Castello Maniace), but in 1693 a violent earthquake reduced large parts of the city to a dusty rubble. The many baroque buildings in the old city date from its rebuilding.

Perhaps the best way to deal with Syracuse, as a sightseer, is to divide it up into its main quarters and examine each one separately. Ortygia is of course the hub of the city, its character predominantly medieval and baroque. To the north-west, on the mainland, is Achradina which has always been its commercial quarter. To the north is Tyche which contains the all-important Museo Archeologico Paolo Orsi and the catacombs. West of Achradina is Neapolis with the 'archaeological park' and some of the stone quarries where the hapless Athenians met their end. Further to the north-west is Epipolae with the Castello Euryalus.

One of Ortygia's most impressive monuments is without doubt the Duomo whose façade has no match in Sicily for monumental plasticity. Its profile changes, twisting and turning as you walk around it. Begun in 1728 to the designs of Andrea Palma, it is in fact a much earlier building, the scale of Palma's work being defined by the proportions of the Greek Doric Temple of Athena of the 5th century BC that forms its skeleton. It is not terribly difficult to disentangle the two once you have located the Norman additions and the infill that transformed the original building into a church in early Christian times.

The Temple of Athena is thought to have been started by Gelon in thanksgiving for his victory over the Carthaginians at Himera in 480 BC. Cicero wrote that this great temple – the richest in Syracuse – was lavishly decorated with a series of fine paintings depicting the battles of Agathocles against the Carthaginians. These were stolen by Verres (see Chapter 6) in the 1st century BC. Cicero also records that the temple doors were extremely splendid: 'doors more exquisitely wrought in ivory and gold have never existed in any temple at all'. The massive Doric columns that perhaps he leaned against still survive down the aisles, while the temple's cella occupied by the present nave and a part of the choir is not difficult to discern (a part of the cella wall still exists unbroken on the southern section of the apse in the north aisle, while the arches of the nave itself, curious flat cut-outs, are nothing more than openings made down the cella's length). When you walk through the outer baroque portal of the Duomo's entrance, you are in fact going through the point at which the temple's external row of columns would have stood, so that facing you, at the inner main entrace to the nave, was the columned front of the cella – the columns still exist but can only be seen from the nave – over whose threshold Gelon, Dionysius and all the other tyrants must have stepped.

The building (it became the Cathedral in the 7th century) has been much altered over the years; it was badly damaged in the earthquake of 1693 and rebuilt. During this century much of its internal baroque overlay was removed when the earliest structures were rediscovered, though happily the façade, which is its best 18th century feature, still remains with its robust overlay of carving and the strange chiaroscuro of its screen-like entrance portal.

The most noteworthy, post-classical, elements of its interior are the Gagini statues in the north aisle, in particular Antonello Gagini's *Madonna of the Snows* in the north apse (whose beautifully cut brickwork is a remnant of the Byzantine period). The baptistery, which is at the west end of the south aisle (to the immediate right of the main entrance) contains a Norman font made from a marble block, on which you can still see a Greek inscription, supported by bronze lions. Another area to note is the Chapel of the Holy Sacrament in the south aisle: it is thought to have been designed by Giovanni Vermexio around 1650. See the polychrome marble tabernacle by Vanvitelli – the designer of the vast palace at Caserta outside Naples. The Chapel of the Crucifix, to the right of the main altar, normally displays a painting of St Zosimus which is attributed to Antonello da Messina. It was stolen in the 1970s, but has since been recovered, though it is not yet hanging in its old home. In the presbytery is a baroque altar that was constructed using a monolith from the Temple's frieze.

The rest of Ortygia is as much a confusion of different styles as the Duomo. Across the Piazza del Duomo is the Palazzo Beneventano del Bosco, built by Luciano Ali (1779) in the Syracusan baroque style, which is characterised by a very much bolder approach than the baroque of either Palermo or Catania. The Palazzo Beneventano is picked out for favourable criticism by Anthony Blunt, primarily because of the monumental stair in its inner courtyard which, when completed, 'must have been one of the finest open staircases in Sicily'. Its arches, now blocked up or glazed over, once looked through to an inner court, '. . .providing,' says Blunt, 'a dramatic climax to what even now is one of the most complete realisations of Syracusan Baroque.' (*Sicilian Baroque*) Just walk in and have a look.

Still in the baroque vein is the church of Santa Lucia alla Badia built immediately after the 1693 earthquake at the south end of the Piazza Duomo. And while in the Piazza Duomo, facing the Palazzo Beneventano is the Palazzo Vermexio – the Municipio – and, further down the piazza, the Galleria Numismatico which contains an important coin collection documenting the various stages of Syracuse's ever-increasing wealth.

An interesting array of buildings from earlier periods includes the ruins of the Temple of Apollo (or more probably Artemis, since Ortygia was sacred to Artemis, and Pindar called the temple 'the couch of Artemis') at the landward end of Ortygia, facing Piazza Pancali and the Ponte Nuova. This is thought to be the earliest of the big Doric temples in Sicily – built some time in the first half of the 6th century BC. It too became a church later in its history – see the Norman door high up in what was once the wall of its cella. Note that the columns, like those of the Temple of Athena, are monoliths. Not far away, off the Via Resalibera, is the Church of San Pietro, a small basilica thought to have been built in the second half of the 4th century AD by Bishop Germanus and subsequently altered by the Byzantines, the Normans and again in the later Middle Ages.

Moving across the south-west bulge of Ortygia, from north to south, the Palazzo Montalto, just off the Via Montalto, has a wonderful 14th century façade with double and triple Chiaramonte-style windows. (Chiaramonte is the Gothic-Renaissance style of architecture named after the powerful family whose castles and palaces it adorned. See also Chapter 2). In Piazza Archimede is the Palazzo Lanza with some pretty 15th century windows, and just off the Via Maestranza (in the Via Gargallo) is the Palazzo Gargallo which dates from the 15th century. It has a rather strange outside stairway with a Catalan appearance. In the Via Capodieci is the Palazzo Bellomo, a 13th century building with a whole host of 15th century features in a local version of the Catalan-Gothic style. This is now the home of the Museo Regionale d'Arte Mediovale e Moderna whose collection contains the *Annunciation* by Antonello da Messina (see his other works in the gallery in Messina, Chapter 11).

Still in the Via Capodieci, towards the west, is the Fonte Aretusa, the freshwater spring to which classical writers frequently refer. According to Pausanias the nymph Aretusa was changed into a spring by Artemis to help her escape from her lover Alpheus, who himself was changed into a river. She emerged at this spot. Other legends mention the cup that was thrown into the river Alpheus in the Peloponnese, emerging at this fountain on Ortygia. Another tells of the water running red at Ortygia after the sacrifice of oxen at Olympia. You can still gaze into these sacred waters, nowadays filled with ducks, bream and papyrus and protected from the sea by a high wall which most probably replaces the 'massive stone wall' mentioned by Cicero.

Still further south in the Via San Martino is one of Syracuse's oldest churches – the 14th century San Martino – a rebuilding of a 6th century basilica. And at the very tip of Ortygia is the Castello Maniace, a massive fortification built in about 1239 by Frederick II and named after the great Byzantine general George Maniakes who took Syracuse briefly from the Arabs in 1038. Nowadays it is a barracks and hence difficult to enter. Its Gothic marble portal is flanked by two niches which once held Hellenistic bronze rams, one of which can be seen in the archaeological museum in Palermo (see Chapter 3).

Most of the quarter of Achradina was flattened in the last war but one or two ancient edifices stoically resisted the air raids. The oldest is the Foro Siracusano, at the west end of the Corso Umberto, which contain the remains of the agora of the ancient Greek city. Nearby, in Via Elorina, is the Ginnasio Romano, a small Roman theatre built in the 1st century AD, and just north of the Via dell'Arsenale is the Byzantine bath-house in which, so they say, Emperor Constans II, who resided briefly in Syracuse from AD 663 to 668, was assassinated with a soap dish. In the Piazza Santa Lucia is the 17th century church of Santa Lucia del Sepolcro which is supposed to mark the spot where this saint, the patroness of Syracuse, was martyred by the Romans probably during Diocletian's persecution. In paintings you see her carrying two eyes on a dish; it is thought that this is a connection with her name, which means light and is probably the reason she is popularly invoked against diseases of the eye. According to legend, she was denounced as a Christian by her suitor, withstood exposure in a brothel and ordeal by fire, and was finally stabbed in the throat. Whatever the real story, it was begun in 1629 on a plan designed by Giovanni Vermexio who designed an octagonal chapel next to Santa Lucia to house her remains – although they were stolen and taken to Constantinople in the 11th century only to be carried on to Venice in 1204 where they remain to this day in the Church of St Geremia. As if to outdo this monument to saintly virtue the huge modern church of the Madonna delle Lacrime stands in the Via degli Orti San Giorgio. It houses the figure of the Virgin which wept for five days in 1953.

Directly to the north of Achradina is Tyche, which contains most of Syracuse's catacombs, the oldest in Sicily, and second only to those in Rome. Most were hewn from the rock, others made in subterranean water channels disused since Greek days. Sadly, they are unsafe and are now closed but for one smallish group beneath the ruins of the basilica of San Giovanni, just behind the archaeological museum. San Giovanni was Syracuse's cathedral until AD 640 when Bishop Zosimus transferred his seat to Ortygia, to the church housed in the remains of the Temple of Athena.

San Giovanni was built over the Crypt of St Marcian, the first Bishop of Syracuse who was flogged to death in AD 254. The crypt is a strange haphazard arrangement of altars and apses in little chapels, and in one of these an altar marks the spot where St Paul is supposed to have preached (it faces St Marcian's tomb). St Paul came to Syracuse on the *Castor and Pollux* (Acts 28: 12) on his way from Malta to Rome; he stayed for three days.

Perhaps the most interesting place in Syracuse is the Museo Archeologico Paolo Orsi, built in the grounds of the Villa Landolina. It contains the finds from the city as well as those from important sites scattered around the province. It is useless to attempt a description of its contents because they are so varied and so many, but among the most celebrated is the Venus Landolina which dates from the 1st century AD (a much criticized piece condemmed by prudes for its 'immodest modesty', though Vincent Cronin in *The Golden Honeycomb* thought that the milk-white of the marble imparted 'an ineffacable purity'). There is also a great squat headless goddess, suckling twin babies, which came from Megara Hyblaea and which dates from the mid 6th century BC. And there are various *kouroi*, muscular youths, of which the 5th century BC example from Lentini is the most outstanding. There are Hellenistic and Roman portrait busts from Sicily and north Africa, a marble sarcophagus (*c*. mid 4th century AD) which came from the catacombs of San Giovanni, architectural fragments from Syracuse and beyond, pottery from a whole range of periods, and other artefacts from the earliest civilisations up until the Christian and Byzantine periods.

In Neapolis's Parco Archeologico, most of the rest of the remains of Syracuse's classical past are clustered together, making it rather easy to visit them all at once. As you enter, beyond the elliptical Teatro Romano is the Ara di Ierone II, the altar of Hieron II, which was cut from the living rock some time after 241 BC in honour of Zeus Eleutherios. Although the scale of what remains is evidence of a massive structure, the altar is now a total ruin. We do know however that it once consisted of a long raised area approached by ramps at either end up which, on one occasion according to Diodorus, 450 bulls were led between the sacrificial fires to be slaughtered. It must have been like an enormous religious barbecue.

North of the altar is the Teatro Greco, the Greek Theatre, one of the most spectacular monuments in south-eastern Sicily. Like Hieron's altar this was carved out of and not built from the stone – the original slope of the landscape can be estimated from the large rocky outcrop just to the west of the stage area. If Aeschylus did see his plays being produced in Syracuse, then it was here that he saw them. Here too will have been performed the works of Sophocles and Euripides in front of an audience which at times must have included Plato, Theocritus and Archimedes.

The Teatro Greco is a vast place, capable of holding 15,000 spectators. What you see there today dates from the rule of Hieron II, though there has most probably been a theatre on the site since the 5th century BC. Halfway up the auditorium (the cavea) are some inscriptions which date from the 3rd century BC. They tell you, in Greek, to whom the sections of the cavea were dedicated: the central section to Zeus Olympicos, the west side to Hieron, and the east to his wife Philistis.

Beyond the theatre, to the north, is the Nymphaeum, a large artificial grotto sacred to the Muses. To the south-west is the Teatro Lineare, a simple, regular theatre which could have accommodated about 1000 people. Nearby is the Santuario di Apollo Temenites – in Cicero's day a huge statue of Apollo stood here, but it was later taken to Rome by Tiberius. And to the west of the Nymphaeum is the so-called Street of the Tombs, lined with Byzantine tombs and votive niches cut into the sides of the flanking rock.

Moving deeper into the archaeological park, east of Hieron II's altar is the huge eliptical Roman amphitheatre dating from the second half of the 2nd century AD and gouged mostly from the rock itself. This building is only slightly smaller than the one in Verona. To the north of it, east of the Greek Theatre, are the stone quarries, the Latomie del Paradiso, which although now a lush garden were most probably the site of the incarceration of the 7000 Athenian prisoners of war (the Latomie dei Cappuccini in east Syracuse is the other possible location for this horrible episode). Thucydides says that they received a daily ration of half a pint of water and a pint of corn, and that after ten weeks those who had not died were sold as slaves. In the Latomie del Paradiso is an artificial serpentine cave known as the Ear of Dionysus; it has remarkable acoustic properties and according to legend Dionysius had it opened up so that he could eavesdrop on the conversations of the prisoners in the quarry below. Actually, this legend arose after a visit to the cave by the painter Caravaggio (1588) who was struck by its resemblance to the human inner ear. Nobody knows the cave's true origins.

Not far from Syracuse at Epipolae is the Castello Euryalus which is the most important complete Greek fortification to have survived anywhere in the ancient Greek world. It is well worth seeing, perhaps as a special outing from the city. The fortress lies on the Epipolae ridge about 7 km from the city, and most of what you see there dates from the time of Hieron II. With this in mind, it does not seem too far-fetched to suppose that Archimedes was involved in its construction.

Leaving Syracuse for **Pantalica**, the vast cemetery of rock-cut tombs from the 13th to the 8th century BC, take the SS124 via Floridia, and head for the Monti Iblei in the west. Eighteen kilometres beyond Floridia, branch right, crossing the Anapo river, and head for Ferla. Immediately after the crossing, and just before Ferla, a sign points to the Necropolis at Pantalica, a rocky desolate area about 9 km down a rough track at the end of the gorge through which runs the Anapo. The gorge, by contrast, is one of the most beautiful parts of south-eastern Sicily, and is filled with terraces of fruit trees and wild flowers. It is completely hidden, secret and remote.

Pantalica itself was originally populated by refugees from places like Thapsos on the coast. Their village (still unexcavated) stood on a plateau between the Anapo and its northern tributary the Cava Grande, while on the sheer cliffsides all around they buried their dead. As many as 5000 tombs have been discovered – row upon row of them in several tiers, each one a little square opening in the rock face shielding the dead in deep caves gouged roughly into the mountain, and each one originally sealed by a single flat stone. It was a necropolis of colossal proportions, a fact which once apparent, says Vincent Cronin in *The Golden Honeycomb*, makes the whole place take on an even more sinister aspect. 'Here,' says Cronin, 'is Sicily of the Stone Age, intent on nothing higher than the taking of food and the burial of its dead. The pageant of nation after nation which was later to form a continual progress ... [has] not yet arrived: the stage is bare and empty'.

Pantalica was abandoned about 733 BC and remained uninhabited until the Byzantine period when refugees found the tombs of their ancestors a safe haven from the barbarian raiders. From this period dates a little Byzantine Oratory – called San Micidiario – not far from the Anaktoron, the house of the tribal chief of the site's earliest inhabitants.

It takes a day to see and to enjoy this site thoroughly; the Anapo is wide and deep at certain points around Pantalica and, apart from providing a vantage point over a singular prehistoric landscape, is good for swimming and makes a pleasant backdrop to walks. Returning to Ferla, cross the Anapo again and continue along the SS124 to **Palazzolo Acreide**, an extremely pretty country town with some exceptionally lively baroque buildings and the descendant of the old city of Akrai (founded in the 7th century BC by colonists from Syracuse) whose remains lie nearby.

The best of the town's baroque offerings (built after the 1693 earthquake) are scattered, and you must walk the streets to find the oddities; notice the absurdities, and the quirky opulence of some of the more rustic examples of the style. Among the best is the church of the Annunziata, actually a much earlier building reconstructed in the 18th century, which has a very splendid doorway framed by a pair of Salomonic columns (barley-sugar shape, a feature typical of the Spanish baroque) heavily encrusted with vine leaves and festooned with all kinds of fruit and flowers (early 18th century). Antonello da Messina painted his *Annunciation* for this church, but you now have to go to the Museo Regionale d'Arte Mediovale e Moderna in Syracuse to see it. At the other end of the Via Annunziata from this church is the church of San Paolo, a hefty baroque edifice attributed to Vincenzo Sinatra (mid 18th century). While its opulence is on a monumental scale, the façade of the Palazzo Zocco in the Piazza Umberto has a rough-and-tumble baroque ornamentation in which the stone carvers evidently had great fun sculpting the most grotesque faces they could (this sort of carving is more predominant in Noto).

The ruins of **Akrai** have the most magnificent site: just outside the town, high on a summit, they overlook the trade routes from Syracuse to the interior of the island. Yet despite this, and although Akrai quickly became a strategic military outpost, nothing much ever happened here. It enjoyed two moments of prosperity: one was during the reign of Hieron II, the other was in the 4th and 5th centuries AD when, after a period of severe decline under the Romans, it suddenly (and for no clear reason) became an early Christian centre.

There remain the ruins of a theatre, a smallish senate house (the bouleuterion), and the agora which, though hardly excavated, contains bits of a very early Temple of Aphrodite – it dates from the 6th or the 5th centuries BC. Below this are two quarries from which stone for Akrai was taken, each one subsequently converted into a burial ground by the early Christians. In one, the lower, deeper one, you can see a Roman votive wall plaque carved into the stone: it represents heroes offering a sacrifice and it probably dates from the 1st century BC.

Most interesting are the 'Santoni' figures just to the south-east of the site, below the Templi Ferali (another quarry which once held plaques commemorating the dead). These rock-cut figures, twelve in all, are thought to represent Cybele, the fertility goddess, and this site was obviously sacred to her cult. In fact no other site like it has been found in Sicily. The figures date from the 3rd century BC, when that cult spread throughout Magna Graecia from Athens. Their survival is rather remarkable, but you can be sure that their name in recent centuries (*santoni* means great saints) has ensured that their 'powers' are not ignored by the local rural population.

From Palazzolo Acreide, a smallish country road goes west for 14 km to Giarratana through which runs the SS194 going south to **Ragusa**. This is a lovely hilltown in two very distinct parts. Destroyed in the 17th century earthquake, the old town of Ragusa Ibla ('Ibla' records the fact that it occupies the ancient site of Hybla Haerea, scant traces of which have survived) was simply rebuilt. At the same time a new town emerged a short distance away on a higher ridge. The two are linked by immensely long, immensely wearing flights of steps. The walk from the higher town to the lower takes about half an hour, 'the way being . . . not an orderly, continuous stairway, but irregular, erratic goat paths which wind like tangled skeins of wool in and around the houses and sweep under bridges; long flat steps and narrow, steep grace-notes, tumbling down like a cascade, following the line of least resistance to the gorge below. When that is reached, a similar path up the farther slope zigzags through Ragusa Ibla,' says Vincent Cronin. Be warned!

The two parts of Ragusa are very different from each other: the newer town is laid out on a grid while the older town, even though it was largely rebuilt, still more or less follows medieval building lines, and the streets are narrow and convoluted. A busy, commercial place, Ragusa Superiore is not particularly interesting. It is here that life in Ragusa runs its daily course away from the silent, deserted but beautiful streets of Ragusa Ibla down below.

The chief attractions there are the works of the architect Rosario Gagliardi (1698?–1762?, see Appendix II) – the churches of San Giorgio and San Giuseppe. Both are masterpieces of the Sicilian baroque, and owe as much to their siting on a slope as they do to the architect's ingenuity. San Giorgio, begun possibly in 1746, is a great wedding-cake of a place. Nearly every surface of the façade, which dominates a sloping piazza linked to the building by broad flights of steps, is in some way rounded or in the process of 'moving' into another plane. The whole façade builds to a crescendo as the eye moves up to the belfry, centrally placed above the main entrance and in the main bay of the building – unprecedented in Italy. Even before the eye takes in the façade of the church, it is busily engaged in sorting out the planes of the steps and the differences in the heights of the surrounding terrain. All this 'movement', the essence of the baroque style, is unmatched by the interior of the building which is rigid and dull by comparison – a fault for which Gagliardi is often criticised, in Anthony Blunt's case, obliquely: 'Gagliardi's greatest achievement lies in his design for façades'.

San Giuseppe is much smaller than San Giorgio and has not been built on a site with quite such obvious scenic advantages. But it has more subtle dramatic qualities which you will notice if you stand beneath one of the high plinths of the clusters of columns framing the main entrance and look straight upwards. Layers of curves and jagged, broken cornices rush in every direction, each one doing its best to counter its neighbour's movement.

There is one interesting excursion from Ragusa: this is to **Comiso** and **Vittoria**, two smallish towns just to the west of Ragusa. Comiso is a conglomeration of detritus from the Middle Ages and ebullient effusions of the baroque, lumped together in the shadow of the domes of the 18th century Duomo. Its principal attraction is the 15th century church of San Francesco, inside which the Cappella Naselli is the proud possessor of a much photographed oddity: its cupola is joined to the square crossing below using an extraordinary Arab-Norman style pastiche, rather strange considering the date of its construction (1517–55). Along with nearby Vittoria, with its lovely baroque church of the Madonna della Grazia, Comiso is well worth visiting.

Modica is only about 7 km away from Ragusa on the SS115 and is another of the south-east's earthquake-ravaged towns. Like Ragusa, it was comprehensively rebuilt. There are two churches to note here: one is the church of Modica's patron saint, St Peter, erected at the beginning of the 18th century. It is an example of early local baroque and is much more staid than the later church of San Giorgio, by contrast one of south-eastern Sicily's masterpieces of the later, fully developed baroque style. In the absence of any documentary evidence, and on the basis of the various similarities it has with its namesake in Ragusa Ibla, this church is judged to be another of Gagliardi's. What a magnificent place it is – not because it overawes with splendour, but because it is imbued with the most remarkable vitality and plasticity, and its graceful bearing defiantly challenges nature to dare topple it. It also has the most remarkable site on the side of a steep hill flanking the Corso Umberto approach to Modica.

The columns, the concave and convex sweeps of wall, the rich, almost rococo encrustations of ornament on the pediments around the five main doors, are all balanced by the deep, dark openings of the doors themselves and the shadowy window and belfry recesses. The effect is enhanced because you cannot see the bulk of the nave – or even the dome – from the front of the church. Both seem to melt into the clutter of little square houses crammed on to the hillside around the building. The approach to the church from the very bottom of the steps in front of it is dominated by the soaring belfry centrally placed over the main door, this is one of the features that suggests Gagliardi's authorship.

Like the interior of Ragusa's San Giorgio this one is a bit disappointing. But this nave probably survives from an earlier building: there has been a church on this site since the 9th century. The Saracens destroyed the first, an earthquake in 1613 the second, and while the third – a great new building commissioned by the Count of Modica, the Viceroy of Sicily Alfonso Henriquez Cabrera – was underway, the massive 'quake of 1693 left it and the town around it lying in a heap.

In the lower town, the 15th century church of Santa Maria di Betlem is worth a visit; so is the church of the Carmine with its 15th century façade and the Gaginiesque *Annunciation* inside it. And like Ragusa, the town is dotted with a range of fine palaces whose window surrounds, doorways and balcony supports are freely and robustly carved. In both towns you should hunt these out: all are interesting, each with its own array of individual design features.

Not far from Modica – about 10 km to the south – is Scicli. Like Modica and Ragusa, it has a lovely 18th century aspect, and an array of small provincial palaces – though here in Scicli they all seem closed and forgotten. One in particular, the Palazzo Beneventano, which dates from the middle of the 18th century, has fantastic grotesque heads scattered liberally over its façade (in the vein of the Villa Palagonia in Bagheria, see Chapter 8) along with fanciful geometric shapes with interestingly textured surfaces, swags and eccentric patterns. Not on most people's route by any means, this little town is well worth the detour.

Halfway between Modica and Ispica, on the SS115 to Noto, is the Cava d'Ispica, the site of a wide range of tombs from the Neolithic to the early Christian eras. There are also troglodytic dwellings of which some were turned into catacombs and others into Byzantine sanctuaries; the presence of Man on this site can be traced from the earliest times. It is a strange chalky area filled with the ghosts of past communities who took to this gorge in an attempt to carry on their lives unhindered by invasion and persecution. It is easy to get to from Modica: leave the town going east for about 7 km on a very minor country road with some rather helpful signposts.

Twenty-one kilometres from Ispica itself, a small medieval town with the lovely art nouveau Palazzo Bruno by Ernesto Basile, is Noto, a city whose predecessor was another of the victims of the 1693 disaster. Noto, like Ragusa and nearby Avola (whose predecessor, Avola Vecchia, lies about 9 km above it in the mountains) was simply rebuilt on virgin territory because the devastation was so extensive. Noto (perhaps more properly Noto Nuova) must be one of the most enchanting baroque cities in Sicily, indeed one of the most magical embodiments of the style anywhere at all.

Quite distinct is Noto Antica whose ruins moulder away on a rocky outcrop called Monte Alveria in the foothills of the Ibleian mountains just to the east of Syracuse. The site of the old city, which you can still visit – take the SS287 going north from Noto Nuova – had been occupied for millenia; as with any other important provincial city in Sicily, Bronze Age settlers were followed by Greeks,

Romans and the whole range of foreigners who came to make the island their home, right up until the Spaniards unlucky enough to live there at the time of the earthquake. Noto Antica had a rich variety of buildings – churches, palaces, monasteries, convents, a royal fortress, fortifications – from every period; all this was destroyed completely on January 9 and 11 1693. Says one eyewitness: 'Then came an earth quake so horrible, so ghastly that the soil undulated like the waves of a stormy sea, and the mountains danced as if drunk, and the city collapsed in one terrible moment killing more than a thousand people'.

It is very unusual for a community to be transferred lock, stock and barrel from one site to another. Old towns, their sites and urban spaces, all have significance for the inhabitants which cannot be replaced – Catania and Messina were both flattened at least once in their long histories and on each occasion were rebuilt *in situ*. The people of Noto Antica had to move because its site was too narrow to accommodate a new city among the ruins and the hillside was so utterly broken up as to be pretty well inaccessible.

Noto Nuova today is one of the most homogeneous post-earthquake cities in Sicily. Not only is the style of its buildings harmonious from street to street, but its plan (instigated by Giovanni Battista Landolina), on two levels, with all the major buildings at its centre, was developed in a relatively short space of time with an emphasis on symmetry and regularity. The piazzas were designed to afford balanced views, and the churches sited in dominant positions to create vistas and to make the greatest possible impression. Noto is filled with churches, convents, monasteries and a whole clutch of palaces which ravish the eye with exotic external carvings.

The lower town, centred on San Nicolò, was for the clergy and the aristocracy, and in the upper town, on the summit of the site, were the homes of the poorer citizens, clustered around the church of Santissima Crocifisso. Up here, behind the church and squeezed up against various religious foundations, are the warrens of little houses crammed together with haphazard abandon within the blocks imposed by Noto's grid plan. It is as worthwhile to wander about up here as it is to visit the centre; the little dwellings of the contemporary poor of Noto are not so different from those in which their ancestors lived just after the rebuilding of the city. In fact a great many still live in the early buildings, which often consist of merely a single room opening directly on to the street.

The church of San Nicolò at the centre of the town – in the Piazza Municipio – is the latest of Noto's churches, completed in the 1770s. Attributed to Rosario Gagliardi, its plan was altered over the years so that the final result is part baroque, and part (particularly its façade) neo-classical. Immediately to its right, facing on to the Via Gavour which runs east-west behind San Nicolò, is the Palazzo Trigona (1781). On the other side of the street, facing on to the Piazza Municipio, is the 19th century Bishop's Palace. This in turn lies adjacent to the Monastery of SS Salvatore whose tower, with its eccentrically undulating façade, around the back of the church, is also thought to be by Rosario Gagliardi. The Trigona building is rather an ambitious one, and extremely large for a town as small as Noto; according to Stephen Tobriner, some of its rooms have a quality of decoration which matches the building's exterior. This is unusual for Noto where nearly all the elaboration was devoted to the exteriors, since these were intended to demonstrate wealth and status.

A good example is the façade of the palace belonging to the Nicolaci Princes of Villadorata in the second block to the left of San Nicolò, facing on to the Via Corrado Nicolaci. The Nicolaci palace is the biggest noble residence in Noto, and if the effusive, boisterous carving of the balcony supports on its main façade are anything to go by, this family must have been extremely rich. This section of the building dates from the 1730s. The grimacing lions, the horses and the anthropomorphic architectural elements are reminiscent of the architecture of Lecce in Apulia, and also of some buildings in Catania such as the Palazzo Biscari (see Chapter 13), though Noto is a great deal more restrained.

The Landolina palace which lies between the Nicolaci palace and San Nicolò, is less amazing. It dates from the 1740s and is more neo-classical than baroque. But there are many other palaces to admire: the Palazzo Astuto for example, which faces the back of San Nicolò, is another huge one with ornately billowing wrought-iron balconies. It stands next to the Monastery of Montevergine which must be one of the most striking of Noto's churches. Its concave central bay between two towers creates a vista at the north end of the Via Nicolaci.

Perhaps the most beautiful of all of Noto's palaces is the Palazzo Ducezio – the Municipio which faces San Nicolò's front entrance. This, the work of Vincenzo Sinatra who was Gagliardi's assistant, dates from the middle of the 1740s and was built in a remarkably

French style. It is actually modelled on a French 18th century concept of an Italian palace which, according to Léon Dufourney, was taken from a design by Jacques Francois Blondel. The upper storey is a later addition; the building consisted originally of just the lovely, billowing ground floor which was topped by a dome.

On the periphery of central Noto are a wide range of other interesting buildings. There is the Palazzo Impellezzeri, situated at the eastern end of the Via Trigona, opposite the church of San Teodoro. This dates from the early 1750s. And if you go northwards up the Via Sergio Saliciano, which flanks the western end of the Palazzo Impellezzeri, you soon come to the church of SS Crocifisso in the main square at the summit of the town. This is supposed to have been the work of Rosario Gagliardi – certainly its plan is very similar to that of San Giorgio in Ragusa – but it seems to lack the *joie de vivre* of that building. This church possesses two Romanesque lions which came from Noto Antica and a Madonna signed by Francesco Laurana (1471) – the most inspired of all the Laurana Madonnas, according to Bernard Berenson (*The Passionate Sightseer*).

At the western end of the Corso – the central wide street going west out of the Piazza Municipio – is the church and the Convent of San Domenico. Of all the churches in Noto this must be the most exciting. It is the work of Gagliardi (*c.* 1732), and the style of its architecture is that of the full-blown high baroque of the Roman type. It is quite different from his other buildings at Ragusa and Modica. Another interesting church, Santa Maria dell'Arco (begun in 1713 with work still underway in 1779), immediately south of the Palazzo Ducezio on the Via Ducezio, is Gagliardi's first commission in Noto. This church is quite different, again, from San Domenico. One thing is certain: Gagliardi was an immensely versatile architect and designer. Not only do his designs vary from church to church, but they vary even on a single building. For example, see Santa Maria dell'Arco's beautiful entrance portal: its door, flanked by two Salomonic columns, could not be more different from the doors on the south and the north façades of this church: the one decorated with carvings of angels heads, the other flanked by Doric pilasters and topped by a strange little curlicue placed at the pinnacle of its arch.

The buildings of Noto are deteriorating fairly rapidly; the honey-coloured limestone from which they were built, while easy to carve, is too soft to withstand pollution and erosion. A few monuments are currently being restored, and others are closed. Even so, Noto is by far the most interesting town in this region, and merits a stay of at least a couple of days.

Perhaps the nicest thing about Noto, Ragusa and Modica is that once you have passed out of their gates, you are in open countryside almost immediately. There is hardly any bedraggled peripheral development, no meaningless sliproads, and above all no confusion – something increasingly rare in Sicily. These three towns are in my opinion the loveliest on the island.

To Goethe Sicily was a unique and beautiful place, 'clear, authentic and complete'. He also regarded it as a foretaste of what to expect on the Italian mainland. In a way this is still true, in spite of the many predators who have been attracted to Sicily and who have exploited it. In the end, however, its conquerors came to love and beautify it and today if you can see beyond the squalor and violence, you will find a sentimental and soft-hued land. In a way it is the most typically Italian region of Italy, magnifying both its faults and its virtues.

APPENDICES

I

Chronological Outline of the History of Sicily

GREEK

8th century BC - 215 BC
(8th century BC Phoenician colonization in north-west Sicily)

c. 570–*c.* 549 Phalaris (tyrant) at Akragas (Agrigento).
491–478 Gelon (tyrant) at Syracuse.
478–467 Hieron (tyrant) I at Syracuse.
467–405 Period of democratic rule at Syracuse.
405–367 Dionysius I at Syracuse, 415–413 Athenian Invasion.
367–344 Dionysius II at Syracuse.
345–*c.* 338 Timoleon at Syracuse.
317–289 Agathocles at Syracuse.
265–215 Hieron II at Syracuse, 264–241 First Punic War.

ROMAN

241 BC - AD 318
73–71 Governorship of Gaius Verres

VANDALS/GOTHS

AD 318–535

BYZANTINE

535–827

ARAB

827–1061

NORMAN

1061–1194
1071 (capture of Palermo)–1101 Count Roger
1101–1154   King Roger II
1154–1166   King William I, the Bad
1166–1189   King William II, the Good

1189–1194   Tancred
    1194   King William III

HOHENSTAUFEN

1194–1268
1194–1197   Emperor Henry VI (Holy Roman Emperor)
1197–1250   Emperor Frederick II ('Stupor Mundi', Holy Roman Emperor and
King of Sicily)
1250–1254   Conrad
1254–1266   Manfred

ANGEVIN

1268–1282 Charles of Anjou
1282   Sicilian Vespers

ARAGONESE

1282–1516

HABSBURG (Spanish)

1516–1713
1701–1714   War of the Spanish Succession

PIEDMONTESE

1713–1720

HABSBURG (Austrian)

1720–1734

BOURBON (Spanish)

1734–1860
1734–1759   Charles III
1759–1825   Ferdinand III (Ferdinand I, King of the Two Sicilies)
1825–1830   Francis I (King of the Two Sicilies)
1830–1859   Ferdinand II (King of the Two Sicilies)
    1848   Sicilian Revolution
1859–1860   Francis II
    1860   Garibaldi captures Sicily

HOUSE OF SAVOY

1861–1946
1861–1878   Vittorio Emanuele II

1870   Unification of Italy
1878–1900   Umberto I
1900–1946   Vittorio Emanuele III
1943   Allied invasion of Sicily
1946   Republic of Italy
1946   Regional autonomy for Sicily
1947   First Assembly elected

II

Painters, Sculptors and Architects

This appendix lists the foremost painters, sculptors and architects mentioned in the text. Their dates are included where known, and their principal works mentioned in the text.

Amato, Giacomo   The most important architect in Palermo at the end of the 17th century; b. Palermo 1643, d. 1732; was a lay brother in the Ministri degli Infermi which called him to Rome in the 1670s. Here he studied the work of Rainaldi and Fontana both of whom were particularly influential in the subsequent formation of a Sicilian baroque style. While the façades of Amato's churches (Madonna della Pietà, and Santa Teresa, see Chapter 2) use the language of the High Roman baroque, the results were never quite orthodox – which is what makes Sicilian baroque so exciting. Amato also designed church interiors (choir, Santa Caterina, Chapter 2), palaces (Cutò, Chapter 4, Cattolica, Chapter 2) and furniture. Unlike most Sicilian architect's drawings, Amato's have survived and are a unique record for the island's architectural history.

Amato, Paolo   Architect; b. Ciminna, Sicily, 1634, d. 1714 (no relation to Giacomo Amato); most prominent works in Palermo are the altars, chapels and church interiors which he embellished with rich marble ornament in very high relief. His decoration tends to cover every available surface and, although he was only the latest exponent of what was a local tradition, he was more brilliant and showed greater versatility than his peers.

Amico, Giovanni Biagio   An innovative architect who was also a priest; b. Trapani 1685, d. 1754; his churches (San Lorenzo, Trapani, see Chapter 6, Sant'Anna, Palermo, see Chapter 2) present an interesting version of the Sicilian baroque style. His façades tend to be very lively, rippling with 'movement': canted columns, curves. Amico wrote the only complete architectural treatise to be published in the 18th century in Sicily: *L'Architetto pracctico*, Palermo 1726 and 1750.

Antonello da Messina   Painter; 1430–79; the major Sicilian painter of his day and the only one to have entered the mainstream of Italian painting in the 15th century (see Messina, Chapter 11, Palermo, Chapter 2, Syracuse, Chapter 14). A

228

pioneer of the oil painting technique – in fact Vasari claims he introduced it to Italy.

Basile, Ernesto Architect; b. Palermo 1857, d. 1932; one of the leading modern Italian architects. He began by working for his father Giovanni Battista Filippo Basile, executing designs for the Vittorio Emanuele monument, the Palace of Justice and the Houses of Parliament, all in Rome. His work in Sicily is conspicuous by its eclectic style. Much of it is in the 'Liberty' style: the kiosks in the Piazza Verdi, Palermo, the Villa Igiea and the Villino Florio (see Chapter 4).

Battaglia, Francesco Architect; b. 1710, d. 1788; not much is known about him except that he vented sudden and inexplicable bursts of energy on his projects, such as the Palazzo Biscari (see Chapter 13). His usual style was more in the neo-classical vein than the baroque; in fact, as the century progressed his work became more severely classicizing.

Carnelivari, Matteo A little known architect (and native of Noto) but one of the most important *capo-maestri* in Sicily in the 15th century. His most important work is in Palermo: the Palazzo Abatellis (see Chapter 2). He attempted a reconciliation between the prevailing Spanish late-Gothic style and the Italian Renaissance tradition. Other works are the Palazzo Aiutamicristo, Palermo (see Chapter 2) and the Castello di Miselmeri.

Gagliardi, Rosario Architect; b. Syracuse 1698?, d. 1762?; the most important architect (and one of Sicily's best) working in south-east Sicily in the 18th century. He was responsible for much of the rebuilding of Noto (see Chapter 14). He also worked at Ragusa and Modica (see Chapter 14) and is one of the principal exponents of the southern Sicilian baroque style. His buildings display a robust mixture of the local provincial tradition of overwrought ornamentation with the hefty grandeur to some of the baroque buildings of Rome, Palermo and Catania. He was most adept at handling his materials; his buildings are like gigantic sculptures. All his efforts went into façade at the expense of interior and the planning of his buildings.

Gagini, Antonello Sculptor; son of Domenico, and father of Fazio (d. 1569) and Vincenzo, Giacomo and Antonino. More finely in tune with the Quattrocento Florentine style than his father, this prolific sculptor is responsible for bringing to even the remotest of churches an inkling of the great Renaissance traditions of the mainland.

Gagini, Domenico Sculptor and architect; first recorded in Palermo in 1463, d. Palermo 1492. The eldest of the Gagini, arrived in Palermo in 1463 from Naples. He worked in a style deriving from his native Lombardy and from late Quattrocento Florence (where he is thought to have worked in the studio of Brunelleschi). Establishing this style in Sicily, it was carried on with certain stylistic variations throughout the 16th century by his family and assistants. In fact craftsmen of this dynasty were still active in the first decades of the 17th century. Not much by Domenico seems to have survived (see the attributions in San Francesco, Palermo, see Chapter 2).

Giganti, Andrea Architect; 1731–87. Although not much that is his has survived, he appears to have been a master of a fully developed baroque style (Palazzo Bonagia staircase, see Chapter 2) and, by the time he died, was beginning to work in a classical style.

Ittar, Stefano Architect; d. Malta 1790; brought up in Rome, and greatly influenced by the circle of Carlo Fontana. He worked in Catania and after the death of Vaccarini was the leading architect in the city. His works are rather ponderous (San Placido and the Collegiata, see Chapter 13) with sophisticated, restrained decoration, and his personal style tends towards the neo-classical.

Laurana, Francesco Sculptor; b. La Vrana, Dalmatia *c*. 1430, d. *c*. 1502; was at one time in Urbino, and may have been related to Luciano Laurana. Best known for his busts of women: Battista Sforza (*c*. 1472) in the Bargello in Florence, and Eleanora of Aragon (late 15th century) in the Galleria Nazionale della Sicilia (Chapter 2). A contemporary of Domenico Gagini, but vastly superior to him, his style (particularly that of the Chapel of Mastrantonio in San Francesco, Palermo, Chapter 2) was too advanced and far too brilliant to take root in Sicily: the Sicilians were not ready for it. The Gagini with their (by comparison) inferior version of the Quattrocento style were left to introduce it. See also the Laurana Madonna (signed) in SS Crocifisso, Noto (see Chapter 14).

Marvuglia, Venanzio The most distinguished architect of the early neo-classical movement in Sicily; b. Palermo 1729, d. 1814; was in Rome in the middle of the 18th century and there influenced by the neo-classicism of Cardinal Albani and the late baroque of Luigi Vanvitelli. In Palermo he is known mostly for his civil architecture; his palaces and villas show an inventive and simple mixture of baroque and neo-classical elements (Palazzo Costantino, Chapter 3; Palazzo Belmonte-Riso, Chapter 4; Tepidarium, Botanical Gardens, Palermo, Chapter 2; Villa Villarosa, Bagheria, Chapter 8). He was responsible for the Benedictine Monastery of San Martino delle Scale (Chapter 5).

Masuccio, Natale Architect; b. Messina 1561; a precursor of the baroque style, he spent some time in Rome where he absorbed some influences of the Mannerist style of architecture, particularly of Ammanati. Vigorous surface decoration and a monumentality characterizes his work (Jesuit Noviciate, Trapani, see Chapter 6) which was in the same tradition as that of Paolo Amato.

Messina, Vincenzo *Stuccatore* in the Giuseppe and Giacomo Serpotta circle. His style is highly exuberant, and almost fantastical. His work (see the Oratorio del

Sacramento, Carini, Chapter 5) is less sophisticated than the Serpottas' which Donald Garstang (op. cit.) puts down to the fact that he was never guided by an architect.

Napoli, Tommaso Maria   Dominican monk and architect; c. 1655–1725. Not much is known about this figure which is a pity because his known works are highly inventive and remarkably ingenious in their planning and the articulation of the building masses (Villas Valguarnera and Palagonia, Bagheria, see Chapter 8). His work fits into a late baroque phase. See also San Domenico, Palermo, Chapter 3.

Novelli, Pietro   Painter; 1603–47; called the Monrealese since he was born in Monreale. One of the principal painters of his day.

Palma, Andrea   Architect and painter; b. Trapani 1664, d 1730; closely associated with Giacomo Amato and one of the main exponents of a fully mature Sicilian baroque style characterized by ebullience and finely tuned individuality. His work (Chapel of St Catherine, Santa Caterina, Palermo, see Chapter 2, Cathedral, Syracuse, see Chapter 14), like Gagliardi's at Noto, Ragusa and Modica, shows a brilliant handling of materials creating an almost sculptural mass which is full of energy.

Ragusa, Giambattista   Sculptor; d. 1727 but active from 1711; received some training in Rome which he put to good effect in the Chapel of the Immaculate Conception in San Francesco, Palermo (see Chapter 2). His masterpiece is the statue of St Peter outside the Cathedral, Palermo (see Chapter 4). See also the column in the centre of Piazza San Domenico (Chapter 3).

Salerno, Giuseppe   Painter; 1570–1632; known as Lo Zoppo di Gangi, the Cripple of Gangi. His works can be seen in churches all over Sicily.

Serpotta, Giacomo   *Stuccatore*; b. 1656 Palermo, d. Palermo 1732. Rarely working outside his medium, Serpotta represents the full flowering of a local tradition of sculpture. The medium in which he worked was stucco made of lime and marble dust added to which, in Sicily, was plaster. Each piece has an underlying framework of wood, wire and rags held together by sand and lime. Because of the fast-drying nature of the medium, the artist had to work very rapidly indeed, improvising as he went along, and working to accurately estimated measurements. One must assess the quality of his work in this context: the ornamental detail, the expressions, the textures – all brilliantly rendered. What makes them magical is that Serpotta added marble dust to the wet stucco, giving each piece a porcelain-like quality. Without it – and on several stuccos it has worn off – his figures seem by comparison lifeless. His work in stucco is as much an expression of the Sicilian love of overwrought decorative richness as the technique of inlaid and coloured marbles found scattered about Sicily's churches. (Palermo – Oratorio di San Lorenzo, Chapter 2, Oratorio di Santa Zita, Oratorio di San Domenico,

Chapter 3). Giacomo's brother, Giuseppe, and the latter's son Procopio, are often found working with him, though the latter was more worthy of the master's talent. For a full and extremely comprehensive examination of his work see Donald Garstang's *Giacomo Serpotta*.

Smiriglio, Mariano   Painter and architect; b. Palermo 1561; as an architect he was involved in a variety of projects: civic, military and ecclesiastical buildings as well as fountains.

Vaccarini, Giovanni Battista   Architect; b. Palermo 1702, d. 1768; worked most prominently in Catania (in fact his work shaped the built environment of the city – see Chapter 13) though he trained in Rome in the 1720s where he absorbed ideas based on the work of Borromini and Bernini. He launched the full throttle of 1720s Roman baroque on Catania. His buildings are lively, massive with a certain Roman grandeur, and towards the end of his life they show a definite classicising tendency.

III

Festivals

It is important to check the dates of these with the local Italian State Tourist Office before you depart (they change mysteriously, often without warning). Those marked with an asterisk are the best.

JANUARY

6 **Piana degli Albanesi** Albanian Epiphany; the principal feature of this, apart from the Byzantine rites of the occasion, are the elaborate costumes worn by the women.

20 ***Acireale** Festival of San Sebastiano, an orgy of devotion to this saint whose effigy is carried around the town under a huge silver canopy.

FEBRUARY

3-5 ***Catania** Festa di Sant'Agata, in honour of the patron saint of the city.

1st or 2nd week **Agrigento** Sagra del Mandorlo in Fiore, Festival of the Almond Blossom.

22-27 **Taormina** Carnevale, processions in strange costumes, exhibitions – one of the rare occasions when Taormina is full of Sicilians only.

APRIL (EASTER)

Easter festivals all over the island are often an elaborate series of rituals that have their origins in the pagan past – but feature an overlay of Christian ritual. Colourful, often richly evocative of magic and superstition, and including dramatic displays of penitence and mourning, the following are some of the best:

Palm Sunday ***Gangi** Procession of the Confraternaties carrying palms.
*Piana degli Albanesi Procession with the bishop riding through the town on a donkey (evoking Christ's arrival in Jerusalem). Wonderful, decorative costumes, particularly the womens'.
Palermo Look out for the plaited palm branches adorning the doors of the churches.
Petralia Sottana Colourful 'meeting' between Christ and the Madonna.

Holy Thursday   *Caltanissetta Procession of the Mysteries.
                  *Marsala Procession of the living Mysteries – people instead of
                  statues are used; wonderful costumes.

Good Friday   Enna Confraternal processions carrying the Urn of the Dead Christ
                and the sorrowing Mary; it would be interesting to be in Enna for
                the entire Holy Week.
                *Gangi Procession of the confraternaties carrying on their shoul-
                ders statues (tableaux) of the Easter events.
                Palermo The urn carrying Christ's 'dead body' is carried around
                the city in procession by young men in the livery of local aristocratic
                households.
                *Ragusa Procession of the Mysteries.
                *San Fratello Carnival-like occasion at which demonic masked
                'Jews' are present dressed in colourful costumes.
                *Trapani Procession of the Mysteries.

Easter Sunday   Aidone Pantomime-like 'meeting' between Christ and His
                  Mother at which the Apostles are present.
                  *Barrafranca There is a 'meeting' between Christ and His Mother
                  at which eleven giants are present. More like a pantomime than
                  an Easter festival.
                  Caltagirone There is a 'meeting' between the two 18th century
                  statues of the Addolorata and Christ. 'St Peter' spreads the news
                  to the faithful.
                  *Prizzi The Dance of the Devils and Death.

APRIL

3   Adrano La Diovalata: a fierce battle enacted in the main square between five
    devils headed by Lucifer and a child who impersonates an angel; in the end
    Good beats Evil.

JULY

1st and 2nd Sunday of the month   Agrigento Feast of San Calogero, thanks-
                                    giving for the harvest. Characteristic of this
                                    event are the bread rolls in the shape of the
                                    saint, thrown during the procession.

15   *Palermo Festival of Santa Rosalia. Procession up Monte Pellegrino.

AUGUST

13-14   *Piazza Armerina Palio dei Normanni, a very colourful pageant with
        jousting which recalls the coming of Count Roger 1st in the 11th century.

15   Messina Parade of the Giants Mata and Grifone, in which the like-
     nesses of these founders of Messina are wheeled around the city.

SEPTEMBER

8   **Tindari** Birth of the Virgin (celebrated all over the island but this is one of the best places to come to.)

NOVEMBER

1   **All Saints' Day** Presents are given by 'the dead' to children. Events all over Sicily.

2   **Il Giorno dei Morti** Visits to the dead at the local cemeteries or catacombs. Graves and tombs are decorated all over Sicily.

DECEMBER

Christmas Day Most churches throughout Sicily will have a crib in them; some of these are very elaborate (Trapani and Acireale in particular).

IV

Recommended Reading

SOCIETY

Dolci, Danilo   *Inchiesta a Palermo*, 1956, published in English as *To Feed the Hungry*, MacGibbon, 1959
   Waste, MacGibbon 1963
Lewis, Norman   *The Honoured Society*, Collins, London, 1964, reprinted by Eland Books, London, 1984
Maxwell, Gavin   *The Ten Pains of Death*, Longmans, 1959
   God Protect me from my Friends, Pan, 1958
Servadio, Gaia   *To a Different World (In the Land of the Mafia)*, Hamish Hamilton, London, 1979
   Angelo La Barbera - a Profile of a Mafia Boss, Quartet, 1974
Shawcross, Tim and Martin Young   *Mafia Wars*, Fontana, London, 1988

HISTORICAL

Correnti, Santi   *Storia di Sicilia*, Longanesi & Co, Milano, 1989
Finlay, M.I. & D. Mack Smith   *A History of Sicily*, London, 1968, 3 vols.
Ginsborg, Paul   *A History of Contemporary Italy: Society and Politics 1943-1988*, Penguin, London, 1990
Hibbert, Christopher   *Garibaldi and his Enemies*, Penguin, London, 1987
Masson, Georgina   *Frederick II*, Secker & Warburg, 1957
Norwich, John Julius   *The Normans in the South, 1016-1130*, Longmans, Green & Co Ltd, 1967
   Kingdom in the Sun, 1130-94, 1970
Runciman, Stephen   *The Sicilian Vespers*, Cambridge University Press, Cambridge, 1988
Trevelyan, Raleigh   *Princes Under the Volcano*, Macmillan, London, 1972

GENERAL

Buttitta, Antonino   *Easter in Sicily*, Sicilian Tourist Service, Palermo, 1990
Cronin, Vincent   *The Golden Honeycomb*, Rupert Hart Davis, London, 1954
Fulco (Duca Fulco di Santo Stefano della Cerda di Verdura)   *The Happy Summer Days*, Weidenfeld & Nicolson, London, 1976
Lewis, Norman   *The March of the Long Shadows*, Arena, London, 1986

Taylor Simeti, Mary   *On Perspehone's Island*, Penguin, London, 1989
    Sicilian Food, Random Century Group Ltd, 1989 (first published as
    Pomp and Sustenance)

LITERATURE AND BIOGRAPHY

Levi, Carlo   *The Words are Stones*, Victor Gollancz, London, 1959
Gilmour, David   *The Last Leopard: A life of Giuseppe di Lampedusa*, Quartet,
    London, 1988
di Lampedusa, Giuseppe Tomasi   *The Leopard*, Collins, 1962
Verga, Giovanni   *Short Sicilian Novels*, Dedalus, London, 1985
    Cavalleria Rusticana, Dedalus, London, 1987
    I Malavoglia (the House by the Medlar Tree), Dedalus, London, 1985
    Maestro Don Gesualdo, Dedalus, London, 1984

ART AND ARCHITECTURE

Blunt, Anthony   *Sicilian Baroque*. Weidenfeld & Nicolson, London, 1968
Boscarino, Salvatore   *Sicilia Barocca: Architettura e Città 1610-1760*, Officina
    Edizione, 1986
Garstang, Donald   *Giacomo Serpotta*, Zwemmer Ltd., London, 1984
Guido, Margaret   *Sicily: An Archaeological Guide*, Faber & Faber, 1967
Lanza Tomasi, Gioacchino   *Le Ville di Palermo*, Palermo, 1974
De Seta, Giorgio and Leonardo Di Mauro   *Palermo*, Editori Laterza, Bari,
    1981
Tobriner, Stephen   *The Genesis of Noto*, Zwemmer Ltd., London, 1982

TRAVEL

Giuseppe Bellafiore   *Palermo*, Azienda Autonoma di Turismo di Palermo e
    Monreale, 1974
Berenson, Bernard   *The Passionate Sightseer*, Thames & Hudson, London,
    1988
Brydone, Patrick   *A Tour through Sicily and Malta in a Series of Letters to
    William Beckford*, London, 1790.
Goethe, J.W.   *Italian Journey, 1786-1788* (translated by W.H. Auden and
    Elizabeth Mayer), Penguin, London, 1985
Hutton, Edward   *Cities of Sicily*, Methuen & Co., London, 1926
Lawrence, D.H.   *D.H. Lawrence and Italy: Twilight in Italy, Sea and Sardinia,
    Etruscan Places* (Introduction by Anthony Burgess), Viking Penguin,
    1972
Murray, John   *Southern Italy and Sicily*, John Murray Ltd, London, 1892
Touring Club Italia   *Sicilia*, T.C.I., Milan, 1989

Index